PSYCHOBIOLOGICAL APPROACHES FOR ANXIETY DISORDERS

Wiley Series in

CLINICAL PSYCHOLOGY

Adrian Wells   *School of Psychological Sciences, University*
(Series Advisor)   *of Manchester, UK*

For other titles in this series please visit www.wiley.com/go/cs

PSYCHOBIOLOGICAL APPROACHES FOR ANXIETY DISORDERS

Treatment Combination Strategies

Edited by Stefan G. Hofmann

A John Wiley & Sons, Ltd., Publication

This edition first published 2012
© 2012 John Wiley & Sons, Ltd.

Wiley-Blackwell is an imprint of John Wiley & Sons, formed by the merger of Wiley's global Scientific, Technical and Medical business with Blackwell Publishing.

Registered Office
John Wiley & Sons Ltd, The Atrium, Southern Gate, Chichester, West Sussex, PO19 8SQ, UK

Editorial Offices
350 Main Street, Malden, MA 02148-5020, USA
9600 Garsington Road, Oxford, OX4 2DQ, UK
The Atrium, Southern Gate, Chichester, West Sussex, PO19 8SQ, UK

For details of our global editorial offices, for customer services, and for information about how to apply for permission to reuse the copyright material in this book please see our website at www.wiley.com/wiley-blackwell.

The right of Stefan G. Hofmann to be identified as the author of the editorial material in this work has been asserted in accordance with the UK Copyright, Designs and Patents Act 1988.

All rights reserved. No part of this publication may be reproduced, stored in a retrieval system, or transmitted, in any form or by any means, electronic, mechanical, photocopying, recording or otherwise, except as permitted by the UK Copyright, Designs and Patents Act 1988, without the prior permission of the publisher.

Wiley also publishes its books in a variety of electronic formats. Some content that appears in print may not be available in electronic books.

Designations used by companies to distinguish their products are often claimed as trademarks. All brand names and product names used in this book are trade names, service marks, trademarks or registered trademarks of their respective owners. The publisher is not associated with any product or vendor mentioned in this book. This publication is designed to provide accurate and authoritative information in regard to the subject matter covered. It is sold on the understanding that the publisher is not engaged in rendering professional services. If professional advice or other expert assistance is required, the services of a competent professional should be sought.

Library of Congress Cataloging-in-Publication Data

Psychobiological approaches for anxiety disorders : treatment combination strategies / edited by Stefan G. Hofmann.
   p. ; cm.
 Includes bibliographical references and index.
 ISBN 978-0-470-97181-9 (cloth) – ISBN 978-0-470-97180-2 (pbk.)
 I. Hofmann, Stefan G.
 [DNLM: 1. Anxiety Disorders–therapy. 2. Combined Modality Therapy–methods. WM 172]

 616.85'22–dc23

2011043015

A catalogue record for this book is available from the British Library.

Wiley also publishes its books in a variety of electronic formats. Some content that appears in print may not be available in electronic books.

Set in 10/12pt Palatino by Thomson Digital, Noida, India
Printed in Singapore by Ho Printing Singapore Pte Ltd

1   2012

CONTENTS

About the Contributors vii
About the Editor. xi
Introduction 1
Stefan G. Hofmann

    Chapter 1   The Biology and Efficacy of Combination Strategies for Anxiety Disorders 5
                      Keith A. Ganasen and Dan J. Stein

    Chapter 2   Benzodiazepines 25
                      Bridget A. Hearon and Michael W. Otto

    Chapter 3   Tricyclic Antidepressants and Monoamine Oxidase Inhibitors 41
                      Franklin R. Schneier

    Chapter 4   Selective Serotonin Reuptake Inhibitors, Reversible Inhibitors of Monoamine Oxidase-A, and Buspirone 61
                      Borwin Bandelow, Markus Reitt, and Dirk Wedekind

    Chapter 5   D-Cycloserine. 75
                      Adam J. Guastella and Gail A. Alvares

    Chapter 6   Yohimbine Hydrochloride 91
                      Samantha G. Farris, Michelle L. Davis, Lindsey B. DeBoer, Jasper A. J. Smits, and Mark B. Powers

    Chapter 7   Cortisol. 109
                      Leila Maria Soravia and Dominique J.-F. de Quervain

    Chapter 8   Oxytocin 123
                      Markus Heinrichs, Frances S. Chen, and Gregor Domes

Chapter 9   Dietary Supplements. 145
            Lindsey B. DeBoer, Michelle L. Davis,
            Mark B. Powers, and Jasper A. J. Smits

Chapter 10 A Roadmap for the Research and Practice
            of Combination Strategies 181
            Stefan G. Hofmann

Index 195

ABOUT THE CONTRIBUTORS

Gail Alvares is a PhD student at the Brain and Mind Research Institute, University of Sydney, working in the field of social anxiety and decision making. Her research explores some of the fundamental ways in which stress and anxiety influences learning and habit formation.

Dr Borwin Bandelow is Professor at the Department of Psychiatry and Psychotherapy at the University of Göttingen, Germany. He is the Managing Director of the clinic and head of the Anxiety Disorders Unit. As a psychiatry and neurology specialist, a psychologist, and a psychotherapist, Borwin Bandelow specializes in anxiety disorders (panic disorder, generalized anxiety disorder, and social phobia), schizophrenia, depression, psychotherapy, and psychopharmacology. He has authored or co-authored over 200 publications internationally in both books and scientific journals. Borwin Bandelow is President of the German Society for Anxiety Research. He is Editor-in-Chief of the German Journal of Psychiatry, one of the first on-line psychiatric journals.

Frances S. Chen, PhD, is a postdoctoral fellow at the University of Freiburg, Germany. She completed her PhD in psychology at Stanford University. From 2009 to 2010, she was a Visiting Professor of Psychology at Deep Springs College in California. She currently conducts research at the University of Freiburg as a Fulbright Scholar and Alexander von Humboldt Postdoctoral Fellow. Her research focuses on neurobiological and psychological factors influencing social relationships, in particular attachment behavior and behavior within negotiation and conflict settings.

Michelle L. Davis is a research assistant for the Anxiety Research and Treatment Program at Southern Methodist University. She received a BSc in Biology at Texas Tech University. She is currently a project coordinator for a study funded by the National Institute of Drug Abuse examining exercise as an augment to cognitive behavioral treatment for smoking cessation.

Lindsey B. DeBoer is a clinical psychology doctoral candidate at Southern Methodist University. She received a BA in Psychology and in Child Development at The University of Texas at Dallas and an MA in clinical psychology at SMU. Ms. DeBoer is currently a research assistant for the

Anxiety Research and Treatment Program at SMU. Her research focuses on the interplay between anxiety and health behaviors including eating behavior, exercise, and substance use, as well as augmenting empirically supported psychotherapy with exercise and dietary interventions.

Dr Dominique de Quervain is a full professor at the Faculty of Medicine and Faculty of Psychology and Director of the Division of Cognitive Neuroscience, University of Basel, Switzerland. He studied medicine at the University of Berne, Switzerland, and was a Postdoctoral Fellow at the University of California Irvine, USA, and at the universities of Basel and Zurich, Switzerland. He is interested in the effects of stress hormones on memory in health and disease and in the identification of memory-related genes in humans using behavioral genetics approaches together with neuroimaging techniques.

Dr Gregor Domes completed his PhD in psychology at the University of Tübingen, Germany, and his postdoctoral research at the University of Rostock, Germany and the University of Zurich, Switzerland. Currently, he is an assistant professor at the University of Freiburg, Germany and a member of the Freiburg Brain Imaging Center. His research focuses on the behavioral and neural effects of steroid hormones and neuropeptides in health and mental disorders.

Samantha G. Farris is a clinical psychology doctoral student at the University of Houston. She received her Bachelor's degree in psychology from Rutgers University, while working at the Center of Alcohol Studies. After completing her degree, Ms Farris worked as a research coordinator at the Center for the Treatment and Study of Anxiety, at the University of Pennsylvania. Her current research interests include the relationship between anxiety and substance use disorders, and dissemination of empirically-supported treatments.

Keith Ganasen, MD, is a resident in psychiatry. He has, during his training in psychiatry, embarked on research in the anxiety disorders, and is planning a career in academic psychiatry.

Dr Adam Guastella is Associate Professor, a clinical psychologist, and principal research fellow at the Brain and Mind Research Institute, University of Sydney. He manages the youth anxiety services at the institute. His research focuses on using translational models to improve social function in disorders of social deficit and to develop novel methods to reduce anxiety.

Bridget A. Hearon, MA, is a doctoral student in the Clinical Psychology Program at Boston University. Her research interests include the treatment of anxiety and substance use disorders as well as factors which influence health behaviors.

Dr Markus Heinrichs is a full Professor at the Faculty of Economics and Behavioral Sciences and at the Faculty of Medicine, Director of the Laboratory for Biological and Personality Psychology, and Director of the Outpatient Clinic for Stress-Related Disorders at the University of Freiburg, Germany. He received his PhD from the University of Trier, Germany, where he began his studies on oxytocin and social behavior. Prior to his position at the University of Freiburg, he spent 10 years at the University of Zurich, Switzerland, where he was a professor of clinical psychology and psychobiology from 2007 to 2009. His research topics include experimental therapy research on mental disorders with social deficits, neurobiology of social interaction, and stress- and anxiety-protective factors.

Michael W. Otto, PhD, is Professor of Psychology at Boston University. Michael Otto specializes in the cognitive-behavioral treatment of anxiety, mood, and substance use disorders. An enduring theme across these disorders is the role of exposure-based emotional tolerance/acceptance strategies in improving mental health and activity levels. His research focuses on difficult-to-treat populations, including interventions for patients who have failed to respond to previous treatments. He also focuses on health behavior promotion ranging from medication adherence to engagement in exercise, and has published over 300 articles, chapters, and books spanning his research interests.

Mark B. Powers, PhD, is Assistant Professor and Co-Director of the Anxiety Research and Treatment Program at Southern Methodist University. He received a BA at the University of California at Santa Barbara, an MA at Pepperdine University, and a PhD from the University of Texas at Austin. He also completed a pre-doctoral fellowship at Boston and Harvard universities and a residency at the University of Washington. He has over 70 publications and his current research focuses on mechanisms of change in anxiety disorders.

Markus Reitt is a clinical psychologist at the Department of Psychiatry and Psychotherapy at the University of Göttingen. He is trained in Cognitive Behavioral Therapy. In his research, he cooperates with the East China Normal University, Shanghai, China. He is currently working with the Task Force for Germany National Guidelines for Anxiety Disorders.

Franklin R. Schneier, MD, is Professor of Clinical Psychiatry at the Department of Psychiatry at Columbia University in New York and

Research Psychiatrist in the Anxiety Disorders Clinic of New York State Psychiatric Institute. His research has focused on psychobiology, and cognitive-behavioral and pharmacological treatments for anxiety and mood disorders.

Jasper J. A. Smits, PhD, is Associate Professor and Co-director of the Anxiety Research and Treatment Program at Southern Methodist University. He is a federally funded investigator of intervention strategies to improve outcomes for adults suffering from anxiety and related disorders.

Dr Leila Maria Soravia is a Postdoctoral Fellow at the Department of Psychiatric Neurophysiology of the University Hospital of Psychiatry, University of Berne, Switzerland. She studied Psychology at the University of Berne, and obtained her PhD at the Department of Clinical Psychology and Psychotherapy of the University of Zürich, Switzerland. She has focused on the investigation of the neuroendocrinological mechanisms of anxiety disorders and the development of new treatment approaches, especially for social phobia and spider phobia. Her main interest is in the exploration of the HPA-axis, the glucocorticoid cortisol, and its influence on fear memory in phobic patients.

Dan J. Stein's MD, PhD, is Professor and Chairman of the Department of Psychiatry at the University of Cape Town in South Africa. His research focuses on the psychobiology of anxiety disorders, ranging from animal models, through clinical research, and on to epidemiological work.

Dr Dirk Wedekind is a senior consultant psychiatrist at the Department of Psychiatry at the University of Göttingen, Germany. He attended medical school in Göttingen, Germany and studied affective neuroscience in Maastricht, The Netherlands. His scientific work has focused on the neurobiology and neuropharmacology of anxiety disorders. He also worked on clinical and biological aspects of addiction disorders and did research on personality- and somatoform disorders. He has authored and co-authored more than 60 articles in scientific journals and books and is a frequent national speaker on pharmacological and clinical topics.

ABOUT THE EDITOR

Stefan G. Hofmann, PhD, is Professor of Psychology at Boston University and the Director of the Psychotherapy and Emotion Research Laboratory. He is president-elect of the Association for Behavioral and Cognitive Therapies and president-elect of the International Association for Cognitive Psychotherapy. He is also a Board Member of the Academy of Cognitive Therapy and of the Anxiety Disorders Association of America. He is an advisor to the DSM-V Development Process. He is widely published with more than 200 peer-reviewed journal articles and book chapters, and 10 books, including "An Introduction to Modern CBT" (Wiley-Blackwell, 2012). His primary research interests center on treatment of anxiety disorders for which he has received many research awards. Weblink: http://www.bostonanxiety.org/

INTRODUCTION

Stefan G. Hofmann
Department of Psychology, Boston University, Boston, MA, USA

Individuals with anxiety disorders show excessive fear when confronted with specific objects, situations, physical sensations, or other external or internal cues in the absence of any actual danger. As a consequence, people with these debilitating conditions often avoid these cues or endure their anxiety under great distress. This often leads to great personal suffering, diminished quality of life, and high economic cost to society (Olatunji *et al.* 2007).

Epidemiological studies indicate that the group of anxiety disorders, which includes specific phobias, social anxiety disorder, generalized anxiety, obsessive compulsive disorder, panic disorder, agoraphobia, and post-traumatic stress disorder, are the most prevalent class of mental disorders, with 12-month and lifetime prevalence rates of 18.1 and 28.8%, respectively (Kessler *et al.* 2005a; b).

A large body of work supports the efficacy of cognitive behavioral therapy (CBT) (Hofmann and Smits 2008) and anxiolytic medication for treating anxiety disorders (Roy-Byrne and Cowley 2002). CBT combines cognitive strategies to target maladaptive beliefs about the fear-eliciting cues and exposure techniques aimed at helping patients reacquire a sense of safety around cues associated with anxiety disorders. In contrast to CBT, pharmacological interventions aim to directly target biochemical pathways underlying the anxiety elicited by disorder-specific cues (Bourine and Lambert 2002). Pharmacological agents that have demonstrated efficacy for a variety of anxiety disorders include benzodiazepines, tricyclic antidepressants, monoamine oxidase inhibitors, selective serotonin reuptake inhibitors (SSRIs), reversible inhibitors of monoamine oxidase-A (RIMA), and buspirone (Baldwin *et al.* 2005; Bourine and Lambert 2002). There is some evidence to suggest that CBT may be more tolerable and

---

Psychobiological Approaches for Anxiety Disorders: Treatment Combination Strategies, First Edition.
Edited by Stefan G. Hofmann.
© 2012 John Wiley & Sons, Ltd. Published 2012 by John Wiley & Sons, Ltd.

more cost-effective, especially in the long-term, than some of these traditional anxiolytic agents (Otto *et al.* 2006). Although both treatment modalities are efficacious, there is clearly room for improvement (Hofmann and Smits 2008; Roy-Byrne and Cowley 2002).

Because these treatment modalities are less than perfect when administered as monotherapies, investigators have examined whether combining pharmacotherapy and psychotherapy is more effective than either of the monotherapies for reducing anxiety symptoms. Many of these studies show that combination strategies are not substantially more effective than monotherapies in the short term and may even be worse in the long term for some anxiety disorders. Thus some cases, adding conventional pharmacotherapy can even be detrimental to the success of psychological treatments, such as when using benzodiazepines in combination with exposure therapy for panic disorder (see Otto *et al.*, 2006, for a review).

A more recent approach toward combination therapy is to enhance the mechanism of CBT using pharmacological agents. Some of these approaches are highly promising and support such augmentation strategies to further enhance the efficacy of CBT. Examples of those agents include D-cycloserine, yohimbine, cortisol, oxytocin, propranolol, and various nutritional supplements. Some of these agents appear to act as cognitive enhancers based on the mechanism through which they augment CBT (Hofmann *et al.* 2011).

The goal of this book is to discuss the evidence from the existing literature on conventional and novel combination therapies for anxiety disorders. For this purpose, a number of leading investigators were invited to present the evidence of combination strategies for treating anxiety disorders. The first chapter gives an overview of the biology and efficacy of combination strategies, which points to some of the limitations of the contemporary literature and recommends that future research should embrace a translational research approach. The following chapters 2, 3, and 4 discuss traditional combination strategies using benzodiazepines, tricyclic antidepressants, monoamine oxidase inhibitors, SSRIs, RIMA, and buspirone. Chapter 5 discusses the evidence of D-cycloserine as a cognitive enhancer of CBT. Similarly, yohimbine (Chapter 6), cortisol (Chapter 7), and oxytocin (Chapter 8) offer new combination strategies born out of a translational research approach. Chapter 9 discusses dietary supplements, which offer promising options that are worthy of further investigation. Chapter 10 provides a general roadmap for future research in combination treatments for anxiety disorders and recommends that the field of psychiatry and pharmacology should:

- move beyond the traditional horse race comparison of clinical trials and toward translational research from 'bench to bedside;'
- move closer toward understanding the mechanism of treatment change; and

- move closer toward personalized medicine by tailoring the treatment to the client based on certain biomarkers.

I hope that this volume will inspire researchers, clinicians, policy makers, funding agencies, and the pharma industry to move beyond conventional paradigms of combination therapies for anxiety disorders.

REFERENCES

Baldwin, D. S., Anderson, I. M., Nutt, D. J. *et al.* (2005). British Association for Psychopharmacology: Evidence-based guidelines for the pharmacological treatment of anxiety disorders: recommendations from the British Association for Psychopharmacology. *Journal of Psychopharmacology*, 19: 567–596.

Bourine, M. and Lambert, O. (2002). Pharmacotherapy of anxiety disorder. *Human Psychopharmacology*, 17: 383–400.

Hofmann, S. G. and Smits, J. A. J. (2008). Cognitive-behavioral therapy for adult anxiety disorders: A meta-analysis of randomized placebo-controlled trials. *Journal of Clinical Psychiatry*, 69: 621–632.

Hofmann, S. G., Smits, J. A. J., Asnaani, A., Gutner, C. A., and Otto, M. W. (2011). Cognitive enhancers for anxiety disorders. *Pharmacology, Biochemistry, and Behavior*, 99: 275–284.

Kessler, R. C., Berglund, P. A., Demler, O., Jin, R., and Walters, E. E. (2005a). Lifetime prevalence and age-of-onset distributions of DSM-IV disorders in the National Comorbidity Survey Replication (NCS-R). *Archives of General Psychiatry*, 62, 593–602.

Kessler, R. C., Chiu, W. T., Demler, O., Merikangas, K. R., and Walters, E. E. (2005b). Prevalence, severity, and comorbidity of 12-month DSM-IV disorders in the National Comorbidity Survey Replication. *Archives of General Psychiatry*, 62: 617–627.

Olatunji, B. O., Cisler, J. M., and Tolin, D. F. (2007). Quality of life in the anxiety disorders: A meta-analytic review. *Clinical Psychology Review*, 27: 572–581.

Otto, M. W., Smits, J. A. J., and Reese, H. E. (2006). Combined psychotherapy and pharmacotherapy for mood and anxiety disorders in adults: Review and analysis. *Clinical Psychology: Science and Practice*, 12: 72–86.

Roy-Byrne, P. P. and Cowley, D. S. (2002). Pharmacological treatments for panic disorder, generalized anxiety disorder, specific phobia, and social anxiety disorder. In P. E. Nathanand J. M. Gorman (eds), *A Guide To Treatments that Work*, 2nd edn. New York, Oxford University Press: 337–365.

Chapter 1

THE BIOLOGY AND EFFICACY OF COMBINATION STRATEGIES FOR ANXIETY DISORDERS

Keith A. Ganasen and Dan J. Stein

Department of Psychiatry, University of Cape Town, Cape Town, South Africa

INTRODUCTION

Optimal treatment of anxiety disorders is important as they are the most prevalent psychiatric disorders in community studies, and generalized anxiety disorder is the most prevalent psychiatric disorder in primary care (Kessler *et al.* 2010). In addition, anxiety disorders begin early in life, and predispose to the development of comorbid disorders such as depression and substance use disorders; early and robust treatment may therefore be important in secondary prevention (Goodwin and Gorman 2002). Anxiety disorders are not only associated with significant suffering in affected individuals and families, but also contribute enormously to the societal burden of disease; a number are among the most disabling of all medical conditions (Lopez *et al.* 2006).

Fortunately, there have been significant advances in the treatment of anxiety disorders. A range of medications have been approved in the past few decades for the major anxiety disorders on the basis of randomized controlled trials showing efficacy and safety. Similarly, during the same period, a number of psychotherapies have been rigorously studied, and shown to have both short-term and longer-term efficacy. Expert guidelines, often incorporating systematic meta-analyses of the research literature, have been developed, and highlight the evidence base for first-line interventions, such as selective serotonin uptake inhibitors (SSRIs) and cognitive behavioral therapy (CBT) (Ipser and Stein 2009). The majority of patients with anxiety disorders can be expected to respond to such first-line interventions.

Psychobiological Approaches for Anxiety Disorders: Treatment Combination Strategies, First Edition.
Edited by Stefan G. Hofmann.
© 2012 John Wiley & Sons, Ltd. Published 2012 by John Wiley & Sons, Ltd.

At the same time, underdiagnosis and undertreatment of, and resistance to treatment in, anxiety disorders remain significant problems. Underdiagnosis and undertreatment may reflect a range of structural and attitudinal barriers, including insufficient numbers of well-trained therapists and insufficient mental health literacy in both the general population and primary care practitioners. First-line treatments may work in the majority of cases, but even when appropriately diagnosed and treated, 40% or more of patients may fail to respond (Pallanti et al. 2002; Bandelow and Ruther 2004). There is a relative lack of effectiveness trials in anxiety disorders, but in real-world settings, where patients may have increased comorbidity, and where clinicians are required to be generalists rather than specialists, treatment response rates may be lower, and tolerability concerns more obvious, particularly over the longer term.

Combination treatment is an important consideration in attempts to improve the efficacy and effectiveness of intervention in anxiety disorders. Given the multiple factors, including neurobiological and psychological variables, involved in anxiety disorder pathogenesis, there is a prima facie case for a comprehensive treatment approach including pharmacotherapy and psychotherapy. Indeed, early thinking suggested pharmacotherapy was useful for a rapid treatment response, while psychotherapy was valuable for a maintained response, even after discontinuation of short-term intervention (Riba and Ballon 2005). It has therefore been surprising to see a growing evidence base suggesting relatively little advantage in combining pharmacotherapy and psychotherapy for anxiety disorders (Foa et al. 2002; Otto et al. 2005; Black 2006; Bandelow et al. 2007; Hofmann et al. 2009).

Perhaps one of the most exciting developments in combination treatment of anxiety disorders, if not in all of medicine, has been the adoption of a rigorous translational neuroscience approach (Davis et al. 2006; Otto et al. 2007; Hofmann et al. 2011; Kaplan and Moore 2011). Advances in a range of basic neuroscience areas, including animal models of anxiety disorders, have allowed combination interventions to be studied in the laboratory. Rather than relying on standard first-line pharmacotherapies, such work has focused on targets (e.g. in glutamatergic systems) that may be specifically relevant to enhancing cognitive-behavioral interventions. Such work provides a rigorous foundation for moving findings through to the bedside, in the form of proof-of-principle clinical studies. This approach appears to have significant potential and has therefore attracted considerable interest from researchers, making this book extremely timely.

This chapter will briefly focus on a number of background issues relevant to combination treatment in anxiety disorders. First, we will review some of the psychobiology relevant to an understanding of how combined treatments work. Second, we will review some of the findings addressing, and issues concerning, the efficacy of such combined treatments.

PSYCHOBIOLOGY OF COMBINATION TREATMENTS

There is a growing understanding of the neurocircuitry underlying the fear response in animals and anxiety disorders in humans. Advances in structural and functional neuro-imaging have been key in developing our understanding of such circuitry in clinical conditions (Shin and Liberzon 2010). Thus, a growing body of evidence suggests that anxiety disorders are characterized by abnormalities in both prefrontal and sub-cortical (e.g. amygdala, hippocampus) circuitry (Grillon 2002; Anderson and Insel 2006). Neurotransmitters involved in such pathways include serotonergic, noradrenergic, glutamatergic, gamma-aminobutyric acid (GABA)ergic, and neuropeptide systems, and many available pharmacotherapies act on such systems (Charney 2003).

One approach to understanding the psychobiology of combined pharmacotherapy and psychotherapy is to argue that pharmacotherapy acts predominantly on bottom-up neurotransmitter-mediated mechanisms, while psychotherapy acts mainly on top-down cognitive-affective processes. Medications, such as SSRIs, may act on the amygdala and its efferent pathways (e.g. to hypothalamus and brainstem) to reduce panic attacks, which in turn leads to reduced anticipatory anxiety and phobic avoidance (Gorman et al. 2000). However, interventions such as CBT, may act upstream of the amgydala, strengthening the ability of medial prefrontal areas to inhibit sub-cortically mediated processes, by decreasing cognitive misattributions and deconditioning the fear response (Mayberg 2002).

While such an approach may be heuristically useful, it may entail some over-simplification. First, neurocircuitry alterations following psychotherapy are not limited to prefrontal areas; instead they may be widespread (Roffman et al. 2005; Frewen et al. 2008). Conversely, the effects of pharmacotherapy are unlikely to be limited to sub-cortical neurotransmitter activity; rather they may lead to significant changes in high-level cognitive and affective processing. Furthermore, such an approach does not explain why certain combinations of pharmacotherapy and psychotherapy appear ineffective or even contra-indicated (Otto et al. 2005). Indeed, both pharmacotherapy and psychotherapy are interventions that have complex and interactive effects on the brain-mind.

Another question that requires a more complex approach is whether combination strategies are likely to be similar across different anxiety disorders, or whether specific combined treatment approaches will be needed for each disorder. On the one hand, imaging studies suggest that there are a number of overlapping mechanisms that cut across different anxiety disorders. A recent meta-analysis of brain imaging studies in anxiety disorders, for example, found an increase in the activity of the amygdala and insula in participants with post-traumatic stress disorder (PTSD), social anxiety disorder, and with specific phobia, relative to healthy control subjects (Etkin and Wager 2007). Thus, it may be predicted that SSRIs act to decrease insula activity, while CBT acts to decrease amygdala activity, in a number of these conditions (Furmark *et al.* 2002; Carey *et al.* 2004). On the other hand, there is also involvement of distinctive neurocircuitry in different anxiety disorders (Etkin and Wager 2007). Furthermore, within a particular disorder, different neuronal circuitry may be involved in different symptom presentations (Lueken *et al.* 2011). Thus, it is possible that different forms of combined treatment may be effective, not only for different anxiety disorders, but also for different subtypes of particular anxiety disorders.

Imaging studies in humans will no doubt continue to be important in answering such questions. For example, particular neurocircuitry findings predict response to pharmacotherapy, while others predict response to psychotherapy, or to combined treatment (Brody *et al.* 1998; Furmark *et al.* 2002; 2005). Data from studies that address the impact of particular gene variants on neuro-imaging findings are also likely to be important in developing more integrative models. Also, in order to develop more complex models of combined treatments, it would be helpful to have good laboratory models of anxiety disorders and interventions. Fortunately, there is a range of ongoing work in this area. We briefly review some of the relevant work targeting neurotransmitter systems (e.g. glutamatergic, noradrenergic, and adenosine systems), neuroendocrine systems (e.g. glucorticorticoids), and social neuropeptides (e.g. oxytocin (OT)).

Neurotransmitter Systems

Laboratory research has suggested the glutamatergic system as a target for combined pharmacotherapy and psychotherapy; this research demonstrated that the *N*-methyl-D-aspartate (NMDA)-glutamate receptor of the lateral and basolateral amygdaloid nuclei was involved in fear conditioning and fear extinction in rodents (Davis *et al.* 1993). Given that antagonists of the NMDA receptor prevented both the acquisition and extinction of fear (Lee and Kim 1998), the question arose of whether an NMDA agonist would facilitate the extinction of conditioned fear (Walker *et al.* 2002). Indeed, rats that received the partial NMDA agonist D-cycloserine (DCS), in combination with repeated exposure to the conditioned stimulus, had enhanced extinction of their fear as compared to the rats that received DCS alone (Walker *et al.* 2002). The work provided a solid foundation for clinical trials of combined DCS and CBT; the first of these seminal proof-of-principle clinical studies was undertaken in acrophobia (Ressler *et al.* 2004), and several others soon followed.

Animal research has also questioned the extent to which the effects of DCS on fear extinction are generalized. Rats given DCS and fear extinction training to one stimulus, also exhibited reduced fear to another stimulus (Ledgerwood *et al.* 2005). Furthermore, some animal work has indicated that DCS may prevent the relapse of learned fear (Ledgerwood *et al.* 2004).

However, it has also been suggested that if DCS enhances fear extinction by improving learning, then it may also facilitate recall of aversive memories (Lee et al. 2006). Perhaps, to reduce the potential for sensitization of negative memories, it will prove preferable to administer DCS after an exposure session that is determined by the clinician to be successful (Hofmann et al. 2011).

There is also some concern about developing tolerance to DCS, thereby reducing efficacy of combined treatment over time. Perhaps DCS should be used on an acute rather than chronic basis (Hofmann et al. 2006). Indeed, poorer results have been found in studies that used DCS at higher or more frequent doses (Kushner et al. 2007; Wilhelm et al. 2008; Storch et al. 2010). Ultimately, additional clinical research is needed to determine the extent of precise benefits and risks of using DCS in combined treatments (Krystal 2007). Combination strategies using DCS are further discussed in Chapter 5 of this book.

Ongoing animal research has provided additional insight into the specific mechanisms whereby DCS exerts its effects. DCS acts on the NMDA receptor complex's strychnine-insensitive glycine-recognition binding site, facilitating the movement of calcium, which in turn initiates intracellular processes that are involved in learning. The effects of DCS appear to be mediated in particular by intra-amygdala signaling cascades involving mitogen-activated protein kinase (MAPK), phosphatidylinositol 3-kinase (PI-3K), both of which are known to play a role in fear conditioning (Yang and Lu 2005). Such work may ultimately lead to additional pharmacological interventions for use in clinical employment of combined treatment.

A range of neurotransmitter systems, other than the glutamatergic system, are also likely involved in facilitating prefrontally-mediated fear extinction. The noradrenergic system, for example, plays a key role in prefrontal processes. Yohimbine hydrochloride is a selective competitive alpha2-adrenergic receptor antagonist that stimulates c-Fos expression in the medial prefrontal cortex (Singewald 2003). Administration of yohimbine hydrochloride in rats enhanced extinction learning and improved the time needed to reduce conditioned fear, providing a foundation for subsequent translation to human studies (Cain 2004; Powers 2009). Combination strategies using yohimbine hydrochloride in the treatment of anxiety disorders are further discussed in Chapter 6.

Various neutraceuticals may also act on neurotransmitters mediating fear and anxiety. Caffeine, a psychostimulant that acts on adenosine receptors, is one of the most widely used. It induces positive feelings such as alertness and increased mental performance. However, individuals with a history of anxiety disorders, particularly panic disorder, experience more unpleasant physical symptoms, suggesting adenosine receptor sensitivity; hence the hypothesis that administration of caffeine during exposure based treatment might enhance and sustain fear extinction. Neutraceutical combination treatments are discussed further in Chapter 9.

Neuroendocrine Systems

Glucocorticoids are steroid hormones that are synthesized in the adrenal cortex, and are released along with catecholamines as part of the hypothalamic-pituitary-adrenal neuroendocrine response to stress. Laboratory research has shown that adrenalectomy and administration of corticosteroid synthesis inhibitors reduces the unconditioned startle response and increases time spent in a fearful environment (Cordero 1998; Takehashi 1998). Conversely, administration of GR agonists prior to fear extinction facilitates fear extinction on repeated exposure of the stimulus, an effect that is blocked by co-administration of a GR antagonist (Yang et al. 2006). This work again provides a foundation for clinical trials of GR agonists together with psychotherapy (see below).

Laboratory research again suggests particular clinical research directions. For example, administration of a GR agonist after the extinction phase continues to have a facilitatory effect, suggesting that glucocorticoids influence memory consolidation (Yang et al. 2006), a finding that may be particularly relevant in the context of a condition such as PTSD. Further extensions of laboratory research may ultimately lead to additional clinical targets. It is notable, for example, that it is glucocorticoid receptors, rather than mineralocorticoid receptors, which are associated with memory consolidation (Oitzl and de Kloet 1992; Roozendaal and McGaugh 1996). As the neurobiology of these receptors becomes increasingly better understood, so additional clinical routes of investigation open up (Cahill and McGaugh 1996; Lupien and McEwen 1997). A broad range of other neuroendocrine targets (e.g. gonal hormonal systems) may also be relevant to combined treatments.

One important area of glucorticorticoid research lies in developmental psychobiology. The effects of early adversity of the developing brain-mind, for example, are mediated by a range of neurochemical and neuroendocrine pathways, including the glucocorticoid system (Stein et al. 2005). Administration of an SSRI may reverse some of these effects in rodent models of early life trauma (Uys et al. 2006). Although there has been some literature on both the pharmacotherapy and psychotherapy of patients presenting with psychopathology in the context of a history of early adversity (Nemeroff et al. 2003; Stein et al. 2003), much further work is needed to establish optimal combined treatments for such patients. Combination strategies using glucocorticoids are further discussed in Chapter 7.

Social Neuropeptides

OT and arginine vasopressin (AVP) are highly conserved neuropeptides that play an important role in social interaction, including parental care, pair-bonding, sexual behavior, and social memory. Across species, OT often mediates female-specific behavior such as parturition and lactation, while AVP often mediates male-specific behavior including aggression (Donaldson and Young 2008). Both OT and AVP appear critical for linking social signals to mesocorticolimbic reward circuitry (Insel 2003). These basic scientific findings raise the question of whether such social neuropeptides may be usefully incorporated into combined treatments of clinical disorders. A broad range of other peptide systems (e.g. opioid system) may also be relevant to the clinical setting (Stein *et al.* 2007).

In humans, intranasal administration of OT increases feelings of trust (Kosfeld *et al.* 2005) and enhances emotion recognition (Domes *et al.* 2007). OT attenuates behavioral or amygdala responses to breaches of trust, aversive stimuli, or fear-conditioned responses to social stimuli (Kirsch *et al.* 2005; Domes *et al.* 2007; Baumgartner *et al.* 2008; Petrovic *et al.* 2008). Depending on the paradigm studied, there may also be reduced coupling of amygdala to brainstem regions involved in the fear response (Kirsch *et al.* 2005), or decreased activation in regions involved in facial recognition (Petrovic *et al.* 2008). However, further work is needed to determine whether such effects are also seen during combined treatment of clinical disorders.

While laboratory studies give insight into general cognitive-affective processes, they may not necessarily be devised with specific clinical conditions in mind. Given the role of OT and AVP in social interaction, these peptides have been postulated to play a role in autism (Hammock and Young 2006). OT may be decreased in autism and association studies have suggested a role for OT receptor variants in autism (Israel *et al.* 2008). Arginine vasopressin 1a receptor (AVPR1a) knockout mice have social dysfunction that is redolent of autism, and both linkage and association data in clinical samples have pointed to involvement of AVPR1a in autism (Hammock and Young 2006). However, there is also some evidence that these neuropeptides or their receptors may play a role in a broad range of other psychiatric conditions, including schizophrenia, post-traumatic stress disorder, obsessive-compulsive disorder, depression, and substance use disorders (Stein 2009). Thus, should OT be found useful as part of combined treatment, study of a broad range of conditions may be relevant. Combination strategies using OT are further discussed in Chapter 8.

EVIDENCE FOR COMBINATION THERAPY IN ANXIETY DISORDERS

Although a psychobiological perspective may be used to support the combination of some pharmacotherapies and psychotherapies, and although laboratory research has provided a basis for the development of specific agents to augment exposure based therapies in the clinic, ultimately the proof of the pudding is, of course, in the eating. In this section, we briefly review some of the clinical data on combined treatments in anxiety disorders, in order to draw some general conclusions regarding work in this area. Later chapters in this book will discuss combination strategies with specific agents in further detail; Chapter 2 will discuss benzodiazepines, Chapter 3 will discuss tricyclics and monoamine oxidase inhibitors, and Chapter 4 will discuss selective serotonin re-uptake inhibitors, reversible inhibitors of monomine oxidase-A, and buspirone.

Panic Disorder

A relatively large number of studies of combined pharmacotherapy (i.e. antidepressants or benzodiazepines, plus CBT) have been undertaken in panic disorder. An early meta-analysis indicated that 20 studies provided data on the efficacy of combined treatment compared to psychotherapy. Combined treatment was found to be slightly more effective than CBT alone. However, in those studies which included a follow-up, there was no significant difference between a combination approach and CBT alone (Mitte 2005). A subsequent meta-analysis reviewing trials, combining antidepressants with CBT for panic disorder (Furukawa *et al.* 2007), confirmed that during short-term treatment, combination therapy was more effective than single modality treatment, and found that during long-term follow-up, combined treatment was as effective as psychotherapy alone, and was more effective than pharmacotherapy alone.

Bandelow *et al.* (2007) have emphasized that by using different methods, meta-analyses of treatments in anxiety disorders may reach different conclusions. In their meta-analysis of combined treatments for different anxiety disorders, they restricted their analysis to studies which directly compared pharmacotherapy, psychotherapy, or the combination of these therapeutic modalities. Furukawa *et al.* concluded that combined pharmacological and psychological treatment was superior to monotherapy for panic disorder. Effect sizes range between $d = 0.23$ and $d = 0.61$ (which corresponds to small to medium effect sizes, Cohen 1988), thus indicating that combined therapy is the most effective treatment strategy.

Medications studied in combination with CBT for panic disorder are, however, heterogenous, including various antidepressants, buspirone, and benzodiazepines (Marks *et al.* 1993; Cottraux *et al.* 1995; Barlow *et al.* 2000). Although there are arguably too few studies of combined benzodiazepines and CBT in panic disorder to draw definitive conclusions (Watanabe *et al.* 2009), a study with alprazolam showed that improvements made early in combined treatment were lost when alprazolam was tapered off (Barlow *et al.* 2000). However, improvements made in the groups receiving CBT alone, or placebo alone, were maintained. This finding suggests that alprazolam weakens the effects of CBT, perhaps due to interference with learning or suppression of affect during exposure therapy (Black 2006; Hofmann 2006; Otto *et al.* 2010).

More recently, DCS has been combined with exposure-based CBT for panic disorder (Otto et al. 2010). The results indicated large effect sizes for the additive benefit of DCS augmentation, consistent with the view that DCS consolidates extinction memory. The authors also emphasized that this was the first DCS study to have emphasized exposure to feared internal sensations (i.e. interoceptive exposure). Furthermore, the treatment targeted participants who in most cases were refractory to previous pharmacotherapy. A more recent trial was unable to show a significant additive benefit of DCS to panic disorder due to the fact that patients responded well to CBT; however, there was evidence that in more severely measure ill patients, DCS accelerated symptom reduction in the primary outcome (Siegmund et al. 2011).

Social Anxiety Disorder

Sertraline, fluoxetine, phenelzine, and moclobemide are some of the medications that have been studied in combination with CBT for the treatment of social anxiety disorder (Blomhoff et al. 2001; Davidson et al. 2004; Prasko et al.2006; Blanco et al. 2010). Early meta-analysis found that there was insufficient data to demonstrate an advantage for combined over unimodal treatment (Bandelow et al. 2007). However, in the largest of the comparative studies, combined phenelzine and CBT treatment was superior to either treatment alone (Blanco et al. 2010). Furthermore, as discussed below, combined treatment is more effective than unimodal therapy in children and adolescents with social anxiety disorder (Walkup et al. 2008).

However, few of these studies of combined treatment for social anxiety disorder have compared outcomes in acute and long-term treatment. The sertraline study suggested that a combination of treatment and exposure therapy had enhanced efficacy (Blomhoff et al. 2001), but this did not hold true over a 1-year follow-up (Haug et al. 2003). The moclobemide study followed-up participants over 2 years (Prasko et al.2006). Although there were no significant advantages between the groups in the first 3 months, the combined treatment group had quicker onset of symptom reduction. The moclobemide group showed a greater reduction in subjective anxiety over the 3 months, while the CBT group showed a greater reduction in avoidant behavior. However, by 6 months, there was no significant difference in outcomes between the groups.

Social anxiety disorder, like other anxiety disorders, is a heterogeneous condition. Most pharmacotherapy studies have focused on patients with generalized social anxiety disorder. Nevertheless, there are reports of the efficacy of both pharmacotherapy and psychotherapy in patients with specific performance phobia, and it would be useful to assess the relative efficacy of combined treatments in this condition.

Of particular interest to translational medicine, two studies have now found that DCS has an additive advantage to exposure-based CBT for social anxiety disorder (Hofmann *et al.* 2006; Guastella *et al.* 2008). Controlled effect sizes in this work were in the medium to large range. In their meta-analysis of the early literature on DCS in the augmentation of CBT, Norberg *et al.* (2008) suggested that DCS may be useful early in treatment. However, further work with larger samples is clearly needed to fully demonstrate the therapeutic profile of DCS in social anxiety disorder, and to determine predictors of response.

Generalized Anxiety Disorder

There are too few studies that have combined psychotherapy and pharmacotherapy in the treatment of generalized anxiety disorder to reach definitive conclusions (Bandelow *et al.* 2007). In a study of buspirone and various forms of anxiety treatment, combined treatment conferred some additional benefits (Lader and Bond 1998). In one study of diazepam and CBT, the combined treatment was superior to the drug alone, but with a smaller effect in comparison to CBT plus placebo, and inconsistent findings for the combined treatment in comparison to CBT alone (Power *et al.* 1990). Additional work is clearly needed in this area.

Walkup *et al.* (2008) conducted a study of combination treatment in children and adolescents with various anxiety disorders, including GAD, separation anxiety disorder, and social anxiety disorder. In this study, the combination of CBT and sertraline was significantly more effective than either treatment modality alone for each of these anxiety disorders. This finding raises the important question of whether combined treatments are equally effective at different development stages; it may, for example, be hypothesized that combined treatments are most effective at developmental periods when neuroplasticity is highest.

The literature on combined treatment for GAD also questions the use of an integrated approach to help improve outcomes of benzodiazepine discontinuation. Cognitive-behavioral treatment has shown efficacy in preventing relapse and facilitating BZ discontinuation in panic disorder (Otto *et al.* 1993; 2002; Spiegel *et al.* 1994). CBT provides specific efficacy for the successful discontinuation from BZs, even when controlling for therapist contact and relaxation training (Otto *et al.* 2010). Similarly, CBT appears useful in preventing relapse and increasing the tolerability of withdrawal in patients with GAD (Gosselin *et al.* 2006).

Post-traumatic Stress Disorder

A meta-analysis of trials of combined pharmacotherapy and psychotherapy for post-traumatic stress disorder found four trials eligible for inclusion (Hetrick et al. 2010). All used an SSRI and prolonged exposure or a cognitive behavioral intervention. Two trials compared combination treatment with pharmacological treatment and two compared combination treatment with psychological treatment. There was no strong evidence to show group differences. The authors concluded that there is not enough evidence available to support or refute the effectiveness of combined psychological therapy and pharmacotherapy compared to either of these interventions alone.

The literature on combined treatment in PTSD also questions how the sequencing of combined treatments affects outcome. In one study, CBT was added to sertraline in PTSD subjects who had already demonstrated a poor response to sertraline alone, and combined treatment was effective in these treatment-refractory patients (Otto et al. 2003). However, in PTSD patients who were symptomatic after prolonged exposure therapy, the addition of paroxetine was no more effective than placebo (Simon et al. 2008). Further work is needed to determine what specific individual factors predict response to combined and sequenced treatments. In the interim, when combining modalities, clinicians need to weigh up a range of considerations, including issues of counter-transference, and the possible symbolic meaning of medications for both therapists and patients (Southwick and Yehuda 1993).

The developmental of good animal models of PTSD will hopefully facilitate the translation of combined treatment approaches from 'bench to bedside' (Harvey et al. 2004; Cohen and Zohar 2004). Clearly, there is a prima facie case for considering the use of DCS in the combined treatment of PTSD (Choi et al. 2010; Ganasen et al. 2010). In addition, approaches which focus on the use of glucorticoid and other neuroendocrine and neuropeptide targets are worthy of further investigation in the clinical setting (Cohen et al. 2008; Kaplan and Moore 2011).

Obsessive-Compulsive Disorder

Medications studied in combination with CBT in treatment of obsessive-compulsive disorder include clomipramine and fluvoxamine (Marks et al. 1980; Cottraux et al. 1990; Hohagen et al. 1998; van Balkom et al. 1998; Foa et al. 2005). The combined results from these studies provide little evidence that combined treatment is better than monotherapy in obsessive-compulsive disorder (OCD). Nevertheless, individual studies have suggested that combined treatment, perhaps with more intensive CBT, may be more effective (Hohagen et al. 1998; Foa et al. 2005). As with PTSD, it may be particularly relevant to consider the use of an augmentation approach in those patients who are treatment-refractory.

Unfortunately, studies of DCS in OCD have also not been entirely persuasive (Kushner et al. 2007; Storch et al. 2007; Wilhelm et al. 2008). Obsessive-compulsive disorder arguably has different psychobiologic underpinnings from other anxiety disorders. Perhaps the investigation of more specific animal models of OCD at the bench, will ultimately lead to specific targets for combined treatments at the bedside (Joel et al. 2008).

As with PTSD, another important possible target of CBT in combination therapy for OCD is in addressing cognitive distortions about medication (Julius et al. 2009). For example, patients with OCD may view their medication as somehow 'contaminated.' Or some patients with religious obsessions may view their medications as somehow contributing to their inability to remain 'pure.' In general, there is little literature on how schemas and their products (cognitions, affects) may influence patients' attitudes toward medication, and therapeutic responses to pharmacotherapy (Pontoski 2010).

CONCLUSION

Anxiety disorders can take pride in a number of aspects of research on combined treatments for these conditions. First, there is a long tradition of systematically comparing pharmacotherapy, psychotherapy, and their combination in anxiety disorders (Westra 1998). This work is arguably more rigorous and extensive for anxiety disorders than for most other psychiatric disorders. Second, the first work comparing the mediating functional neuro-anatomy of pharmacotherapy versus psychotherapy was undertaken in an anxiety disorder (Baxter et al. 1992). This tradition of research continues, and there is data on the comparative effects of pharmacotherapy and psychotherapy on a number of anxiety disorders. Third, laboratory discoveries on fear extinction led to the first exemplar of a translational approach to combined treatments in psychiatry (Davis et al. 2005). A range of ongoing work is attempting to move from bench to bedside to optimize combined treatment approaches in anxiety disorders (Hofmann et al. 2011).

However, the number of trials comparing pharmacotherapy, psychotherapy, and combined treatments remains rather limited. In addition, almost all of this work has been undertaken in highly specialized centers with adult patients with a single disorder, and there is a real need for extension to more complex populations, including different age groups, with effectiveness and cost-efficiency trials in real-world settings. Second, our understanding of the psychobiological mechanisms underlying pharmacotherapy and psychotherapy of anxiety disorders remains limited. More work is needed in order to understand fully the relevant neurocircuitry and molecular mechanisms, as well as contributing genetic and epigenetic variance, so that additional targets for the full range of anxiety disorders and their subtypes are developed. Finally, translational work is at an early stage with many questions regarding which disorders respond best to which augmenting agents, optimal timing and dosing of these agents, and long-term efficacy and effectiveness in real-world settings.

Finding resources for conducting larger trials, in the absence of industry support, will be a challenge.

From a practical perspective, meta-analysis of combined pharmacotherapy and psychotherapy treatments are perhaps disappointing, in that they show only limited benefits for combined treatments. However, meta-analyses are only as good as the contributing studies, and given the heterogeneity of this work, the conclusions are perhaps not surprising. Furthermore, a number of clinically relevant conclusions also flow from this literature. First, not all pharmacotherapies and psychotherapies should be combined; there is some reason, for example, to be cautious about using benzodiazepines with CBT. Second, the effects of combined treatments may vary at different points in time, both during development and during the course of an illness; the early clinical rule of thumb that medications work quicker, while CBT lasts longer, may have some truth, although not all data are supportive (Bandelow *et al.* 2007). Third, it is important to consider the optimal sequencing of pharmacotherapy and psychotherapy. Although there are admittedly few research data that support particular sequences of pharmacotherapy and psychotherapy in anxiety disorders (Fava *et al.* 2005; Simon *et al.* 2009), it may be hypothesized, for example, that some patients respond better to CBT once their anxiety is somewhat diminished by pharmacotherapy.

A particularly important lesson, from the work on combined treatment, is that an integrated approach to understanding patients and their disorders is needed. Clearly, advances at the intersection of gene x environmental studies, or studies of the association between gene variants and brain imaging, have emphasized the importance of understanding the contribution of multiple causal mechanisms to psychopathology. Translational neuroscience of combined treatment has provided proof-of-principle evidence that, as we better understand the psychobiology of psychiatric disorders, we will be able to optimize the development of integrated treatments. A translational approach to understanding the placebo effect may further contribute to enhanced treatments (Stein and Mayberg 2005; Furukawa *et al.* 2007). Taken together, although we clearly need to be cautious about the extent of our progress to date, we can be hopeful that over time, there will be further developments in the crucially important area of anxiety disorders. The remaining chapters provide a comprehensive overview of current progress and future directions.

REFERENCES

Anderson, K. C. and Insel, T. R. (2006). The promise of extinction research for the prevention and treatment of anxiety disorders. *Biological Psychiatry*, 60: 319–321.

Bandelow, B. and Ruther, E. (2004). Treatment-resistant panic disorder. *CNS Spectrums*, 9: 725–739.

Bandelow, B., Seidler-Brandler, U., Becker, A., Wedekind, D., and Ruther, E. (2007). Meta-analysis of randomized controlled comparisons of psychopharmacological and psychological treatments for anxiety disorders. *World Journal of Biological Psychiatry*, 8: 175–187.

Barlow, D. H., Gorman, J. M., Shear, M. K., and Woods, S. W. (2000). Cognitive-behavioral therapy, imipramine, or their combination for panic disorder: A randomized controlled trial. *JAMA*, 283: 2529–2536.

Baumgartner, T., Heinrichs, M., Vonlanthen, A., Fischbacher, U., and Fehr, E. (2008). Oxytocin shapes the neural circuitry of trust and trust adaptation in humans. *Neuron*, 58: 639–650.

Baxter, L.R., Schwartz, J.M., Bergman, K.S., Szuba, M.P., Guze, B.H. (1992). Caudate Glucose Metabolic Rate Changes With Both Drug and Behavior Therapy for Obsessive-Compulsive Disorder. *Arch Gen Psychiatry*, 49: 681–689.

Black, D. W. (2006). Efficacy of combined pharmacotherapy and psychotherapy versus monotherapy in the treatment of anxiety disorders. *CNS Spectrums*, 11: 29–33.

Blanco, C., Heimberg, R. G., Schneier, F. R. *et al.* (2010). A placebo-controlled trial of phenelzine, cognitive behavioral group therapy, and their combination for social anxiety disorder. *Archives of General Psychiatry*, 67: 286–295.

Blomhoff, S., Haug, T. T., Hellstrom, K. *et al.* (2001). Randomised controlled general practice trial of sertraline, exposure therapy and combined treatment in generalised social phobia. *British Journal of Psychiatry*, 179: 23–30.

Brody, A. L., Saxena, S., Schwartz, J. M. *et al.* (1998). FDG-PET predictors of response to behavioral therapy and pharmacotherapy in obsessive compulsive disorder. *Psychiatry Research*, 84: 1–6.

Cahill, L. and McGaugh, J. L. (1996). The neurobiology of memory for emotional events: adrenergic activation and the amygdala. *Proceedings of the West Pharmacological Society*, 39: 81–84.

Cain, C.K., Blouin, A.M., Barad, M. (2004). Adrenergic transmission facilitates extinction of conditional fear in mice. *Learn. Mem.*, 11: 179–187.

Carey, P. D., Warwick, J., Niehaus, D. J. *et al.* (2004). Single photon emission computed tomography (SPECT) of anxiety disorders before and after treatment with citalopram. *BMC Psychiatry* 4: 30.

Charney, D. S. (2003). Neuroanatomical circuits modulating fear and anxiety behaviors. *Acta Psychiatria Scandinavica, Supplement* 38–50.

Choi, D.C., Rothbaum, B.O., Gerardi, M., Ressler, K.J. (2010). Pharmacological enhancement of behavioral therapy: focus on posttraumatic stress disorder. *Curr. Top. Behav Neurosci.*, 2: 279–299.

Cohen, J. (1988). *Statistical Power Analysis for the Behavioral Sciences*, 2nd edn. Hillsdale, NJ: Lawrence Erlbaum Associates.

Cohen, H. and Zohar, J. (2004). An animal model of post-traumatic stress disorder: the use of cut-off behavioral criteria. *Annals of the New York Academy of Science*, 1032: 167–178.

Cohen, H., Matar, M. A., Buskila, D., Kaplan, Z., and Zohar, J. (2008). Early poststressor intervention with high-dose corticosterone attenuates post-traumatic stress response in an animal model of posttraumatic stress disorder. *Biological Psychiatry*, 64: 708–717.

Cordero, M.I., Sandi, C. (1998). A role for brain glucocorticoid receptors in contextual fear conditioning: dependence upon training intensity. *Brain Res*, 786: 11–17.

Cottraux, J., Mollard, E., Bouvard, M. et al. (1990). A controlled study of fluvoxamine and exposure in obsessive-compulsive disorder. *International Clinical Psychopharmacology*, 5: 17–30.

Cottraux, J., Note, I. D., Cungi, C. et al. (1995). A controlled study of cognitive behaviour therapy with buspirone or placebo in panic disorder with agoraphobia. *British Journal of Psychiatry*, 167: 635–641.

Davis, M., Falls, W. A., Campeau, S., and Kim, M. (1993). Fear-potentiated startle: a neural and pharmacological analysis. *Behavorial Brain Research*, 58: 175–198.

Davis, M., Myers, K. M., Ressler, K. J., and Rothbaum, B. O. (2005). Facilitation of extinction of conditioned fear by D-cycloserine – Implications for psychotherapy. *Current Directions in Psychological Science*, 14: 214–219.

Davis, M., Ressler, K., Rothbaum, B. O., and Richardson, R. (2006). Effects of D-cycloserine on extinction: Translation from preclinical to clinical work. *Biological Psychiatry*, 60: 369–375.

Domes, G., Heinrichs, M., Glascher, J., Buchel, C., Braus, D. F., and Herpertz, S. C. (2007). Oxytocin attenuates amygdala responses to emotional faces regardless of valence. *Biological Psychiatry*, 62: 1187–1190.

Domes, G., Heinrichs, M., Michel, A., Berger, C., and Herpertz, S. C. (2007). Oxytocin improves 'mind-reading' in humans. *Biological Psychiatry*, 61: 731–733.

Donaldson, Z. R. and Young, L. J. (2008). Oxytocin, vasopressin, and the neurogenetics of sociality. *Science*, 322: 900–904.

Etkin, A. and Wager, T. D. (2007). Functional neuro-imaging of anxiety: a meta-analysis of emotional processing in PTSD, social anxiety disorder, and specific phobia. *American Journal of Psychiatry*, 164: 1476–1488.

Fava, G. A., Ruini, C., and Rafanelli, C. (2005). Sequential treatment of mood and anxiety disorders. *Journal of Clinical Psychiatry*, 66: 1392–1400.

Foa, E. B., Franklin, M. E., and Moser, J. (2002). Context in the clinic: How well do cognitive-behavioral therapies and medications work in combination? *Biological Psychiatry*, 10: 987–997.

Foa, E. B., Liebowitz, M. R., Kozak, M. J. et al. (2005). Randomized, placebo-controlled trial of exposure and ritual prevention, clomipramine, and their combination in the treatment of obsessive-compulsive disorder. *American Journal of Psychiatry*, 162: 151–161.

Frewen, P. A., Dozois, D. J., and Lanius, R. A. (2008). Neuro-imaging studies of psychological interventions for mood and anxiety disorders: Empirical and methodological review. *Clinical Psychology Review*, 28: 228–246.

Furmark, T., Tillfors, M., Marteinsdottir, I. et al. (2002). Common changes in cerebral blood flow in patients with social phobia treated with citalopram or cognitive-behavioral therapy. *Archives of General Psychiatry*, 59: 425–433.

Furmark, T., Appel, L., Michelgard, A. et al. (2005). Cerebral blood flow changes after treatment of social phobia with the neurokinin-1 antagonist GR205171, citalopram, or placebo. *Biological Psychiatry*, 58: 132–142.

Furukawa, T. A., Watanabe, N., Churchill, R. (2007). Combined psychotherapy plus antidepressants for panic disorder with or without agoraphobia. *Cochrane. Database. Syst. Rev.*, CD004364.

Furukawa, T., Watanabe, N., Omori, I., and Churchill, R. (2007). Can pill placebo augment cognitive-behavior therapy for panic disorder? *BMC Psychiatry*, 7: 73.

Ganasen, K.A., Ipser, J.C., Stein, D.J. (2010). Augmentation of cognitive behavioral therapy with pharmacotherapy. *Psychiatr Clin North Am*, 33: 687–699.

Guastella, A. J., Richardson, R., Lovibond, P. F. et al. (2008). A randomized controlled trial of D-cycloserine enhancement of exposure therapy for social anxiety disorder. *Biological Psychiatry*, 63(6): 544–549.

Goodwin, R. M. and Gorman, J. M. (2002). Psychopharmacologic treatment of generalized anxiety disorder and the risk of major depression. *American Journal of Psychiatry*, 159: 1935–1937.

Gorman, J.M., Kent, J.M., Sullivan, G.M., Coplan, J.D. (2000). Neuroanatomical hypothesis of panic disorder, revised. *Am J Psychiatry*, 157: 493–505.

Gosselin, P., Ladouceur, R., Morin, C. M., Dugas, M. J., and Baillargeon, L. (2006). Benzodiazepine discontinuation among adults with GAD: a randomized trial of cognitive-behavioral therapy. *Journal of Consulting and Clinical Psychology*, 74: 908–919.

Grillon, C. (2002). Startle reactivity and anxiety disorders: aversive conditioning, context, and neurobiology. *Biological Psychiatry*, 52: 958–975.

Hammock, E. A. D., and Young, L. J. (2006). Oxytocin, vasopressin and pair bonding: implications for autism. *Philosophical Transactions of the Royal Society B-Biological Sciences*, 361: 2187–2198.

Harvey, B. H., Oosthuizen, F., Brand. L., Wegener, G., and Stein, D. J. (2004). Stress-restress evokes sustained iNOS activity and altered GABA levels and NMDA receptors in rat hippocampus. *Psychopharmacology* 175: 494–502.

Haug, T. T., Blomhoff, S., Hellström, K. et al. (2003). Exposure therapy and sertraline in social phobia: 1-year follow-up of a randomised controlled trial. *British Journal of Psychiatry*, 182: 312–318.

Hetrick, S. E., Purcell, R., Garner, B., and Parslow, R. (2010). Combined pharmacotherapy and psychological therapies for post-traumatic stress disorder (PTSD). *Cochrane Database Sysems Review 2010*; CD007316.

Hofmann, S. G., Meuret, A. E. Smits, J. A. J. et al. (2006). Augmentation of exposure therapy with D-cycloserine for social anxiety disorder. *Archives of General Psychiatry*, 63: 298–304.

Hofmann, S. G., Sawyer, A. T., Korte, K. J., and Smits, J. A. J. (2009). Is it beneficial to add pharmacotherapy to cognitive-behavioral therapy when treating anxiety disorders? A meta-analytic review. *International Journal of Cognitive Therapy*, 2: 160–175.

Hofmann, S. G., Smits, J. A. J., Asnaani, A., Gutner, C. A., and Otto, M. W. (2011). Cognitive enhancers for anxiety disorders. *Pharmacology, Biochemistry, and Behavior*, 99: 275–284.

Hohagen, F., Winkelmann, G., Rasche-Ruchle, H. et al. (1998). Combination of behaviour therapy with fluvoxamine in comparison with behaviour therapy and placebo. Results of a multicentre study. *British Journal of Psychiatry*, Supplement 71–78.

Insel, T. R. (2003). Is social attachment an addictive disorder? *Physiology & Behavior*, 79: 351–357.

Ipser, J. C. and Stein, D. J. (2009). A systematic review of the quality and impact of anxiety disorder meta-analyses. *Current Psychiatry Reports*, 1: 302–309.

Israel, S., Lerer, E., Shalev, I. et al. (2008). Molecular genetic studies of the arginine vasopressin 1a receptor (AVPR1a) and the oxytocin receptor (OXTR) in human behaviour: From autism to altruism with some notes in between. In: Inga DNaR (ed.), *Progress in Brain Research Advances in Vasopressin and Oxytocin – From Genes to Behaviour to Disease*. Amsterdam, Elsevier: 435–449.

Joel, D., Stein, J., and Schreiber, R. (2008). Animal models of obsessive-compulsive disorder: from bench to bedside via endophenotypes and biomarkers. In: A. M. Robert and B. Franco (eds), *Animal and Translational Models for CNS Drug Discovery*. San Diego, Academic Press: 133–164.

Julius, R. J., Novitsky, M. A., and Dubin, W. R. (2009). Medication adherence: a review of the literature and implications for clinical practice. *Journal of Psychiatric Practice*, 15: 34–44.

Kaplan, G. B. and Moore, K. A. (2011). The use of cognitive enhancers in animal models of fear extinction. *Pharmacological Biochemical Behavior*, 99: 217–228.

Kessler, R. C., Ruscio, A. M., Shear, K., and Wittchen, H. U. (2010). Epidemiology of anxiety disorders. *Current Topics in Behavioral Neuroscience*, 2: 21–35.

Kirsch, P., Esslinger, C., Chen, Q. *et al.* (2005). Oxytocin modulates neural circuitry for social cognition and fear in humans. *Journal of Neuroscience*, 25: 11489–11493.

Kosfeld, M., Heinrichs, M., Zak, P. J., Fischbacher, U., and Fehr, E. (2005). Oxytocin increases trust in humans. *Nature*, 435: 673–676.

Krystal, J.H. (2007). Neuroplasticity as a target for the pharmacotherapy of psychiatric disorders: new opportunities for synergy with psychotherapy. *Biol. Psychiatry*, 62: 833–834.

Kushner, M. G., Kim, S. W., Donahue, C. *et al.* (2007). D-cycloserine augmented exposure therapy for obsessive-compulsive disorder. *Biological Psychiatry*, 62(8): 835–838.

Lader, M. H. and Bond. A. J. (1998). Interaction of pharmacological and psychological treatments of anxiety. *British Journal of Psychiatry*, Supplement 42–48.

Ledgerwood, L., Richardson, R., and Cranney, J. (2004). D-cycloserine and the facilitation of extinction of conditioned fear: Consequences for reinstatement. *Behavioral Neuroscience*, 118: 505–513.

Ledgerwood, L., Richardson, R., and Cranney, J. (2005). D-cycloserine facilitates extinction of learned fear: Effects on reacquisition and generalized extinction. *Biological Psychiatry*, 57(8): 841–847.

Lee, H. and Kim, J. J. (1998). Amygdalar NMDA receptors are critical for new fear learning in previously fear-conditioned rats. *Journal of Neuroscience*, 18: 8444–8454.

Lee, J. L., Milton, A.L., and Everitt, B. J. (2006). Reconsolidation and extinction of conditioned fear: Inhibition and potentiation. *Journal of Neuroscience*, 26: 10051–10056.

Lopez, A. D., Mathers, C. D., Ezzati, M., Jamiso, D. T., and Murray, C. J. L. (2006). *Global Burden of Disease and Risk Factors*. New York: Oxford University Press and the World Bank.

Lueken, U., Kruschwitz, J. D., Muehlhan M., Siegert, J., Hoyer, J., and Wittchen, H. U. (2011). How specific is specific phobia? Different neural response patterns in two subtypes of specific phobia. *Neuroimage*, May. 1: 363–372.

Lupien, S. J. and McEwen, B. S. (1997). The acute effects of corticosteroids on cognition: integration of animal and human model studies. *Brain Research Review*, June: 1–27.

Marks, I. M., Stern, R. S., Mawson, D., Cobb, J., and McDonald, R. (1980). Clomipramine and exposure for obsessive-compulsive rituals. *British Journal of Psychiatry*, 136: 1–25.

Marks, I. M., Swinson, R. P., Basoglu, M. *et al.* (1993). Alprazolam and exposure alone and combined in panic disorder with agoraphobia. A controlled study in London and Toronto. *British Journal of Psychiatry*, 162: 776–787.

Mayberg, H. (2002). Depression, II: Localization of pathophysiology. *American Journal of Psychiatry*, 159: 1979–1979.

Mitte, K. (2005). A meta-analysis of the efficacy of psycho- and pharmacotherapy in panic disorder with and without agoraphobia. *J Affect. Disord.*, 2005: 27–45.

Nemeroff, C. B., Heim, C. M., Thase, M. E. *et al*. (2003). Differential responses to psychotherapy versus pharmacotherapy in patients with chronic forms of major depression and childhood trauma. *Proceedings of the National Academy of Science USA*, 100: 14293–14296.

Norberg, M. M., Krystal, J. H., and Tolin, D. F. (2008). A meta-analysis of D-cycloserine and the facilitation of fear extinction and exposure therapy. *Biological Psychiatry*, 63: 1118–1126.

Oitzl, M. S. and de Kloet, E. R. (1992). Selective corticosteroid antagonists modulate specific aspects of spatial orientation learning. *Behavioral Neuroscience*, February: 62–71.

Otto, M. W., Pollack, M. H., Sachs, G. S., Reiter, S. R., Meltzer-Brody, S., and Rosenbaum, J. F. (1993). Discontinuation of benzodiazepine treatment: efficacy of cognitive-behavioral therapy for patients with panic disorder. *American Journal of Psychiatry*, 150: 1485–1490.

Otto, M. W., Hong, J. J., and Safren, S. A. (2002). Benzodiazepine discontinuation difficulties in panic disorder: Conceptual model and outcome for cognitive-behavior therapy. *Current Pharmaceutical Design*, 8: 75–80.

Otto, M. W., Smits, J. A. J., and Reese, H. E. (2005). Combined psychotherapy and pharmacotherapy for mood and anxiety disorders in adults: Review and analysis. *Clinical Psychology: Science and Practice*, 12: 72–86.

Otto, M. W., Basden, S. L., Leyro, T. M., McHugh, R. K., and Hofmann, S. G. (2007). Clinical perspectives on the combination of D-cycloserine and cognitive-behavioral therapy for the treatment of anxiety disorders. *CNS Spectrums*, 12: 51–61.

Otto, M.W., Hinton, D., Korbly, N.B., Chea, A., Ba, P., Gershuny, B.S., Pollack, M. H. (2003). Treatment of pharmacotherapy-refractory posttraumatic stress disorder among Cambodian refugees: a pilot study of combination treatment with cognitive-behavior therapy vs sertraline alone. *Behav Res Ther*, 41: 1271–1276.

Otto, M. W., Smits, J. A. J., and Reese, H. E. (2010). Combined pharmacotherapy and cognitive-behavioral therapy for anxiety Disorders: medication effects, glucocorticoids, and attenuated treatment outcomes. *Clinical Psychology: Science and Practice*, 17: 91–103.

Pallanti, S., Hollander, E., Bienstock, C. *et al*. (2002). Treatment non-response in OCD: methodological issues and operational definitions. *International Journal of Neuropsychopharmacology*, 5: 181–191.

Petrovic, P., Kalisch, R., Singer, T., and Dolan, R. J. (2008). Oxytocin attenuates affective evaluations of conditioned faces and amygdala activity. *Journal of Neuroscience*, 28: 6607–6615.

Pontoski, K. E. H. R. (2010). The Myth of the Superiority of Concurrent Combined Treatments for Anxiety Disorders. *Clin Psychol Sci Prac*, 17: 107–111.

Power, K.G., Simpson, R.J., Swanson, V., Wallace, L.A., Feistner, A.T.C., Sharp, D. (1990). A controlled comparison of cognitive- behaviour therapy, Diazepam, and placebo, alone and in combination, for the treatment of generalised anxiety disorder. *J Anxiety. Disord.*, 4: 267–292.

Powers, M.B., Smits, J.A., Otto, M.W., Sanders, C., Emmelkamp, P.M. (2009). Facilitation of fear extinction in phobic participants with a novel cognitive enhancer: a randomized placebo controlled trial of yohimbine augmentation. *J Anxiety. Disord.*, 23: 350–356.

Prasko, J., Dockery, C., Horacek, J. *et al.* (2006). Moclobemide and cognitive behavioral therapy in the treatment of social phobia. A six-month controlled study and 24 months follow-up. *Neuro Endocrinology Letters*, 27: 473–81.

Ressler, K. J., Rothbaum, B. O., Tannenbaum, L. *et al.* (2004). Cognitive enhancers as adjuncts to psychotherapy – Use of D-cycloserine in phobic individuals to facilitate extinction of fear. *Archives of General Psychiatry*, 61: 1136–1144.

Riba, M. B., Balon, R. (2005). Competency in Combining Pharmacotherapy and Psychotherapy: Integrated and Split Treatment. Washington; London: American Psychiatric Publishing.

Roffman, J. L., Marci, D., Glick, D. M., Dougherty, D. D., and Rauch, S. L. (2005). Neuro-imaging and the functional neuroanatomy of psychotherapy. *Psychological Medicine*, 35: 1385–1398.

Roozendaal, B. and McGaugh, J. L. (1996). Amygdaloid nuclei lesions differentially affect glucocorticoid-induced memory enhancement in an inhibitory avoidance task. *Neurobiology of Learning and Memory*, January: 1–8.

Shin, L. M. and Liberzon, I. (2010). The neurocircuitry of fear, stress, and anxiety disorders. *Neuropsychopharmacology*, 35: 169–191.

Siegmund, A., Köster, L., Meves, A. M., Plag, J., Stoy, M., and Ströhle, A. (2011). Stress hormones during flooding therapy and their relationship to therapy outcome in patients with panic disorder and agoraphobia. *Journal of Psychiatric Research*, 45: 339–346.

Simon, N. M., Connor, K. M., Lang, A. J., Rauch, S. *et al.* (2008). Paroxetine CR augmentation for posttraumatic stress disorder refractory to prolonged exposure therapy. *J Clin Psychiatry*, 69: 400–405.

Simon, N. M., Otto, M. W., Worthington, J. J., Hoge, E. A. *et al.* (2009). Next-step strategies for panic disorder refractory to initial pharmacotherapy: a 3-phase randomized clinical trial. *J Clin Psychiatry*, 70: 1563–1570.

Singewald, N., Salchner, P., Sharp, T. (2003). Induction of c-Fos expression in specific areas of the fear circuitry in rat forebrain by anxiogenic drugs. *Biol. Psychiatry*, 53: 275–283.

Southwick, S. M. and Yehuda, R. (1993). The interaction between pharmacotherapy and psychotherapy in the treatment of posttraumatic stress disorder. *American Journal of Psychotherapy*, 47: 404–410.

Speigel, D. A., Bruce, T. J., Gregg, S. F., and Nuzzarello, A. (1994). Does cognitive behavior therapy assist a slow-taper alprazolam discontinuation in panic disorder? *American Journal of Psychiatry*, 151: 876–881.

Stein, D. J. (2009). Oxytocin and vasopressin: social neuropeptides. *CNS Spectrums*, 14: 602–606.

Stein, D. J. and Mayberg, H. (2005). Placebo: The best pill of all. *CNS Spectrums* 10: 440–442.

Stein, D. J., Van der Kolk, B., Austin, C., Fayyad, R., and Clary, C. (2003). Efficacy of sertraline in post-traumatic stress disorder secondary to interpersonal trauma or childhood abuse. *European Neuropsychopharmacology*, 13: S363–S364.

Stein, D. J., Harvey, B. H., Uys, J., and Daniels, W. (2005). Suffer the children: The psychobiology of early adversity. *CNS Spectrums*, 10: 612–615.

Stein, D. J., van Honk, J., Ipser, J., Solms, M., and Panksepp, J. (2007). Opioidse: From physical pain to the pain of social isolation. *CNS Spectrums* 12: 675.

Storch, E. A., Merlo, L. J., Bengtson, M. *et al.* (2007). D-cycloserine does not enhance exposure-response prevention therapy in obsessive-compulsive disorder. *International of Clinical Psychopharmacology*, 22(4): 230–237.

Storch, E. A., Murphy, T. K., Goodman, W. K. *et al.* (2010). A preliminary study of D-cycloserine augmentation of cognitive-behavioral therapy in pediatric obsessive-compulsive disorder. *Biological Psychiatry*, 68(11): 1073–1076.

Takahashi, L.K., Goh, C.S. (1998). Glucocorticoid facilitation of cholinergic development in the rat hippocampus. *Neuroscience*, 83: 1145–1153.

Uys, J. D. K., Marais, L., Faure, J. *et al.* (2006). Developmental trauma is associated with behavioral hyperarousal, altered HPA axis activity, and decreased hippocampal neurotrophin expression in the adult rat. *Psychobiology of Post-traumatic Stress Disorder: A Decade of Progress*, 1071: 542–546.

van Balkom, A. J., de Haan, E., van Oppen, P., Spinhoven, P., Hoogduin, K. A., and van Dyck, R. (1998). Cognitive and behavioral therapies alone versus in combination with fluvoxamine in the treatment of obsessive compulsive disorder. *Journal of Nervous and Mental Disease*, 186: 492–499.

Walker, D. L., Ressler, K. J., Lu, K. T., and Davis, M. (2002). Facilitation of conditioned fear extinction by systemic administration or intra-amygdala infusions of D-cycloserine as assessed with fear-potentiated startle in rats. *Journal of Neuroscience*, 22: 2343–2351.

Walkup, J. T., Albano, A. M., Piacentini, J. *et al.* (2008). Cognitive behavioral therapy, sertraline, or a combination in childhood anxiety. *New England Journal of Medicine*, 359: 2753–2766.

Watanabe, N., Churchill, R., Furukawa, T.A. (2009). Combined psychotherapy plus benzodiazepines for panic disorder. Cochrane. Database. *Syst. Rev.*, CD005335.

Westra, H. A. (1998). Cognitive behavioral therapy and pharmacotherapy: complimentary or contradictory approaches to the treatment of anxiety. *Clinical Psychology Review*, 18: 307–340.

Wilhelm, S., Buhlmann, U., Tolin, D. F. *et al.* (2008). Augmentation of behavior therapy with D-cycloserine for obsessive-compulsive disorder. *American Journal of Psychiatry*, 165: 335–341.

Yang, Y. L., Lu, K. T. (2005). Facilitation of conditioned fear extinction by d-cycloserine is mediated by mitogen-activated protein kinase and phosphatidylinositol 3-kinase cascades and requires *de novo* protein synthesis in basolateral nucleus of amygdala. *Neuroscience*, 134: 247–260.

Chapter 2

BENZODIAZEPINES

Bridget A. Hearon and Michael W. Otto

Department of Psychology, Boston University, Boston, MA, USA

Benzodiazepines (BZs) represent one of the most widely prescribed classes of medications for the treatment of anxiety disorders over the past 50 years (Macaluso *et al.* 2010). Their rapid onset of action and efficacy coupled with a reasonable side-effect profile has contributed to their use in both the acute and chronic phases of anxiety disorder treatment (Worthington *et al.*1998; Davidson 2004; Cloos and Ferreira 2009). Yet some of the many benefits of BZ medication have been tempered by difficulties with discontinuing chronic treatment (Otto *et al.* 2002), as well as specific concerns about their use in combination with cognitive-behavior therapy (CBT; Otto *et al.* 2010a). These concerns include issues of impairment in learning, impairment in the retention of treatment effects, attribution of treatment gains, as well as medication discontinuation difficulties. In this chapter, we consider the role of BZs in combined treatment with CBT, with attention given to reviewing each of these issues of concern.

THE EFFICACY OF BZ TREATMENT FOR THE ANXIETY DISORDERS

Some of the advantages of BZ treatment include clear efficacy as well as early onset of action (e.g. with initial anxiolytic effects emerging soon after taking the first pill). For example, for the treatment of social anxiety disorder, effects for the benefits of BZ treatment have been particularly strong, and tend to be above those for alternative pharmacotherapies, including antidepressants (Hidalgo *et al.* 2001). For other disorders, such as generalized anxiety disorder, BZs are more recommended during the acute phase of treatment, but appear not to be as effective as antidepressants

---

Psychobiological Approaches for Anxiety Disorders: Treatment Combination Strategies, First Edition.
Edited by Stefan G. Hofmann.
© 2012 John Wiley & Sons, Ltd. Published 2012 by John Wiley & Sons, Ltd.

in the long term (Rickels *et al.* 1993; Lydiard *et al.* 1997; Rocca *et al.* 1997). Indeed, it is the early onset of action of BZ medications that lead to its use in pharmacologic combination treatment – using a BZ for early onset of action while awaiting the onset of anxiety effects from antidepressant medication, typically serotonin-selective reuptake inhibitors (SSRIs). Use of BZs during this time period is also applied to the anxiogenic side effects of SSRIs during the first 2 weeks of treatment. This combination of BZs and SSRIs is popular (Bruce *et al.* 2003; Vasile *et al.* 2005), and often treatment with both pharmacologic agents remains ongoing, despite evidence that any additive benefit may best be realized in the first 2 months of treatment, with equal benefit for patients who had their BZ medication tapered and discontinued compared to those who did not (Goddard *et al.* 2001; Pollack *et al.* 2003).

Indeed, some of the strongest concerns about BZ medication are associated with difficulties during discontinuation, where taper-related withdrawal effects can emerge. For instance, panic patients treated with BZs reported relapse rates greater than 70% upon discontinuation of medication, and even in cases of slow taper, patients still reported considerable difficulties and symptom relapse (Salzman 1993; Michelini *et al.* 1996). Another concern is the abuse potential of BZs, particularly in those with pre-existing substance use disorders (Nunes *et al.* 1995; Michelini *et al.* 1996; Westra *et al.* 2002). These and other concerns about BZ use have led to other treatments (i.e. SSRIs and CBT) to be considered as first-line treatments over BZs by the American Psychiatric Association (APA 1998) and the National Institute for Health and Clinical Excellence (NICE 2004).

COMBINATION TREATMENT: THE WISH AND THE REALITY

There has long been a desire for a combination treatment strategy that takes the strengths of pharmacotherapy and combines it with the efficacy of CBT to provide a particularly powerful intervention. As reviewed elsewhere, this strategy has met with disappointment for combinations of anxiolytics and CBT (Otto *et al.* 2005; 2010a; Hofmann *et al.* 2009). That is, whereas combination treatment does often lead to higher effects than either monotherapy, these combination effects are often disappointing in magnitude (Foa *et al.* 2002; Watanabe *et al.* 2007), are often lost upon medication discontinuation (Otto *et al.*, 2005), and are far from cost effective (e.g. for cost efficacy data for the treatment of panic disorder, see Otto *et al.* 2000; McHugh *et al.* 2007).

Understanding why the combination of CBT and BZs is not a more powerful treatment directs us to important issues in the mechanism of therapeutic learning offered by CBT. Whereas the effects of BZ are specific to the pharmacologic dampening of anxiety, with a return of symptoms upon discontinuation (Heimberg *et al.* 1993; Noyes *et al.* 1991;

Pollack and Smoller 1996), CBT acts by working to change the perceived safety of anxiety cues through the application of informational, cognitive, and experiential (exposure) strategies. One account of these learning effects of CBT attends to the network of associations that characterize feared stimuli. In exposure-based treatment, Foa and Kozak (1986) hypothesize that this fear network becomes activated so that new information can be integrated into this network of meaning – when that new information is incompatible with the fear meaning stored in the memory structure, safety in relation to these feared cues is (re)learned (emotional processing theory. Foa and Kozak (1986) hypothesize that better safety learning will occur with better activation of the fear network combined with stronger integration of incompatible (safety-related) information. Avoidance of fear cues, or the use of anxiolytic medications is hypothesized to interfere with activation of the fear network and incorporation of new information. As a consequence, a patient in combination treatment may experience the benefit of anxiolysis, but may lose some of the benefit of full learning from exposure, thereby producing some additive benefit, but far from the true additive combination of the efficacy of each strategy applied alone.

SPECIFIC BZ EFFECTS ON MEMORY FOR CBT

Recent evidence suggests that impairing effects of anxiolytics on CBT outcome may have additional sources. First, dampening of arousal alone may have few negative effects, given that high anxious arousal is not necessary for exposure efficacy (Pitman *et al.* 1996; Hayes *et al.* 2008;). Second, Otto *et al.* (2010a) have hypothesized that medications commonly used in combination with CBT may affect glucocorticoid activity, which in turn may lead to attenuation of recall of therapeutic learning (extinction) from CBT. Although it was initially believed that cortisol was detrimental to cognition (Newcomer *et al.* 1999; Heffelfinger and Newcomer 2001), more recent evidence suggests that this relationship is far more complex (Lupien *et al.* 2007), and that acute increases in glucocorticoids may play a role in enhancing emotional consolidation and extinction learning. In particular, research in human populations suggests that cortisol is linked to enhanced consolidation of verbal and pictorial memory, especially in the case of emotional stimuli (Buchanan and Lovallo 2001; Cahill *et al.* 2003; Putnam *et al.* 2004; Abercrombie *et al.* 2006; Beckner *et al.* 2006), in addition to facilitation of fear extinction (Soravia *et al.* 2006). A specific facilitative effect of cortisol on extinction learning has recently received additional support in a clinical trial (de Quervain *et al.* 2011) and in observation of the degree of response in patients undergoing treatment (Siegmund *et al.* 2011). For further discussion of the use of cortisol in treatment, see Chapter 7 of this book.

However, BZs are associated with the suppression of cortisol as well as reduced stress-related increases in cortisol (Gram and Christensen 1987; Rohrer *et al.* 1994; Pomara *et al.* 2005; Fries *et al.* 2006), with cortisol decreases noted in both anxiety disordered (Roy-Byrne *et al.* 1991; Abelson *et al.* 1996; Curtis *et al.* 1997) and non-clinical samples (Santagostino *et al.* 1996). Furthermore, animal studies have shown that BZs acting on the amygdala and hippocampus are disruptive to memory consolidation (Tomaz *et al.* 1991; Dickinson-Anson and McGaugh 1997; Da Cunha *et al.* 1999). For example, Evans and Viola-McCabe (1996) noted an inhibition of long-term potentiation, a process important in memory formation, in hippocampal slices following administration of the BZ, midazolam. Therefore, while BZs may provide relief from anxiety-related symptoms in the short term, they are also likely to have detrimental effects on memory consolidation and extinction learning, hindering CBT in the long term.

Disruption of cortisol activity is a concern that extends to both antidepressant and BZ treatments, and hence Otto *et al.* (2010a) identify cortisol suppression as one possible explanation of the way in which combination treatment may hinder some of the effects of CBT. For BZ treatment, there are other memory effects as well.

Acute treatment with BZs has been associated with anterograde amnesia, such that material presented after drug administration is remembered less well in subjects receiving the actual drug as compared to those receiving placebo with deficits shown in both explicit (consciously recalled material) and implicit (remembered without awareness) memory (Sellal *et al.* 1992; Bishop *et al.* 1996; Buffett-Jerrott *et al.* 1998).

Research has documented that BZs can impair memory of personally experienced events as well as episodic memory (Curran 1991; Hommer 1991). For example, Buffett-Jerrott *et al.* (1998a;b) showed movie clips to participants who had ingested either a BZ or placebo. Those in the BZ treatment group showed significant memory impairments when compared to those in the placebo group, indicating possible memory deficits which are not limited to experimental memory paradigms such as recall of stories and word lists, but also include real-life situations such as recalling the details of a popular movie. Likewise, in a study examining the effects of BZ use on memory of psycho-educational material presented in CBT, Westra *et al.* (2004) compared 16 PD patients taking a daily BZ to 16 demographically and severity matched, non-medicated PD patients. Results of this study showed significantly poorer memory performance for those taking BZs, indicating that use of such medications may contribute to the impairment of both the psycho-education and behavioral learning aspects of CBT.

Such memory impairment has been shown to vary by type of BZ used, dose, as well as the timing of memory encoding in relation to dose, with evidence suggesting that higher potency BZs and higher doses lead to greater memory impairment (Weingartner *et al.* 1992; Curran and

Gorenstein 1993). In addition, peak impairment tended to occur for information encoded during peak blood concentration of the drug (Ghoneim et al. 1983; Curran, 1991, 1992). As such, the use of BZs concomitant with exposure therapy may ensure that the degree of learning during CBT is attenuated. Although memory impairment due to BZs may dissipate over time (Curran et al. 1994; Deckersbach et al. in press), their acute use in conjunction with CBT would still be expected to attenuate CBT effects in a combination treatment paradigm. Accordingly, BZs, as used in combination treatment, can be seen as offering the benefit of anxiety management, while also contributing complicating factors due to potential inhibition of therapeutic memories from the CBT. This nicely fits clinical data provided by van Minnen et al. (2002); they examined predictors of treatment outcome and dropout for prolonged exposure treatment of PTSD. In this sample, BZ use predicted a lower rate of patient drop-out but also a lower rate of treatment response.

ADDITIONAL NEGATIVE EFFECTS OF COMBINATION TREATMENT – DISCONTINUATION EFFECTS

So far in this chapter, we have focused on the positive and negative effects of BZs and CBT when they are used in an ongoing fashion together. Additional negative effects may be evident when BZs are later stopped. Under these conditions, the cessation of BZ treatment appears to take with it some of the beneficial effects of CBT, so that in the long term combination treatment fares less well than with CBT alone.

This effect has perhaps been best documented in a multi-site study by Marks et al. (1993), where patients were randomly assigned to combination treatment (the BZ, alprazolam, combined with exposure therapy), exposure therapy plus placebo, alprazolam plus relaxation training (considered psychological placebo), or placebo plus relaxation training (considered a double placebo condition). Eight weeks of these treatment strategies were applied, followed by taper of the study pills. Prior to taper, there was evidence of some enhanced benefits of combination treatment, but following medication taper, many of these gains were lost. Overall, when the loss of benefit with medication discontinuation was considered, exposure had twice the effect size of alprazolam treatment. Moreover, patients in the treatment trial who attributed their gains to alprazolam, had greater loss of treatment effects after discontinuation of the pill. Similar findings for loss of efficacy with medication discontinuation and the attribution of treatment gains are evident for obsessive-compulsive disorder (Başoğlu et al. 1988), post-traumatic stress disorder (PTSD) (Ehlers et al. 1998), and other studies of panic disorder (Biondi and Picardi 2003).

In a particularly clear demonstration of the power of attributions about treatment, Powers et al. (2008) randomized 95 individuals with claustrophobic fears to a single-session exposure treatment alone, a psychological placebo condition, or the single-session exposure treatment in conjunction with a placebo that they were led to believe was:

- a sedating herbal supplement with anxiety-dampening effects;
- a stimulating herbal supplement with anxiogenic effects; or
- a placebo pill with no expected effects on exposure.

Two important results emerged. First, participants in the 'sedating herb' condition rated the pill as being more helpful than participants in the 'stimulating herb' condition. Second, those in the sedating herb condition had a significantly higher return of fear at 1-week follow-up, enough so that they no longer showed benefits relative to the wait-list or psychological placebo conditions. All other conditions (i.e. exposure alone, exposure plus the pill described as stimulating, and exposure plus the pill described as a placebo) maintained their improvement at follow-up. Accordingly, expectation and attribution of medication effects can attenuate the value of therapeutic learning during exposure.

Furthermore, combination treatment appears to sap CBT efficacy by means other than the attribution of gains. In the relearning of safety to phobic cues, both the external and internal context appears to be important. That is, extinction of fear cues does not appear to be global, but to be learned in relation to a context, so that a cue no longer elicits fear under a set of environmental conditions. Relevant contexts can include time of day, physical environment, the presence of important objects or people, as well as internal cues such as emotional or physiological states (Bouton 2002). Animal research indicates that internal states, such as the reduction in anxiety caused by an anxiolytic medication, is a powerful enough contextual cue that extinction (the learning of safety) may only be achieved in that context (Bouton *et al.* 1990). In addition, research in humans has also demonstrated that exposure-based CBT is sensitive to changes in context. For example, Mineka *et al.* (1999) randomly assigned spider phobic individuals to undergo a single session of graded exposure therapy followed 1 week later by an assessment of fear during which context was manipulated. Results indicated increases in self-reported fear when patients were asked to approach a spider in a context different from where exposure therapy took place. Taken together, such results indicate the important role of context in behavioral learning for both animals and humans. Similar results have been achieved with manipulation of internal context with caffeine – a shift in context brought more return fear than remaining in a high or low arousal condition due to caffeine (Mystkowski *et al.* 2003).

In the case of combination treatment, when an internal state is altered due to withdrawal from a BZ, the newly learned safety response that a patient may have acquired through CBT is no longer accessible in the absence of the medication and so the fear response re-emerges. Conversely, for patients who learned safety responses in the context of CBT without medication, internal context does not change and treatment gains are maintained (for clinical examples consistent with this effect, see Marks *et al.* 1993; Barlow *et al.* 2000; Haug *et al.* 2003). Hence, distinct from any memory attenuation effects due to ongoing BZ use, combination treatment efficacy may suffer after the discontinuation of the BZ treatment due to the effects of a shift in internal context.

A MODEL OF COMBINED BZ AND CBT

Given this evidence for limited combined treatment effects and an apparent cost to CBT of the change in context brought by BZ discontinuation, the question arises about how to best use combination treatment. Certainly one model is to use it for patients who otherwise may be reluctant to engage inCBT. For these patients, informational and motivational interventions represent one strategy of facilitating engagement of patients in CBT (Bonner and Everett 1982; Maltby and Tolin 2005; for review see Halperin *et al.* 2010), as are strategies to adjust exposure exercises to individual components to allow acquisition of an initial sense of accomplishment, followed by a more traditional increasing hierarchy of exposures (Murray *et al.* 2010). These strategies are free of drug-related challenges. Nonetheless, combination treatment with BZs continues to be recommended clinically to help patients to feel less overwhelmed by exposure experiences – using the anxiolytic to help the patient become comfortable with and begin to respond differently to cues for anxiety, without an overwhelming anxiety drive. In this use, BZ treatment is applied analogously to nicotine replacement therapy (NRT) in smoking cessation attempts. For smoking cessation, NRT is used to manage the physiological craving brought by smoking cessation (Pollak *et al.* 2007). With the physiological drive for smoking attenuated by NRT, the therapist is free to attend to the behavioral habit aspects of smoking, helping the smoker to develop alternative responses to cues for smoking. As with BZ treatment, with NRT, clinician and patient face the second step of having to later fade the NRT, while trying to maintain adaptive responses to the smoking cues.

Applying the full analogy, a BZ can be used to attenuate the behavioral drive of anxiety during initial exposure exercises, and the therapist can help the patient re-establish an adaptive behavioral repertoire in relation to phobic cues. Second, the clinician needs to help the patient fade their BZ use, while working to maintain and extend their gains from the behavioral therapy. The cost/benefit ratio of this approach depends on both the patient's fearfulness and hesitancy to engage in exposure, the availability of other alternatives or highly skilled CBT clinicians, and the degree of subsequent difficulties fading the BZ use. It is around the fading of BZ use, that a final type of combination treatment needs to be considered.

CBT FOR BZ DISCONTINUATION

As noted, withdrawal symptoms associated with BZ discontinuation are characterized by anxiety-like symptoms similar to those that motivate treatment seeking in the first place (Roy-Byrne and Hommer 1988; Tryer *et al.* 1990). Moreover, for some disorders, these withdrawal symptoms are especially distressing and appear to interact with core fears inherent in the disorder, such as panic disorder (Otto *et al.* 2002; for PTSD, see Risse *et al.* 1990). One strategy to aid successful discontinuation has been the use of short-term CBT to provide patients with specific skills to help cope with the symptoms of withdrawal and signs of disorder relapse. Several studies have provided consistent evidence for success in this area (Otto *et al.* 1993; 2010b; Spiegel *et al.* 1994), with all emphasizing the use of interoceptive exposure (exposure to feared internal sensations) to help patients become resilient to fears of anxiety and withdrawal sensations.

In an initial trial investigating the use of CBT to aid BZ discontinuation, Otto *et al.* (1993) randomized 33 patients with panic disorder to supportive taper or supportive taper plus 10 sessions of CBT specifically targeted at both panic sensations and symptoms associated with BZ withdrawal. Results showed a clear advantage for taper plus CBT augmentation, with only 25% of patients in the taper alone condition maintaining abstinence from medication as opposed to 76% in the CBT condition. Similar results were noted in a study conducted by Speigel *et al.* (1994), in which 20 patients treated successfully with a BZ for panic disorder were randomized to either slow taper or taper plus CBT. At post treatment, there were no differences between the two groups in rates of BZ discontinuation; however, by 6-month follow-up, a significant difference between the two groups emerged, with greater than 75% of patients in the CBT condition successfully discontinued and only 40% of the taper alone condition successfully discontinued. This effect remained intact through long-term follow-up (2–5 years; Bruce *et al.* 1999; see also Hegel *et al.* 1994).

As previous studies had not controlled for differences in therapist contact between conditions, Otto *et al.* (2010b) compared CBT for BZ discontinuation with taper alone and taper plus relaxation training in 47 patients with panic disorder. Results again showed that a significantly greater proportion of patients from the CBT group were able to maintain BZ discontinuation as compared to both the taper alone and relaxation conditions by 6-month follow-up. Taken together, these studies provide support for the use of CBT in BZ discontinuation for panic disorder. Other studies support the application of CBT for other BZ discontinuation targets, including the treatment of generalized anxiety disorder (Gosselin *et al.* 2006) and insomnia (Morin *et al.* 2005).

SUMMARY AND CONCLUSIONS

Although both CBT and BZ treatment demonstrate efficacy in isolation, research to date has not been able to show a dramatic advantage for combined treatment with this approach. Possible reasons for this failure include the attenuation of extinction learning due to effects of BZs on memory and glucocorticoids during combined treatment, and the attribution of treatment gains and context effects impacting treatment outcome during subsequent taper of BZ use. With these multiple sources of negative influences, combination treatment needs to be considered carefully. A model for the judicious use of combined BZ treatment was introduced that includes both an active and a taper phase of BZ treatment. However, this approach may be cost effective only when alternative CBT approaches are not available. Nonetheless, more research is needed on the action of anxiolytics on cortisol-related memory mechanisms, as well as the time course of these effects relative to both acute and chronic use of BZs. That is, negative effects of BZ use on memory may be most evident during acute phase treatment; both cortisol and memory effects appear to subside with time.

Aside from traditional models of combination treatment, much more consistent evidence of success is linked with the use of CBT to help patients who want to discontinue their BZ medication. To date, these approaches as applied to panic disorder, generalized anxiety disorder, and insomnia can help patients maintain or extend their gains while discontinuing chronic BZ treatment. These strategies provide clinicians and patients with a greater number of treatment options, including the use of CBT at later stages of treatment for patients who have already initiated BZ treatment. These strategies may also provide a broader model of treatment of withdrawal symptoms, with the potential for some of these strategies (i.e. interoceptive exposure and cognitive restructuring) to ease sensitivity to withdrawal-related distress for both licit and illicit substances (Otto *et al.* 2004; Feldner *et al.* 2008).

REFERENCES

Abelson, J. L., Curtis, G. C., and Cameron, O. G. (1996). Hypothalamic-pituitary-adrenal axis activity in panic disorder: Effects of alprazolam on 24 h secretion of adrenocorticotropin and cortisol. *Journal of Psychiatric Research*, 30: 79–93.

Abercrombie, H. C., Speck, N. S., and Monticelli, R. M. (2006). Endogenous cortisol elevations are related to memory facilitation only in individuals who are emotionally aroused. *Psychoneuroendocrinology*, 31: 187–196.

American Psychiatric Association (1998). Practice guideline for the treatment of patients with panic disorder. *American Journal of Psychiatry*, 155: 1–34.

Barlow, D. H., Gorman, J. M., Shear, M. K., and Woods, S. W. (2000). Cognitive-behavioral therapy, imipramine, or their combination for panic disorder: a randomized controlled trial. *Journal of the American Medical Association*, 283: 2529–2536.

Başoğlu, M., Marks, I. M., Kiliç, C., Brewin, C. R., and Swinson, R. P. (1994) Alprazolam and exposure for panic disorder with agoraphobia. Attribution of improvement to medication predicts subsequent relapse. *British Journal of Psychiatry*, 164: 652–659.

Başoğlu, M., Lax T., Kasvikis, Y., and Marks, I. M. (1988). Predictors of improvement in obsessive-compulsive disorder. *Journal of Anxiety Disorders*, 2: 299–317.

Beckner, V. E., Tucker, D. M., Delville, Y., and Mohr, D. C. (2006). Stress facilitates consolidation of verbal memory for a film but does not affect retrieval. *Behavioral Neuroscience*, 120: 518–527.

Biondi, M. and Picardi A. (2003). Increased probability of remaining in remission from panic disorder with agoraphobia after drug treatment in patients who received concurrent cognitive behavioural therapy: a follow-up study. *Psychotherapy and Psychosomatics*, 72: 34–42.

Bishop, K. I., Curran, H. V., and Lader, M. (1996). Do scopolamine and lorazepam have dissociable effects on human memory systems? A dose-response study with normal volunteers. *Experimental and Clinical Psychopharmacology*, 4: 292–299.

Bonner, B. L. and Everett, F. L. (1982). Influence of client preparation and therapist prognostic expectations on children's attitudes and expectations of psychotherapy. *Journal of Clinical Child Psychology*, 11, 202–208.

Bouton, M. E. (2002). Context, ambiguity, and unlearning: Sources of relapse after behavioral extinction. *Biological Psychiatry*, 52: 976–986.

Bouton, M. E., Kenney, F. A., and Rosengard, C. (1990). State dependent fear extinction with two benzodiazepine tranquilizers. *Behavioral Neuroscience*, 104: 44–55.

Bruce, S. E., Vasile, R. G., Goisman, R. M. et al. (2003). Are benzodiazepines still the medication of choice for patients with panic disorder with or without agoraphobia? *American Journal of Psychiatry*, 160: 1432–1438.

Bruce, T. J., Spiegel, D. A., and Hegel, M. T. (1999). Cognitive-behavioral therapy helps prevent relapse and recurrence of panic disorder following alprazolam discontinuation: a long-term follow-up of the Peoria and Dartmouth studies. *American Journal of Psychiatry*, 67: 151–156.

Buchanan, T. W. and Lovallo, W. R. (2001). Enhanced memory for emotional material following stress-level cortisol treatment in humans. *Psychoneuroendocrinology*, 26: 307–317.

Buffett-Jerrott, S., Stewart, S. H., Bird, S., and Teehan, M. D. (1998a). An examination of differences in the time course of oxazepam's effect on implicit and explicit memory. *Journal of Psychopharmacology*, 12, 338–347.

Buffett-Jerrott, S., Stewart, S. H., and Teehan, M. D. (1998b). Further evidence for time course influences on the effects of oxazepam and lorazepam on the implicit and explicit memory. *Psychopharmachology*, 138: 344–353.

Cahill, L., Gorski, L. and Le, K. (2003). Enhanced human memory consolidation with post-learning stress: Interaction with the degree of arousal at encoding. *Learning and Memory*, 10, 270–274.

Cloos, J. M. and Ferreira, V. (2009). Current use of benzodiazepines in anxiety disorders. *Current Opinion in Psychiatry*, 22: 90–95.

Curran, H. V. (1991). Benzodiazepines, memory, and mood: a review. *Psychopharmacology*, 105: 1–18.

Curran, H. V. (1992). Memory functions, alertness and mood of long-term benzodiazepine users: A preliminary investigation of the effects of a normal daily dose. *Psychopharmacology*, 6: 69–75.

Curran, H. V. and Gorenstein, C. (1993). Differential effects of lorazepam and oxazepam on priming. *International Clinical Psychopharmacology*, 8: 37–42.

Curran, H. V., Bond, A., O'Sullivan, G., et al. (1994). Memory functions, alprazolam and exposure therapy: a controlled Longitudinal study of agoraphobia with panic disorder. *Psychological Medicine*, 24: 969–976.

Curtis, G. C., Abelson, J. L., and Gold, P. W. (1997). Adrenocorticotropic hormone and cortisol responses to corticotropin-releasing hormone: Changes in panic disorder and effects of alprazolam treatment. *Biological Psychiatry*, 41: 76–85.

Da Cunha, C., Roozendaal, B., Vazdarjanova, A. and McGaugh, J. L. (1999). Microinfusions of flumazenil into the basolateral but not the central nucleus of the amygdala enhance memory consolidation in rats. *Neurobiology of Learning and Memory*, 72: 1–7.

Davidson, J. R. T. (2004). Use of Benzodiazepines in social anxiety disorder, generalized anxiety disorder, and post-traumatic stress. *Journal of Clinical Psychiatry*, 65: 29–33.

Deckersbach, T., Moshier, S. J., and Otto, M. W. (in press). Memory dysfunction in panic disorder: An investigation of the role of chronic benzodiazepine use. *Depression and Anxiety*.

de Quervain, D. J., Bentz, D., Michael, T. et al. (2011). From the cover: Glucocorticoids enhance extinction-based psychotherapy. *Proceedings of the National Academy of Sciences*, 108(16): 6621–6625.

Dickinson-Anson, H. and McGaugh, J. L. (1997). Bicicilline administered into the amygdala after training blocks benzodiazepine induced amnesia. *Brian Research*, 752: 197–202.

Ehlers, A., Mayou, R. A., and Bryant, B. (1998). Psychological predictors of chronic post-traumatic stress disorder after motor vehicle accidents. *Journal of Abnormal Psychology*, 107: 508–519.

Evans, M. S. and Viola-McCabe, K. E. (1996). Midazolam inhibits long-term potentiation through modulation of GABAA receptors. *Neuropharmacology*, 35: 347–357.

Feldner, M. T., Zvolensky, M. J., Babson, K., Leen-Feldner, E. W., and Schmidt, N. B. (2008). An integrated approach to panic prevention targeting the empirically supported risk factors of smoking and anxiety sensitivity: Theoretical basis and evidence from a pilot project evaluating feasibility and short-term efficacy. *Journal of Anxiety Disorders*, 22: 1227–1243.

Foa, E. B. and Kozak, M. J. (1986). Emotional processing of fear: Exposure to corrective information. *Psychological Bulletin*, 99: 20–35.

Foa, E. B., Franklin, M. E., and Moser, J. (2002). Context in the clinic: How well do cognitive-behavioral therapies and medications work in combination? *Biological Psychiatry*, 10: 987–997.

Fries, E., Hellhammer, D. H., and Hellhammer, J. (2006). Attenuation of the hypothalamic-pituitary-adrenal axis responsivity to the Trier Social Stress Test by the benzodiazepine alprazolam. *Psychoneuroendochronology*, 31: 1278–1288.

Ghoneim, M. M., Mewaldt, S. P., Berie, J. L., and Hinrichs, J. V. (1983). Memory performance and effects of single- and three-week administration of diazepam. *Psychopharmacology*, 138: 334–343.

Goddard, A. W., Brouette, T., Almai, A., Jetty, P., Woods, S. W., and Charney, D. (2001). Early co-administration of clonazepam with sertraline for panic disorder. *Archives of General Psychiatry*, 58: 681–686.

Gosselin, P., Ladouceur, R., Morin, C. M., Dugas, M. J., and Baillargeon, L. (2006). Benzodiazepine discontinuation among adults with GAD: a randomized trial of cognitive-behavioral therapy. *Journal of Consulting and Clinical Psychology*, 74: 908–919.

Gram, L. F. and Christensen, P. (1987). Benzodiazepine suppression of cortisol secretion: a measure of anxiolytic activity? *Pharmacopsychiatry*, 19: 19–22.

Halperin, D. M., Weitzman, M. L., and Otto, M. W. (2010). Therapeutic alliance and common factors in treatment. In M. W.Otto and S. G. Hofmann (eds), *Avoiding Treatment Failures in the Anxiety Disorders*. New York, Springer: 51–66.

Haug, T. T., Blomhoff, S., Hellström, K. *et al.* (2003). Exposure therapy and sertraline in social phobia: I-year follow-up of a randomised controlled trial. *British Journal of Psychiatry*, 182: 312–318.

Hayes, S. A., Hope, D. A., and Heimberg, R. G. (2008). The pattern of subjective anxiety during in-session exposures over the course of cognitive-behavioral therapy for clients with social anxiety disorder. *Behavior Therapy*, 39: 286–299.

Heffelfinger, A. K. and Newcomer, J. W. (2001). Glucocorticoid effects on memory function over the human life span. *Developmental Psychopathology*, 13: 491–513.

Hegel, M. T., Ravaris, C. L., and Ahles, T. A. (1994). Combined cognitive-behavioral and time-limited alprazolam treatment of panic disorder. *Behavior Therapy*, 25: 183–195.

Heimberg, R. G., Salzman, D. G., Holt, C. S., and Blendell, K. A. (1993). Cognitive-behavioral group treatment for social phobia: Effectiveness at five-year follow-up. *Cognitive Therapy and Research*, 17: 325–339.

Hidalgo, R. B., Barnett, S., and Davidson, J. R. (2001). Social anxiety disorder in review: two decades of progress. *International Journal of Neuropsychopharmacology*, 4: 279–298.

Hofmann, S. G., Sawyer, A. T., Korte, K. J., and Smits, J. A. J. (2009). Is it beneficial to add pharmacotherapy to cognitive-behavioral therapy when treating anxiety disorders? A meta-analytic review. *International Journal of Cognitive Therapy*, 2: 160–175.

Hommer, D. (1991). Benzodiazepines: Cognitive and psychomotor effects. In P. P. Roy-Byrne and D. S. Cowley (eds), *Benzodiazepines in clinical practice: Risks and benefits*. Washington, DC, American Psychiatric Press: 113–130.

Lupien, S. J., Maheu, F., Tu, M., Fiocco, A., and Schramek, T. E. (2007). The effects of stress and stress hormones on human cognition: Implications for the field of brain and cognition. *Brain and Cognition*, 65: 209–237.

Lydiard, R. B., Ballenger, J. C., and Rickels, K. (1997). A double-blind evaluation of the safety and efficacy of abecarnil, alprazolam, and placebo in outpatients with generalized anxiety disorder. *Journal of Clinical Psychiatry*, 58: 11–18.

Macaluso, M., Kalia, R., Ali, F., and Khan, A.Y. (2010). The role of benzodiazepines in the treatment of anxiety disorders: a clinical review. *Psychiatric Annals*, 40: 605–610.

Maltby, N. and Tolin, D. F. (2005). A brief motivational intervention for treatment-refusing OCD patients. *Cognitive Behaviour Therapy*, 34: 176–184.
Marks, I. M., Swinson, R. P., Başoğlu, M. *et al.* (1993). Alprazolam and exposure alone and combined in panic disorder with agoraphobia: a controlled study in London and Toronto. *British Journal of Psychiatry*, 162: 776–787.
McHugh, R. K., Otto, M. W., Barlow, D. H., Gorman, J. M., Shear, M. K., and Woods, S. W. (2007). Cost-efficacy of individual and combined treatments for panic disorder. *Journal of Clinical Psychiatry*, 68: 1038–1044.
Michelini, S., Cassano, G. B., Frare, F., and Perugi, G. (1996). Long-term use of benzodiazepines: Tolerance, dependence and clinical problems in anxiety and mood disorders. *Pharmacopsychiatry*, 29: 127–134.
Mineka, S., Mystkowski, J. L., Hladek, D., and Rodriguez, B. I. (1999). The effects of changing contexts on return of fear following exposure therapy for spider fear. *Journal of Consulting and Clinical Psychology*, 67: 599–604.
Morin, C. M., Bélanger, L., Bastien, C., and Vallières, A. (2005). Long-term outcome after discontinuation of benzodiazepines for insomnia: a survival analysis of relapse. *Behavior Research and Therapy*, 43: 1–14.
Murray, H. W., McHugh, R. K., and Otto, M. W. (2010). Avoiding treatment failures in panic disorder. In M. W. Otto and S. G. Hofmann (eds), *Avoiding Treatment Failures in the Anxiety Disorders*. New York, Springer: 103–124.
Mystkowski, J. L., Mineka, S., Vernon, L. L., and Zinbarg, R. E. (2003). Changes in caffeine states enhance return of fear in spider phobia. *Journal of Consulting and Clinical Psychology*, 71: 243–250.
National Institute for Health and Clinical Excellence (2004). Management of anxiety (panic disorder with or without agoraphobia, and generalized anxiety disorder) in adults in primary, secondary and community care. London: NICE guidelines 2004 (amended 2007).
Newcomer, J. W., Selke, G., Melson, A. K. *et al.* (1999). Decreased memory performance in healthy humans induced by stress-level cortisol treatment. *Archives of General Psychiatry*, 56: 527–533.
Noyes, R., Garvey, M. J., Cook, B. L., and Samuelson, L. (1989). Problems with tricyclic antidepressant use in patients with panic disorder or agoraphobia: Results of a naturalistic follow-up study. *Journal of Clinical Psychiatry*, 50: 163–169.
Noyes, R., Garvey, M. J., Cook, B., and Suelzer, M. (1991). Controlled discontinuation of benzodiazepine treatment for patients with panic disorder. *American Journal of Psychiatry*, 148: 517–523.
Nunes, E. V., McGrath, P. J., and Quitkin, F. M. (1995). Treating anxiety in patients with alcoholism. *Journal of Clinical Psychiatry*, Supplement 2, 56: 3–9.
Otto, M. W., Pollack, M. H., Sachs, G. S., Reiter, S. R., Meltzer-Brody, S., and Rosenbaum, J. F. (1993). Discontinuation of benzodiazepine treatment: Efficacy of cognitive-behavioral therapy for patients with panic disorder. *American Journal of Psychiatry*, 150: 1485–1490.
Otto, M. W., Pollack, M. H., and Maki, K. M. (2000). Empirically-supported treatment for panic disorder: Costs, benefits, and stepped care. *Journal of Consulting and Clinical Psychology*, 68: 556–563.
Otto, M. W., Hong, J. J., and Safren, S. A. (2002). Benzodiazepine discontinuation difficulties in panic disorder: Conceptual model and outcome for cognitive-behavior therapy. *Current Pharmaceutical Design*, 8: 75–80.

Otto, M. W., Safren, S. A., and Pollack, M. H. (2004). Internal cue exposure and the treatment of substance use disorders: Lessons from the treatment of panic disorder. *Journal of Anxiety Disorders*, 18: 69–87.

Otto, M. W., Smits, J. A. J., and Reese, H. E. (2005). Combined psychotherapy and pharmacotherapy for mood and anxiety disorders in adults: Review and analysis. *Clinical Psychology: Science and Practice*, 12: 72–86.

Otto, M. W., McHugh, R. K., and Kantak, K. M. (2010a). Combined pharmacotherapy and cognitive-behavioral therapy for anxiety disorders: Medication effects, glucocorticoids, and attenuated treatment outcomes. *Clinical Psychology Science and Practice*, 17: 91–103.

Otto, M. W., McHugh, Farach, F. J., Worthington, J. J., and Pollack, M. H. (2010b). Efficacy of CBT for benzodiazepine discontinuation in patients with panic disorder: Further evaluation. *Behaviour Research and Therapy*, 48: 720–727.

Pitman, R. K., Orr, S. P., Altman, B. et al. (1996). Emotional processing and outcome of imaginal flooding therapy in Vietnam veterans with chronic post-traumatic stress disorder. *Comprehensive Psychiatry*, 37: 409–418.

Pollack, M. H., Simon, N. M., Worthington, J. J. et al. (2003). Combined paroxetine and clonazepam treatment strategies compared to paroxetine monotherapy for panic disorder. *Journal of Psychopharmacology*, 17: 276–282.

Pollack, M. H. and Smoller, J. W. (1996). Pharmacologic approaches to treatment resistant panic disorder. In M. H. Pollack and M. W. (eds), *Challenges in Clinical Practice: Pharmacological and Psychosocial Strategies*. New York: Guildford: 89–112.

Pollak, K. I., Oncken, C. A., Lipkus, I. et al. (2007). Nicotine replacement and behavioral therapy for smoking cessation in pregnancy. *American Journal of Preventative Medicine*, 33: 297–305.

Pomara, N., Willoughby, L. M., Sidtis, J. J., Cooper, T. B., and Greenblatt, D. J. (2005). Cortisol response to diazepam: Its relationship to age, dose, duration of treatment, and presence of generalized anxiety disorder. *Psychopharmacology*, 178: 1–8.

Powers, M. B., Smits, J. A. J., Whitley, D., Bystritsky, A., and Telch, M. J. (2008). The effect of attributional processes concerning medication taking on return of fear. *Journal of Consulting and Clinical Psychology*, 76: 478–490

Putnam, P., Van Honk, J., Kessels, R. P., Mulder, M., and Koppeschaar, H. P. (2004). Salivary cortisol and short- and long-term memory for emotional faces in healthy young women. *Psychoneuroendocrinology*, 29: 953–960.

Rickels, K., Downing, R., Schweizer, E. et al. (1993). Antidepressants for the treatment of generalized anxiety disorder: a placebo-controlled comparison of imipramine, trazodone, and diazepam. *Archives of General Psychiatry*, 50: 884–895.

Risse, S. C., Whitters, A., and Burke, J. (1990). Severe withdrawal symptoms after discontinuation of alprazolam in eight patients with combat-induced post-traumatic stress disorder. *Journal of Clinical Psychiatry*, 51: 206–209.

Rocca, P., Fonzo, V., Scotta, M., *et al.* (1997). Paroxetine efficacy in the treatment of generalized anxiety disorder. *Acta Psychiatrica Scandinavica*, 95: 444–450.

Rohrer, T., von Richthofen, V., Schulz, C. Beyer, J., and Lehnert, H. (1994). The stress-but not corticotropin-releasing hormone-induced activation of the pituitary adrenal axis in man is blocked by alprazolam. *Hormone and Metabolic Research*, 26: 200–206.

Roy-Byrne, P. P., Cowley, D. S., Hommer, D., Ritchie, J., Greenblatt, D., and Nemeroff, C. (1991). Neuroendocrine effects of diazepam in panic and generalized anxiety disorders. *Biological Psychiatry*, 30: 73–80.

Roy-Byrne, P. P. and Hommer, D. (1988). Benzodiazepine withdrawal: Overview and implications for the treatment of anxiety. *American Journal of Medicine*, 84: 1041–1052.
Salzman, C. (1993). Benzodiazepine treatment of panic and agoraphobic symptoms: Use dependence, toxicity, abuse. *Journal of Psychiatric Research*, 27: 97–110.
Santagostino, G., Amoretti, G., Frattini, P. *et al.* (1996). Caetcholaminergic, neuroendocrine and anxiety responses to acute psychological stress in healthy subjects: Influence of alprazolam administration. *Neuropsychobiology*, 34: 36–43.
Sellal, F., Danion, J. M., Kauffmann-Muller, F. *et al.* (1992). Differential effects of diazepam and lorazepam on repetition priming in healthy volunteers, *Psychopharmacology*, 108: 371–379.
Siegmund A., Köster L., Meves A. M., Plag J., Stoy M., and Ströhle A. (2011). Stress hormones during flooding therapy and their relationship to therapy outcome in patients with panic disorder and agoraphobia. *Journal of Psychiatric Research*, 45: 339–346.
Speigel, D. A., Bruce, T. J., Gregg, S. F., and Nuzzarello, A. (1994). Does cognitive behavior therapy assist a slow-taper alprazolam discontinuation in panic disorder? *American Journal of Psychiatry*, 151: 876–881.
Soravia, L. M., Heinrichs, M., Aerni, A. *et al.* (2006). Glucocorticoids reduce phobic fear in humans. *Proceedings of the National Academy of Sciences of the United States of America*, 130: 5585–5590.
Tomaz, C., Dickinson-Anson, H., and McGaugh, J. L. (1991). Amygdala lesions block the amnestic effects of diazepam. *Brain Research*, 568: 85–91.
Tyrer, P., Murphy, S., and Riley, P. (1990). The benzodiazepine withdrawal symptom questionnaire. *Journal of Affective Disorders*, 19: 53–61.
Van Minnen, A., Arntz, A., and Keijers, G. P. J. (2002). Prolonged exposure in patients with chronic PTSD: Predictors of treatment outcome dropout. *Behavior Research and Therapy*, 40(4): 439–457.
Vasile, R. G., Bruce, S. E., Goisman, R. M., Pagano, M., and Keller, M. B. (2005). Results of a naturalistic longitudinal study of benzodiazepine and SSRI use in the treatment of generalized anxiety disorder and social phobia. *Depression and Anxiety*, 22: 59–67.
Watanabe, N., Churchill, R., and Furukawa, T. A. (2007). Combination of psychotherapy and benzodiazepine versus either therapy alone for panic disorder: a systematic review. *BMC Psychiatry*, 7(18): 7–18.
Weingartner, H. J., Hommer, D., Lister, R. G., Thompson, K., and Wolkowitz, O. (1992). Selective effects of triazolam on memory. *Psychopharmacology*, 106: 341–345.
Westra, H. A., Stewart, S. H., and Conrad, B. E. (2002). Naturalistic manner of benzodiazepine use and cognitive behavorial therapy outcome in panic disorder with agoraphobia. *Journal of Anxiety Disorders*, 36: 1–14.
Westra, H. A., Stewart, S. H., Teehan, M., Johl, K., Dozois, D. J. A., and Hill, T. (2004). Benzodiazepine use associated with decreased memory for psycho-education material in cognitive behavioral therapy for panic disorder. *Cognitive Therapy and Research*, 28: 193–208.
Worthington, J. J., Pollack, M. H., Otto, M. W., McLean, R. Y. S., Moroz, G., and Rosenbaum, J. F. (1998). Long-term experience with clonazepam in patients with a primary diagnosis of panic disorder. *Psychopharmacology Bulletin*, 34: 199–205.

Chapter 3

TRICYCLIC ANTIDEPRESSANTS AND MONOAMINE OXIDASE INHIBITORS

Franklin R. Schneier
Columbia University College of Physicians and Surgeons, New York State Psychiatric Institute, New York, USA

INTRODUCTION

Antidepressants that have been shown to be efficacious for anxiety disorders are the medications most studied in combination with psychotherapy for anxiety disorders. These include older medications known as tricyclic antidepressants (TCAs) and monoamine oxidase inhibitors (MAOIs), as well as newer medications of reversible inhibitors of monoamine oxidase A (RIMAs) and serotonin reuptake inhibitors (SRIs). Although TCAs and MAOIs have been largely supplanted by the SRIs as first-line pharmacotherapies for anxiety disorders, there is evidence that TCAs may be at least as efficacious as the newer medications for panic disorder (Bakker *et al.* 2002) and for obsessive-compulsive disorder (OCD) (Piccinelli *et al.* 1995), and that MAOIs may be at least as efficacious in social anxiety disorder (Blanco *et al.* 2003).

This chapter will introduce the rationale for combined treatments of antidepressants with psychotherapy, trace the evolution of research in this area, and consider methodological issues in the development of such studies. It will review the existing literature of randomized controlled trials of combined psychotherapy treatments with TCAs and MAOIs in anxiety disorders. This includes studies of combination treatment with TCAs in panic disorder with agoraphobia and in OCD, and MAOIs in panic disorder and social anxiety disorder (Table 3.1). Notably absent are studies combining these treatments in other anxiety disorders, but neither TCAs nor MAOIs have established efficacy for post-traumatic stress disorder (PTSD), acute stress disorder, or specific phobias. While there is

---

Psychobiological Approaches for Anxiety Disorders: Treatment Combination Strategies, First Edition.
Edited by Stefan G. Hofmann.
© 2012 John Wiley & Sons, Ltd. Published 2012 by John Wiley & Sons, Ltd.

Table 3.1. Panic disorder and agoraphobia: Randomized clinical trials (RCTs) of cognitive behavioral therapy (CBT), exposure therapy or brief psychodynamic therapy combined with TCAs

Source	Efficacy at post-treatment	Daily dose in mg
Zitrin et al. (1980)	Imipramine + Exposure Therapy (29/41) > Placebo + Exposure Therapy (25/35)	Imipramine 150–300
Zitrin et al. (1983)	Imipramine + Exposure Therapy (34/43) = Imipramine + Supportive Therapy (41/53) > Placebo + Exposure Therapy (34/41)	Imipramine 150–300
[a]Marks et al. (1983)	Imipramine + Exposure homework (23/36) = Placebo + Exposure homework (22/36)	Imipramine 100–200
Telch et al. (1985)	Imipramine + Exposure therapy (10/13) > Imipramine + Anti-exposure instructions (10/12) = Placebo + Exposure therapy (9/12)	Imipramine 150–300
[b]Mavissakalian et al. (1986a)	Imipramine + Therapist-assisted exposure (14) = Imipramine + Self-directed exposure (17) = Placebo + Therapist-assisted exposure (17) = Placebo + Self-directed exposure (14)	Imipramine 25–200
[c]Johnston et al. (1995)	Clomipramine (16/26) = Exposure therapy (17/27) = Clomipramine + Exposure therapy (12/28) = Placebo (15/27)	Clomipramine up to 300
[d]Barlow et al. (2000)	CBT + Imipramine (65) = CBT + Placebo (63) = Imipramine (83) > CBT (77) > Placebo (24)	Imipramine up to 300

(Continued)

TRICYCLIC ANTIDEPRESSANTS AND MONOAMINE OXIDASE INHIBITORS 43

[e]Marchand et al. (2008)	Cognitive therapy + Exposure + Imipramine = Cognitive therapy + Exposure + Placebo = Exposure + Imipramine = Exposure + Placebo = Cognitive therapy + Imipramine = Cognitive therapy + Placebo = Supportive therapy + Imipramine = Supportive therapy + Placebo	Imipramine 50–200
Wiborg and Dahl (1996)	Clomipramine + Brief Dynamic Therapy (20/20) > Clomipramine (20/20)	Clomipramine up to 150

Note: '=' = treatments are equally effective on the main efficacy measures, '>' = treatment is significantly superior. In brackets: sample size (evaluable/randomized).

[a] Half of the patients in each group received additional therapist-assisted exposure or relaxation therapy.
[b] 18 patients in unspecified groups failed to return for treatment or dropped out; Efficacy in pooled imipramine groups > pooled placebo groups
[c] Significant main effects for clomipramine > placebo on 6 measures, and for behavior therapy > no therapy on 3 measures (no primary outcome measure specified)
[d] 14 patients in unspecified groups were judged ineligible after randomization
[e] Pooled imipramine groups sample size (63/77), pooled placebo groups sample size (59/77). Sample sizes not reported for individual cells.

some support for TCA efficacy in generalized anxiety disorder, it has not been studied as a combined treatment. Combined treatment with SRIs will be addressed in the next chapter, along with conclusions regarding combination therapy with antidepressants.

WHY COMBINE ANTIDEPRESSANTS AND PSYCHOTHERAPY?

While the most recent approaches to integrating medication and psychotherapies have drawn upon sophisticated translational understanding of neural mechanisms of therapeutic effects, such as facilitation of fear extinction, the original impetus to combine these modalities was less complex: Many of the medications initially developed as antidepressants have been shown to have a broad spectrum of anti-anxiety effects. Neither medications nor psychosocial treatments are fully effective, and the distinctiveness of these approaches suggests that their actions are mediated by different mechanisms. Combining two efficacious treatments with differing mechanisms of action could have additive or synergistic benefits.

Several features of antidepressant medications make them particularly attractive for combined treatment. The delayed onset of action of antidepressants, with clinically evident benefits typically emerging after 2–4 weeks of treatment, has advantages over the rapid action of benzodiazepine medications, in that the treatment effects of medication are less easily distinguishable from those of psychotherapy. This may improve blinding of patients and raters to outcome in research studies, may decrease the risk that immediate relief of symptoms will sap patients' motivation to learn enduring skills in therapy, and may decrease the likelihood that patients will attribute all their gains to the medication (a possible risk factor for post-discontinuation relapse) (Başoğlu *et al.* 1994). The antidepressants' lesser risk of rebound anxiety at the time of discontinuation may further improve chances for prolonged benefit of combined treatment after medication discontinuation. The relatively little cognitive impairment caused by most antidepressants also makes them less likely than benzodiazepines to interfere with cognitive processing of psychotherapy. Whereas benzodiazepines have been shown to cause state dependent learning effects that could further compromise the learning that takes place during CBT (Bouton *et al.* 1990), such effects have not been clearly demonstrated for antidepressants (Arenas *et al.* 2006).

Given the potential advantages for combined treatment with antidepressants, one might wonder why studies of such combinations make up only a small portion of the clinical trial literature. One scientific issue is that the study of combining two independently efficacious treatments requires that each first be established as a monotherapy. Until the past decade, few specific medications or specific CBT packages had reached this threshold of acceptance. Other issues reflect historical differences in the cultures of investigators of medication and psychotherapy. Researchers have tended to be trained in the study of pharmacotherapy or psychotherapy, so study of combined treatments has usually required cross-discipline collaborations. Treatment modalities have sometimes been viewed as competing with others with respect to efficacy and philosophy of approach. Antidepressants have been studied mainly by psychiatrists, and psychotherapies by psychologists, resulting in professional differences in methods and guild allegiance. These factors interfered with the establishment of trust between potential collaborators and the development of well-balanced studies that offered similar quality of treatment for each modality. Finally, combined treatment studies are expensive and difficult to conduct, requiring broad expertise, ability to maintain blind across very different interventions that each have their own set of therapists, and patients who are willing to accept combined treatment or a monotherapy modality that they may not prefer. This chapter's review of combined treatment includes consideration of several landmark studies that helped to bridge this divide and forge the more collaborative approach that prevails today.

TRICYCLIC ANTIDEPRESSANTS FOR PANIC DISORDER AND AGORAPHOBIA

The panic disorder and agoraphobia literature on combined treatment with tricyclics and CBT is by far the largest of any literature on the combination of older medications with CBT for the treatment of anxiety disorders. Imipramine was one of the first psychotropics demonstrated to be efficacious for panic disorder with agoraphobia, initially based on work by Klein (1964), who collaborated on early double-blind randomized controlled trials (RCTs) of the combined treatment of imipramine and exposure therapy (Zitrin et al. 1980; 1983) (Table 3.2). Imipramine dosed up to 300 mg/day + exposure therapy for 26 weeks was superior to placebo + exposure therapy in the treatment of agoraphobia in both studies. The latter study included patients with agoraphobia ($N = 77$), mixed phobias (now likely described as panic disorder with mild agoraphobia) ($N = 60$), and simple (now known as specific) phobias ($N = 81$), and superiority of imipramine was confined to the agoraphobia and mixed phobia groups that reported spontaneous panic attacks. This study also included a combined treatment cell with a control therapy (supportive psychotherapy + imipramine), but results in this group did not differ from those of the imipramine + behavior therapy group.

Other contemporaneous pioneering studies of imipramine in panic disorder were conducted by psychopharmacologist David Sheehan and by Isaac Marks, a leading behavior therapist. Sheehan et al. (1980) reported that 3 months of imipramine + supportive group therapy was superior to

Table 3.2. Obsessive compulsive disorder. RCTs of CBT or exposure therapy combined with the tricyclic antidepressant clomipramine

Source	Efficacy at post-treatment	Daily dose in mg
Marks et al. (1980)	Clomipramine + Exposure (20/20)= Placebo + Exposure (20/20)	Clomipramine up to 225
[a]Marks et al. (1988)	Clomipramine + Therapist-aided exposure (13) = Placebo + Therapist-aided exposure (12) = Clomipramine + Exposure homeowork (12) > Clomipramine + anti-exposure homework (12)	Clomipramine up to 200
Foa et al. (2005)	Exposure therapy + Ritual prevention + Clomipramine (31/33) = Exposure therapy + Ritual prevention (29/37) > Clomipramine(36/47) > Placebo (26/32)	Clomipramine 150–250

Note: '=' = treatments are equally effective on the main efficacy measures, '>' = treatment is significantly superior, 'brackets' = sample size (evaluable/randomized)
[a] *Six subjects dropped out in unspecified groups*

placebo + supportive group therapy in patients reporting spontaneous panic attacks. However, supportive group therapy is not an established independent treatment for panic disorder, so this study did not include a psychotherapy with established efficacy for panic. Marks et al. (1983) compared 4 treatments over 28 weeks in patients with agoraphobia and panic attacks:

1) Imipramine (dosed up to 200 mg/day) + therapist-aided exposure (3 hours total);
2) imipramine + therapist-aided relaxation (3 hours total);
3) placebo + therapist-aided exposure; and
4) placebo + therapist-aided relaxation.

All patients also received systematic self-exposure homework. Outcome for imipramine + psychotherapies did not differ from outcome for placebo + psychotherapies, and there was a small advantage for exposure over relaxation therapy. Naturalistic follow-ups at 2 years (Cohen et al. 1984) and 5 years (Lelliott et al. 1987) also did not find drug-placebo differences.

Limitations of all these early studies include their predating of reliable structured diagnostic interviews and well-validated outcome measures. Similarly, the psychotherapies that were used predated the establishment of cognitive-behavioral therapies for panic disorder that integrate elements of cognitive retraining and interoceptive exposure, and which may therefore be more efficacious.

Given that patients in medication treatment may engage in exposure spontaneously or after informal encouragement from their medicating doctor, several studies have tried to clarify the role of various levels of exposure interacting with imipramine in the treatment of panic. Telch et al. (1985) randomized 37 severely-disabled patients with DSM-III agoraphobia with panic attacks to imipramine + anti-exposure instructions, imipramine + exposure therapy, or placebo + exposure therapy. The imipramine + exposure group improved more than the other 2 groups after 8 weeks of treatment. Patients receiving imipramine with anti-exposure instructions improved in anxiety and dysphoric mood, but not in respect to panic attacks or phobic avoidance. After 26 weeks, the combined imipramine + exposure treatment was also superior to the placebo + exposure group, which did not experience a reduction in panic attacks. These findings support the combination of exposure therapy with imipramine over 26 weeks of treatment. The finding that anti-exposure instructions reduced the efficacy of imipramine suggests that exposure, whether through formal therapy, informal recommendation, or self-initiated, might work in concert with medication to enhance response. The above findings are consistent with an earlier, smaller (N = 18) trial without a placebo control, which suggested that combined imipramine + exposure enhanced improvement in phobic symptoms compared to imipramine alone (Mavissakalian et al. 1983). Mavissakalian and Michelson (1986a;b) further developed this line of research in an RCT comparing imipramine + systematic instructions for self-directed exposure, placebo + self-directed exposure, placebo + therapist-assisted exposure (flooding), and combined imipramine + flooding. They found that all groups improved and that clinical response was particularly robust in patients receiving imipramine doses >150 mg. The combination of imipramine + flooding had little advantage over imipramine + systematic instructions for self-directed exposure. Johnston et al. (1995) found no interactions between clomipramine and *in vivo* exposure therapy in a study that randomized 108 women to 28 weeks of clomipramine alone, exposure alone, clomipramine + exposure, or pill placebo.

The largest and most definitive study of combined tricyclic and CBT treatment in panic disorder to date was conducted by a collaborative team that united experts in psychopharmacology and CBT (Barlow et al. 2000).

The Multicenter Comparative Treatment Study of Panic Disorder randomized 326 patients with panic disorder, without or with mild agoraphobia, to imipramine only (up to 300 mg/d), cognitive-behavioral therapy (CBT) only, placebo only, CBT + imipramine, or CBT + placebo. Patients were treated weekly for 3 months; responders were then seen monthly for 6 months, and then followed up for 6 months after treatment discontinuation.

Responses to imipramine and CBT were each significantly superior to those of the placebo group after 3 months (intent-to-treat response rates of 46, 49, and 22%, respectively). CBT + imipramine and CBT + placebo led to slightly greater, but not significantly greater, response rates (60% and 57%) than monotherapies. After 6 months of maintenance, CBT alone (40%), imipramine alone (38%), CBT + imipramine (57%), and CBT + placebo (47%) were all significantly more effective than placebo alone (13%). Among responders, response quality was greater on imipramine than CBT alone. The response rates of the two combined treatments (CBT + imipramine and CBT + placebo) were not different from each other, but both combined treatments were superior to the monotherapies. Furthermore, all active treatments were superior to placebo. Six months after treatment discontinuation, response rates were 41% for CBT + placebo, 32% for CBT alone, 20% for imipramine alone, 13% for placebo, and 26% for CBT combined with imipramine. In conclusion, a main finding of this study was that the combination of CBT + imipramine and also of CBT + placebo demonstrated a modest advantage over monotherapies that was statistically significant over 9 months of treatment. After treatment discontinuation, CBT, either alone or combined with placebo or imipramine, evidenced trends for the best durability of gains.

Additional reports from this trial have addressed several other issues relevant to combined treatment in panic disorder. Analysis of attrition patterns in the Multicenter Comparative Treatment Study of Panic Disorder did not evidence differences in attrition based on treatment assigned or other features that could jeopardize the validity of the trial (White et al. 2010). Hofmann et al. (2007) examined mechanisms of treatment response, hypothesizing that improvement in CBT should be mediated by reduction in catastrophic cognitions. Evidence for cognitive mediation of treatment response was assessed in a subgroup of 91 patients who received CBT alone, imipramine alone, CBT + imipramine, and CBT + placebo. Multilevel moderated mediation analyses provided preliminary evidence that changes in panic-related catastrophic cognitions from baseline to post-treatment and follow-up did mediate changes in panic severity for treatments that included CBT, but did not mediate changes for imipramine-only treatment.

Despite multiple precautions taken to maintain the blind of independent evaluators in this study, Roll et al. (2004) found that analyses of guesses of treatment group assignment by the independent evaluators of 170 patients revealed a significant relationship between evaluator guesses and which of the 5 treatments was received by a patient at 3 assessment points, across the 15 evaluators, 4 treatment sites, and evaluator professional affiliations (psychology, social work, and medicine). The evaluators were no more accurate in guessing about medication treatment than about behavior therapy. Patients and project staff appear to have inadvertently provided information that compromised the blind. The blind was best protected at a site where consultant independent evaluators had the least awareness of study treatment procedures and which clinicians were providing study treatments. Although there was no evidence that outcome findings were biased or invalidated by this breach, the findings highlight the difficulty of maintaining double-blind conditions in studies with multiple modalities of treatment.

Marcus *et al.* (2007) reported on a side benefit of combined treatment in the subgroup of 172 panic disorder patients who were randomly assigned to receive imipramine alone, CBT + imipramine, or placebo. Treatment with CBT + imipramine resulted in less severe side effects of fatigue/weakness, dry mouth, and sweating, and a lower rate of dropout due to side effects, compared to treatment with imipramine alone. The targeting of physical catastrophic cognitions by CBT may have a side benefit of improving tolerance of adverse effects during combined treatment with imipramine.

Relapse after medication discontinuation was the focus of another report. The finding that after treatment was discontinued, patients who had received CBT + imipramine fared relatively less well than those who had received CBT + placebo, led to an investigation of reasons for this outcome. Raffa *et al.* (2008) hypothesized that participants had correctly deduced their treatment assignments and that those who believed that they had discontinued active medication were more likely to relapse, as had been suggested for a prior study of alprazolam in panic disorder (Başoğlu *et al.* 1994). However, contrary to the hypothesis, there were no group differences in frequency of guessing drug or placebo. Patients did not guess their assignment to imipramine or placebo at a rate better than chance, unlike the findings above for independent evaluators guessing assignment to the five treatment conditions (Roll *et al.* 2004). Differential relapse was not associated with patients' specific beliefs about whether they were taking active drug or placebo, and the gradual time course of relapses suggested that they were also not primarily attributable to withdrawal effects occurring immediately post-discontinuation of imipramine.

A cost-efficacy analysis based on results from the Multicenter Comparative Treatment Study of Panic Disorder estimated the cost per 1-unit improvement in Panic Disorder Severity Scale mean item score for each treatment (McHugh *et al.* 2007). Individual treatments were consistently more cost-effective that combined treatments, with imipramine being the most cost-efficacious treatment option after 3 months of treatment (cost-efficacy ratio = $972) and CBT being the most cost-efficacious option at the end of maintenance treatment (cost efficacy ratio = $1449), and at 6 months after treatment termination (cost-efficacy ratio = $1227).

The Multicenter Comparative Treatment Study of Panic Disorder addressed many important questions about combined treatment of panic disorder, but leaves much to be explored. The most recent addition to the literature of RCTs of combined study with tricyclics in panic disorder (Marchand et al. 2008) further investigated the integration of behavioral and cognitive components of therapy, in combination with medication, among panic disorder patients with moderate to severe agoraphobia. This study compared 4 psychosocial treatments (cognitive therapy + in vivo exposure, in vivo exposure, cognitive therapy, and supportive therapy) that were each combined with imipramine or placebo for a total of 8 experimental conditions in 152 patients. Outcomes at the end of 18 weeks of study treatments and at 1-year follow-up found that all groups improved, and there were no significant differences between treatment groups. The findings highlight the importance (and difficulty) of including placebo and nonspecific therapy control groups in RCTs, given the high rates of response to nonspecific treatments in panic disorder.

While the parallel-groups 'horse race' approach has been the most common design of these combined treatment studies, several researchers have examined the alternative of combining modalities through sequencing of treatments. Mavissakalian (1990) explored sequential treatment with imipramine monotherapy for 8 weeks, followed by imipramine in combination with self-directed exposure for 8 weeks. He found a high response rate in this uncontrolled study and suggested that a sequential approach that reserved combined treatment for nonresponders might be cost-effective. Hoffart et al. (1993) randomized 18 patients with panic disorder with agoraphobia who had not responded to exposure treatment as inpatients to 12 weeks of randomized treatment with clomipramine or placebo, finding significant benefits for clomipramine over this period. Fava et al. (1997) further explored sequential treatment of exposure therapy nonresponders. Twenty-one patients with DSM-IV panic disorder and agoraphobia, who had failed to respond to in vivo exposure, were randomized to exposure alone (continuation), exposure + imipramine, or exposure + cognitive therapy in a cross-over, controlled design. Continuation of exposure alone was unexpectedly superior to each of the combined treatments, suggesting that longer-term behavioral treatment may be sufficient in some patients and superior to combined approaches.

Only one RCT has examined a psychotherapy not based on CBT in a combined treatment with a tricyclic for an anxiety disorder. Brief dynamic psychotherapy in combination with a tricyclic for panic disorder was tested by Wiborg and Dahl (1996). Forty patients with DSM-III-R panic disorder were randomized to clomipramine for 9 months, either alone or combined with 15 weekly sessions of brief dynamic therapy. All dynamic therapy in the study was conducted by a single therapist. While both groups were panic-free after 6 months of treatment, the combined group had superior outcomes after 9 months (at the end of the study treatment), and at naturalistic follow-ups up to 18 months after starting treatment. Findings suggest that brief dynamic psychotherapy combined with clomipramine treatment of panic disorder may enhance outcome during the treatment period and help reduce relapse after treatments are discontinued. However, the use of a single therapist limits the generalizability of these findings.

The body of work on combined treatment of tricyclics and CBT for panic disorder evidences the strengths, weaknesses, and complexities of this approach. The preponderance of evidence suggests a modest advantage for combined treatment over monotherapies but with some important caveats. One issue is what sample of patients should get combined treatment? Prominent spontaneous panic attacks might theoretically favor medication, and prominent agoraphobia might favor exposure-based treatments, but this distinction is not well-established empirically. Reserving combined treatment for nonresponders to monotherapy may be an efficient allocation of resources, but study of sequential treatment requires large initial samples in order to generate sufficient nonresponders for a randomized second phase of treatment. Most RCTs have not even reported the extent to which the patients in their samples previously responded to or failed prior trials of medication or psychotherapy. Another issue is time frame. Combined treatment is most clearly superior in the short term, but the picture is less clear over long-term treatment, and continued superiority of combined treatment is more likely if the medication treatment is maintained rather than discontinued. Another issue is the intensity of each treatment, yet studies vary substantially in respect to the dose of tricyclic and the frequency and duration of CBT. Furthermore, almost all of these studies have been conducted at 'expert' sites, and there is a need to understand how well combined treatments can be transported to community and primary care settings, though preliminary indications in panic and other anxiety disorders are encouraging (Craske *et al.* 2011). Given the number of 'moving parts' in the variety of methods used across this body of work, discrepant findings are not surprising, and the signal in support of combined treatment has been modest.

TRICYCLIC ANTIDEPRESSANTS FOR OBSESSIVE-COMPULSIVE DISORDER

Clomipramine was the first medication demonstrated to be efficacious for OCD, and it remains the only tricyclic antidepressant with established efficacy for this disorder. Studies of combined treatment with clomipramine and CBT have been conducted primarily by two teams of researchers: Isaac Marks' group in London, and the collaboration of Edna Foa's group at the University of Pennsylvania with the New York State Psychiatric/Columbia group of Michael Liebowitz and H. Blair Simpson.

The first study of clomipramine combined with CBT was reported by Marks et al. (1980), who randomized 50 OCD patients to clomipramine or placebo for 8 months. Forty patients who completed and tolerated the first 4 weeks of treatment but remained symptomatic were further randomized to receive inpatient combined treatment with 15 hours of either relaxation therapy or exposure *in vivo* during weeks 4 to 7. All patients then received 15 hours of exposure *in vivo* during weeks 7 to 10. After 8 months, all medication was discontinued. Clomipramine was found superior to placebo only in those patients who initially had depressed mood, and patients often relapsed upon clomipramine discontinuation but improved again on restarting the drug after the study. Relaxation was not significantly helpful, but exposure produced significant improvement in rituals. Clomipramine plus exposure had some additive effects, but this could only be assessed between groups at week 7, before both groups received the additional exposure, and before the full effects of medication were expected. An interaction was noted, in the form of clomipramine enhancing compliance for both exposure and relaxation.

At 2-year follow-up (Mawson et al. 1982) there was improvement in rituals, mood, and social adjustment compared to week 0. Rituals were improved more among patients who had received 30 hours of exposure, but they were equivalent in the drug and placebo groups. At 6-year follow-up of 34 available patients, the sample remained significantly improved on obsessive-compulsive symptoms, work and social adjustment, and depression (O'Sullivan et al. 1991). Randomization to clomipramine or placebo did not affect the long-term outcome, but better outcome continued to be associated with the longer 6-week course of inpatient exposure therapy. The best predictor of long-term outcome was improvement at the end of the original 8-month treatment.

In a second study, Marks et al. (1988) investigated the interaction of various levels of exposure with clomipramine, by randomizing 54 OCD patients to:

- clomipramine + exposure homework;
- clomipramine + anti-exposure homework;
- clomipramine + therapist-aided exposure; and
- placebo + therapist-aided exposure.

Clomipramine and placebo were given for 26 weeks, and exposure homework or anti-exposure homework was given during the first 23 weeks of treatment. The 2 groups receiving therapist-aided exposure received it from weeks 8–23, after receiving only exposure homework for the first

7 weeks. Clomipramine was dosed up to 225 mg/day, although mean doses actually received were approximately 150 mg/day.

Among the patients who received exposure therapy or homework, clomipramine treatment improved some measures of rituals and depression significantly more than did placebo medication during the first 8 weeks, but this effect was no longer present after 26 weeks of treatment. Among the patients who received clomipramine, exposure homework was significantly superior to anti-exposure homework. The addition of therapist-aided exposure (1.3 hours) to self-exposure instructions (3 hours) after 8 weeks of treatment had a significant but transient advantage that was lost at week 23 and at follow-up assessments to week 52.

These studies by Marks *et al.* (1988) extended prior studies of efficacy of exposure therapy for OCD by integrating them with the study of clomipramine – at the time a promising but unproven new pharmacotherapy for OCD. The studies confirmed the centrality of exposure treatment for OCD and suggested that combination with clomipramine had modest advantages that were maximal early in the course of treatment. The potency of exposure homework highlighted the value of adding exposure instructions during pharmacotherapy for OCD.

Two decades later, Foa *et al.* (2005) advanced the methodology of study of combined treatment in OCD through features including use of a manual-based, experimentally validated version of exposure and ritual prevention, an adequate dose of clomipramine treatment, and the collaboration of expert psychopharmacology and CBT research groups and sites. Patients were randomized to one of four treatments:

1) exposure and ritual prevention;
2) clomipramine;
3) exposure and ritual prevention + clomipramine, or
4) placebo.

Exposure and ritual prevention included daily 2-hour sessions, 5 days per week, for 3 weeks, with 2 hours of homework each day. Therapists visited patients' homes twice in week 4 to support generalization of treatment effects and then met patients weekly for the remaining 8 weeks of treatment. Clomipramine was dosed up to 250 mg/day, as tolerated. Independent evaluators rated outcome at 4-week intervals over the 12 weeks of treatment.

Of 149 patients randomized, 27 dropped out of the study after being told of their assignment to therapy or medication, highlighting the challenge of conducting multimodal studies in samples with strong treatment preferences. The remaining 122 patients entered the 4 treatments. Each of the three active treatment groups improved significantly more than the placebo group did, and intensive exposure and ritual prevention was superior to clomipramine treatment. Combined treatment was superior to clomipramine, but did not separate from exposure therapy alone.

Results were consistent across three sites that had differing levels of experience with each of the treatments, and findings for each monotherapy versus placebo comparison were consistent with other monotherapy studies in the literature. However, the authors noted that several design considerations may have limited sensitivity of the study to detect clomipamine effects, including the practice of starting both treatments simultaneously, so that the bulk of the effects of intensive exposure conducted during the first 3 weeks might predate the period during which clomipramine's delayed benefits might have been expected to emerge. The strong effect of exposure therapy as a monotherapy in this study may have resulted in a ceiling effect, with little statistical power to detect potential further benefit of combined treatment.

Simpson et al. (2006) explored remission rates in this study at week 12, using several definitions of response and remission. Exposure and combined treatment again resulted in significantly greater response and remission rates than placebo. Clomipramine produced greater response and remission rates than placebo for some, but not all definitions. When remission was defined by a Yale-Brown Obsessive Compulsive Scale score of 12 or less, remission was achieved by a significantly greater proportion of the combined treatment (58%) and exposure groups (52%) than either clomipramine (25%) or placebo (0%) groups. However, even among study completers, no group achieved a remission rate greater than 71%, suggesting the need for more effective approaches.

Follow-up data were reported on 46 of the study participants who had responded to treatment and were re-assessed blindly 12 weeks after treatment discontinuation (Simpson et al. 2004). Responders in the exposure and ritual prevention group and the exposure and ritual prevention + clomipramine group combined had a significantly lower relapse rate (12%) than responders in the clomipramine-alone group (45%).

In summary, this small amount of literature on combined treatment with exposure and clomipramine has had a powerful effect on the clarification of evidence-based treatment for OCD. Although clomipramine was undoubtedly a breakthrough drug in the treatment of OCD, these studies have demonstrated that for patients who are willing and able to undertake an intensive course of exposure therapy, clomipramine's added value is typically relatively modest and wanes substantially after medication treatment is discontinued.

MONOAMINE OXIDASE INHIBITORS FOR PANIC DISORDER AND AGORAPHOBIA

MAOIs were one of the first medications to be studied for panic disorder, but the literature on combined treatment with these medications is limited to the dual-medication study of Sheehan et al. (1980), reported above for imipramine, that also compared 3 months of phenelzine + supportive group therapy to placebo + supportive group therapy in patients reporting spontaneous panic attacks. Combined treatment with phenelzine was superior to supportive therapy + placebo; however, this study did not include a psychotherapy with established efficacy for panic.

MONOAMINE OXIDASE INHIBITORS FOR SOCIAL ANXIETY DISORDER

MAOIs were among the first medications to be studied for the treatment of social anxiety disorder (also known as social phobia), and controlled trials with the MAOI phenelzine, although few in number, show some of the largest treatment effects in the social anxiety disorder pharmacotherapy literature (Ipser et al. 2008). Phenelzine was also the first medication to be compared directly with CBT for social anxiety disorder in a large-scale collaboration of pharmacologically-oriented and CBT-oriented research groups, led by Michael Liebowitz at New York State Psychiatric Institute/ Columbia and Richard Heimberg of SUNY-Albany (and later of Temple University). An initial collaborative trial (Heimberg et al. 1998) had suggested roughly equivalent response rates for phenelzine and group CBT monotherapies for social anxiety disorder, with some acute advantages for phenelzine and some advantages for CBT during follow-up after treatment discontinuation (Liebowitz et al. 1999) (Table 3.3).

The same investigators subsequently conducted a placebo-controlled study comparing combination treatment to phenelzine and CBT monotherapies. Blanco et al. (2010) randomized 128 patients with social anxiety disorder to 1 of 4 conditions:

Table 3.3. Social anxiety disorder. RCTs of cognitive behavioral therapy combined with MAOIs

Source	Efficacy at post-treatment	Daily dose in mg
[a]Blanco et al. (2010)	Cognitive Behavioral Group Therapy + Phenelzine (32/42) > Phenelzine (35/45) = Cognitive Behavioral Group Therapy (34/40) = Placebo (27/39)	Phenelzine 15–90

Note: '=' = treatments are equally effective on the main efficacy measures, '>' = treatment is significantly superior

[a] Phenelzine was equivalent to cognitive behavioral group therapy, but superior to placebo.

1) Phenelzine;
2) Cognitive-behavioral group therapy (CBT);
3) Combined treatment (CBT plus phenelzine), or
4) Pill placebo.

The study was conducted at a site with particular expertise in medication and a site with particular expertise in CBT treatments, and each expert site supervised the delivery of their treatment at both sites.

Over 12 weeks of acute treatment, this study found a significant gradient of efficacy from combined treatment to each monotherapy to placebo. In pairwise comparisons, combined treatment and phenelzine were each superior to placebo on most outcome measures, but outcomes for CBT did not significantly differ from those of placebo or phenelzine groups. Week 12 response rates in the intention-to-treat sample ranged from 72% for combined treatment to 54% for phenelzine, 47% for CBT, and 33% for placebo. At week 24, the gradient in treatment response from combined treatment to each of the monotherapies to placebo remained significant. Response rates at week 24 were 78% for combined treatment, 49% for phenelzine, 53% for CBT, and 33% for placebo. Remission rates showed a similar gradient of response after both 12 and 24 weeks of treatment.

The authors contrast their findings with other studies in social anxiety disorder that have failed to demonstrate superiority for combined treatment, noting that three of those studies utilized medications that have not been established as efficacious monotherapies for social anxiety disorder (Falloon *et al*. 1981; Clark and Agras 1991; Davidson *et al*. 2004). They note that in the only other study of combined treatment of social anxiety disorder with a medication of established efficacy (sertraline) (Blomhoff *et al*. 2001), may have failed to detect additional benefit of combined treatment due to the use of pairwise comparisons, rather than tests for ordered responses implied in the study design. Reanalysis of the rates of response from the sertraline study, assuming a gradation of response from placebo to monotherapies to combined treatment using a linear-by-linear test, yielded a significant result. These findings highlight both the potential for benefit of combined treatment in social anxiety disorder, and the risk of false negative findings in these studies, which often have low statistical power to detect group differences due to small samples and analyses that must control for multiple comparisons of treatment groups.

CONCLUSION

This chapter has reviewed studies of combined CBT plus medication treatment that have employed TCAs and MAOIs. Early studies with these classes of medication broke new ground in developing methodologies for randomized clinical trials of combined treatment, and later studies represent breakthroughs in collaborative designs that have united research teams with expertise in psychopharmacology and cognitive behavioral therapies, yielding increasingly credible findings. The largest body of evidence exists for combined imipramine and CBT in panic disorder, suggesting a modest advantage for combined treatment. In contrast, clomipramine has not been shown to have added value among patients who receive a course of intensive exposure and response prevention therapy for OCD. A single collaborative study supports the superiority of combined phenelzine plus CBT over monotherapies for social anxiety disorder. Because TCAs and standard MAOIs have largely been supplanted by the better-tolerated serotonin reuptake inhibitors as first-line pharmacotherapies for anxiety disorders, we are unlikely to see many new RCTs of these treatments in combination with CBT. These medications remain among the most efficacious pharmacotherapy options, however, so future research should further investigate their role for the substantial subset of patients with incomplete response to a standard course of CBT and serotonin reuptake inhibitor treatment.

REFERENCES

Arenas, M. C., Vinader-Caerols, C., Monleón, S. et al. (2006). Are the effects of the antidepressants amitriptyline, maprotiline, and fluoxetine on inhibitory avoidance state-dependent? *Behavioural Brain Research*, 166: 150–158.

Bakker, A., van Balkom, A. J., and Spinhoven, P. (2002). SSRIs vs. TCAs in the treatment of panic disorder: a meta-analysis. *Acta Psychiatrica Scandinavica*, 106: 163–167.

Barlow, D. H., Gorman, J. M., Shear, M. K., and Woods, S. W. (2000). Cognitive-behavioral therapy, imipramine, or their combination for panic disorder. A randomized controlled trial. *Journal of the American Medical Association*, 283: 2529–2536.

Başoğlu, M., Marks, I. M., Kiliç, C., Brewin, C. R., and Swinson, R. P. (1994). Alprazolam and exposure for panic disorder with agoraphobia. Attribution of improvement to medication predicts subsequent relapse. *British Journal of Psychiatry*, 164: 652–659.

Blanco, C., Schneier, F. R., Schmidt, A. et al. (2003). Pharmacological treatment of social anxiety disorder: a meta-analysis. *Depression and Anxiety*, 18: 29–40.

Blanco, C., Heimberg, R. G., Schneier, F. R. et al. (2010). A placebo-controlled trial of phenelzine, cognitive behavioral group therapy, and their combination for social anxiety disorder. *Archives of General Psychiatry*, 67: 286–295.

Blomhoff, S., Haug, T. T., Hellstroem, K. et al. (2001). Randomised controlled general practice trial of sertraline, exposure therapy and combined treatment in generalised social phobia. *British Journal of Psychiatry*, 179: 23–30.

Bouton, M. E., Kenney, F. A., and Rosengard, C. (1990). State-dependent fear extinction with two benzodiazepine tranquilizers. *Behavioral Neuroscience*, 104: 44–55.

Clark, D. B. and Agras, W. S. (1991). The assessment and treatment of performance anxiety in musicians. *American Journal of Psychiatry*, 148: 598–605.

Cohen, S. D., Monteiro, W., and Marks, I. M. (1984). Two-year follow-up of agoraphobics after exposure and imipramine. *British Journal of Psychiatry*, 144; 276–281.

Craske, M. G., Stein, M. B., Sullivan, G. et al. (2011). Disorder-specific impact of coordinated anxiety learning and management treatment for anxiety disorders in primary care. *Archives of General Psychiatry*, 68: 378–388.

Davidson, J. R., Foa, E. B., Huppert, J. D. et al. (2004). Fluoxetine, comprehensive cognitive behavioral therapy, and placebo in generalized social phobia. *Archives of General Psychiatry*, 61: 1005–1013.

Falloon, I. R., Lloyd, G. G., and Harpin, R. E. (1981). The treatment of social phobia. Real-life rehearsal with nonprofessional therapists. *Journal of Nervous and Mental Disease*, 169: 180–184.

Fava, G. A., Savron, G., Zielezny, M., Grandi, S., Rafanelli, C., and Conti, S. (1997). Overcoming resistance to exposure in panic disorder with agoraphobia. *Acta Psychiatrica Scandinavica*, 95: 306–312.

Foa, E. B., Liebowitz, M. R., Kozak, M. J. et al. (2005). Randomized, placebo-controlled trial of exposure and ritual prevention, clomipramine, and their combination in the treatment of obsessive-compulsive disorder. *American Journal of Psychiatry*, 162: 151–161.

Heimberg, R. G., Liebowitz, M. R., Hope, D. A. et al. (1998). Cognitive behavioral group therapy vs. phenelzine therapy for social phobia: 12-week outcome. *Archives of General Psychiatry*, 55: 1133–1141.

Hoffart, A., Due-Madsen, J., Lande, B., Gude, T., Bille, H., and Torgersen, S. (1993). Clomipramine in the treatment of agoraphobic inpatients resistant to behavioral therapy. *Journal of Clinical Psychiatry*, 54: 481–487.

Hofmann, S. G., Meuret, A. E., Rosenfield, D. et al. (2007). Preliminary evidence for cognitive mediation during cognitive-behavioral therapy of panic disorder. *Journal of Consulting and Clinical Psychology*, 75: 374–379.

Ipser, J. C., Kariuki, C. M., and Stein, D. J. (2008). Pharmacotherapy for social anxiety disorder: a systematic review. *Expert Review of Neurotherapeutics*, 8: 235–257.

Johnston, D. G., Troyer, I. E., Whitsett, S. F., and Dalby, J. T. (1995). Clomipramine treatment and behaviour therapy with agoraphobic women. *Canadian Journal of Psychiatry*, 40: 192–199.

Klein, D. F. (1964). Delineation of two drug-responsive anxiety syndromes. *Psychopharmacology (Berl.)* 5: 346–354.

Lelliott, P. T., Marks, I. M., Monteiro, W. O., Tsakiris, F., and Noshirvani, H. (1987). Agoraphobics 5 years after imipramine and exposure. Outcome and predictors. *Journal of Nervous and Mental Disease*, 175: 599–605.

Liebowitz, M. R., Heimberg, R. G., Schneier, F. R. et al. (1999). Cognitive-behavioral group therapy versus phenelzine in social phobia: long-term outcome. *Depression and Anxiety*, 10: 89–98.

Marchand, A., Coutu, M. F., Dupuis, G. et al. (2008). Treatment of panic disorder with agoraphobia: Randomized placebo-controlled trial of four psychosocial treatments combined with imipramine or placebo. *Cognitive Behavioral Therapy*, 37: 146–159.

Marcus, S. M., Gorman, J., Shear, M. K. et al. (2007). A comparison of medication side effect reports by panic disorder patients with and without concomitant cognitive behavior therapy. *American Journal of Psychiatry*, 164: 273–275.

Marks, I. M., Stern, R. S., Mawson, D., Cobb, J., and McDonald, R. (1980). Clomipramine and exposure for obsessive-compulsive rituals. *British Journal of Psychiatry*, 136: 1–25.

Marks, I. M., Gray, S., Cohen, D. et al. (1983). Imipramine and brief therapists-aided exposure in agoraphobics having self-exposure homework. *Archives of General Psychiatry*, 40: 153–162.

Marks, I. M., Lelliott, P., Basoglu, M. et al. (1988). Clomipramine, self-exposure and therapist-aided exposure for obsessive-compulsive rituals. *British Journal of Psychiatry*, 152: 522–534.

Mavissakalian, M. (1990). Sequential combination of imipramine and self-directed exposure in the treatment of panic disorder with agoraphobia. *Journal of Clinical Psychiatry*, 51: 184–188.

Mavissakalian, M. and Michelson, L. (1986a). Agoraphobia: relative and combined effectiveness of therapist-assisted *in vivo* exposure and imipramine. *Journal of Clinical Psychiatry*, 47: 117–122.

Mavissakalian, M. and Michelson, L. (1986b). Two-year follow-up of exposure and imipramine treatment of agoraphobia. *American Journal of Psychiatry*, 143: 1106–1112.

Mavissakalian, M., Michelson, L, and Dealy, R. S. (1983). Pharmacological treatment of agoraphobia: imipramine versus imipramine with programmed practice. *British Journal of Psychiatry*, 143: 348–355.

Mawson, D., Marks, I. M., and Ramm, L. (1982). Clomipramine and exposure for chronic obsessive-compulsive rituals: III. Two year follow-up and further findings. *British Journal of Psychiatry*, 140: 11–18.

McHugh, R. K., Otto, M. W., Barlow, D. H., Gorman, J. M., Shear, M. K., and Woods, S. W. (2007). Cost-efficacy of individual and combined treatments for panic disorder. *Journal of Clinical Psychiatry*, 68: 1038–1044.

O'Sullivan, G., Noshirvani, H., Marks, I., Monteiro, W., and Lelliott, P. (1991). Six-year follow-up after exposure and clomipramine therapy for obsessive compulsive disorder. *Journal of Clinical Psychiatry*, 52: 150–155.

Piccinelli, M., Pini, S., Bellantuono, C., and Wilkinson, G. (1995). Efficacy of drug treatment in obsessive-compulsive disorder. A meta-analytic review. *British Journal of Psychiatry*, 166: 424–443.

Raffa, S. D., Stoddard, J. A., White, K. S. et al. (2008). Relapse following combined treatment discontinuation in a placebo-controlled trial for panic disorder. *Journal of Nervous and Mental Disease*, 196: 548–555.

Roll, D., Ray, S. E., Marcus, S. M. et al. (2004). Independent evaluator knowledge of treatment in a multicenter comparative treatment study of panic disorder. *Neuropsychopharmacology*, 29: 612–618.

Sheehan, D. V., Ballenger, J., and Jacobsen, G. (1980). Treatment of endogenous anxiety with phobic, hysterical and hypochondrical symptoms. *Archives of General Psychiatry*, 37: 51–59.

Simpson, H. B., Huppert, J. D., Petkova, E., Foa, E. B., and Liebowitz, M. R. (2006). Response versus remission in obsessive-compulsive disorder. *Journal of Clinical Psychiatry*, 67: 269–276.

Simpson, H. B., Liebowitz, M. R., Foa, E. B. et al. (2004). Post-treatment effects of exposure therapy and clomipramine in obsessive-compulsive disorder. *Depression and Anxiety*, 19: 225–233.

Telch, M. J., Agras, W. S., Taylor, C. B., Roth, W. T., and Gallen, C. C. (1985). Combined pharmacological and behavioral treatment for agoraphobia. *Behaviour Research and Therapy*, 23: 325–335.

White, K. S., Allen, L. B., Barlow, D. H., Gorman, J. M., Shear, M. K., and Woods, S. W. (2010). Attrition in a multicenter clinical trial for panic disorder. *Journal of Nervous and Mental Disease*, 198: 665–671.

Wiborg, I. M. and Dahl, A. A. (1996). Does brief dynamic psychotherapy reduce the relapse rate of panic disorder? *Archives of General Psychiatry*, 53: 689–694.

Zitrin, C. M., Klein, D. F., and Woerner, M. G. (1980). Treatment of agoraphobia with group exposure *in vivo* and imipramine. *Archives of General Psychiatry*, 37: 63–72.

Zitrin, C. M., Klein, D. F., Woerner, M. G., and Ross, D. C. (1983). Treatment of phobias. I: Comparison of imipramine hydrochloride and placebo. *Archives of General Psychiatry*, 40: 125–138.

Chapter 4

SELECTIVE SEROTONIN REUPTAKE INHIBITORS, REVERSIBLE INHIBITORS OF MONOAMINE OXIDASE-A, AND BUSPIRONE

Borwin Bandelow, Markus Reitt, and Dirk Wedekind
Department of Psychiatry and Psychotherapy, The University of Göttingen, Göttingen, Germany

INTRODUCTION

The combination of psychological interventions and drug treatment is a common strategy in the treatment of anxiety disorders. As the etiology of anxiety disorders is multifactorial, such a strategy seems reasonable. Psychological and pharmacological treatment modalities must be seen as partners – not alternatives – in the treatment of anxiety disorders.

Newer antidepressants, including the selective serotonin reuptake inhibitors (SSRIs) and the serotonin norepinephrine reuptake inhibitors (SNRIs), are among the first-line pharmacological treatments for anxiety disorders (Bandelow *et al.* 2008). The efficacy of cognitive-behavioral therapy in the treatment of anxiety disorders has been demonstrated in many controlled studies (Norton and Price 2007; Hofmann and Smits 2008).

METHODOLOGICAL ISSUES

When comparing the efficacy of CBT and SSRIs, we have to consider a number of methodological issues. In contrast to medications, which have to be compared with a pill placebo in order to be considered efficacious for the treatment of anxiety disorders, the requirements for psychological

---

Psychobiological Approaches for Anxiety Disorders: Treatment Combination Strategies, First Edition.
Edited by Stefan G. Hofmann.
© 2012 John Wiley & Sons, Ltd. Published 2012 by John Wiley & Sons, Ltd.

therapies are less strict. In most of the randomized controlled studies, CBT was compared with a wait-list control, whereas the number of studies comparing CBT to a placebo condition is limited for anxiety disorders such as OCD and PTSD (Hofmann and Smits 2008). Demonstrating the superiority of a psychological intervention to a wait-list control is only a first step to validate a new psychotherapeutic method, but not sufficient as efficacy proof. Such studies are not blind and subject to bias, as the patients randomized to a wait-list condition may experience negative demoralizing effects, while those assigned to active treatment may be influenced by positive expectancy effects. Moreover, a wait-list comparison only shows that the treatment is superior to 'no treatment' or the simple passage of time, but in order to demonstrate that a psychological therapy also has effects that go beyond non-specific factors such as attention, evidence is needed to show that the psychotherapeutic intervention is more effective than a 'psychological placebo.' For example, an 'attention placebo' is a control condition that involves a non-directional, neutral discussion between the patient and the treatment provider, in which no specific psychotherapeutic techniques such as 'cognitive restructuring' are applied. Such a control condition does not necessarily require trained psychotherapists. We know that many non-specific factors work in psychotherapy; therefore, it is no surprise that a psychological placebo often leads to substantial improvement in psychiatric disorders. However, if a given psychological therapy does not outperform a psychological placebo and can be delivered by untrained staff, the whole theory behind an elaborated psychotherapy method will have to be questioned.

For anxiety disorders, trials comparing CBT to a wait-list control group found significantly larger differences in effect sizes than those comparing CBT to an attention placebo, while 'psychological placebos' seem to have the same effect size as a pill placebo (Haby *et al.* 2006; Hofmann and Smits 2008). Thus, a credible psychological placebo control is the touchstone for efficacy proofs of psychological therapies.

Even in comparisons with a psychological placebo, there are still other methodological issues. It is difficult, but not impossible, to protect the blind in such studies. A rater who is blind to the treatment condition may reduce expectancy biases on the investigator side, but not on the patient side. Moreover, only a few published studies have provided data that were corrected for attrition (i.e. ITT analysis using the last-observation-carried-forward method) (Hofmann and Smits 2008).

Due to limited financial resources, evaluations of psychological therapies often do not have the optimal sample sizes, which limit their interpretability. Very often, when two or more different active psychological treatments or techniques are compared, the result is 'no difference.' In many cases, this may be due to the use of sample sizes that were far too small for non-inferiority trials. Recent non-inferiority drug trials used between 80 and 300 subjects per arm, and because the average effect sizes obtained with psychological therapy are not higher than with drug treatment, the same sample size requirements apply for psychotherapy trials. Therefore, direct comparisons of psychological and pharmacological therapies are important for an objective assessment of the optimal treatment strategy.

An advantage of psychological treatments is an apparent lack of side effects in the true sense of the word. However, techniques such as exposure and response prevention have high rates of therapy refusal and attrition due to unpleasant feelings during sessions and related anticipatory anxiety. Overdependence on the therapist has also been observed. Like drug treatment, psychological therapy also may show insufficient efficacy. Furthermore, relapses or even deterioration in symptoms is possible. Response may be delayed and usually occurs later than with drug treatment. Prolonged courses of treatment are often needed to maintain an initial treatment response. And finally, demonstrating efficacy of psychotherapy in a trial conducted at an expert site does not guarantee that the same effect sizes are obtained in 'real life' (Nutt and Sharpe 2008).

Follow-Up Studies

It is believed that gains from CBT are maintained after termination of treatment, while patients on drugs immediately have a relapse of anxiety symptoms after medication is stopped. This would offer CBT a considerable advantage over drug treatment. In order to show that CBT has longer lasting effects, it must be shown that treatment gains with CBT still differ significantly from control conditions after a follow-up period without formal treatment, which is usually between 6 and 12 months in the available studies. Control conditions, which may be used in such a comparison, include a psychological placebo condition, a pill placebo, or a medication group, in which the drugs are stopped or tapered off after the acute treatment period. However, in most randomized controlled trials (RCTs) with CBT, the control condition was a wait list. When patients in the wait-list condition are switched to active treatment after this period, there is no control group left for a follow-up comparison. Thus, only few studies remain that can be used as evidence for long-term advantages of CBT.

Some of the few available follow-up studies are hampered by two main problems. First, mostly due to the difficulty in recruiting enough patients for clinical studies, the samples sizes are often already too small for the active treatment phase. As attrition increases with longer study duration, there are often not enough participants left who can be followed-up after the treatment-free period. Therefore, sometimes no significant differences have been found between the various treatment conditions, due to low test power at the follow-up endpoint. The second problem is that it is usually difficult to control the 'purity' of treatments during the follow-up period

For ethical reasons, it is almost impossible to prevent patients in the follow-up period to participate in other treatments. More often than not, participants who are still symptomatic would take drugs in an uncontrolled manner or take part in alternative psychological treatment programs, even though told not to do so by the study investigators. These additional activities level out effect size differences between the original treatments. Therefore, when no differences are found between the CBT-treated patients and the ones in the control group (psychological placebo, pill placebo, or a drug) during the active treatment, it is difficult to say whether this result is due to methodological problems or simply due to the fact that CBT has no longer lasting effects that go beyond spontaneous remission.

META-ANALYSES

As many psychotherapy studies have small sample sizes, meta-analyses have been used in order to pool data from different studies. With meta-analyses, we can not only contrast direct comparisons of psychological and pharmacological interventions, but also compare all other studies in which either a psychological or a drug intervention was studied, thus increasing the total number of studies. However, there are many methodological problems with this method. In the various studies, different scales are used. Although the scale scores are converted into effect sizes in order to compare them across the studies, there is a substantial amount of variation between different scales. Even within a study, effect sizes derived from the Clinical Global Impressions Scale (CGI) and the Hamilton Anxiety Scale differ greatly, although they were obtained from the same patients under the same treatment.

There are two ways to compare effect sizes: the 'relative' method and the 'absolute' method. The relative method measures the difference between the active and control treatment and then compares these differences between psychotherapy and drug studies. However, the difference between active treatment and a wait-list control is much larger than to a psychological placebo, and therefore wait-list control studies with CBT cannot be compared with active drug/placebo contrasts with this method. The other possibility is to compare the absolute effect sizes (i.e. the change from baseline to post-treatment), regardless of the efficacy relative to the respective control group. This method is subject to biases. In a drug study, expectancy to achieve remission is relatively low, as patients have to be informed that they have either received placebo, which has no specific effect, or a new drug, which has probably never been tested before. In contrast, patients who have been assigned to an active treatment with a good reputation, such as CBT, instead of drawing the wait list-lot, have high expectations that they will be well in a few weeks, which might result in higher effect sizes. Moreover, in some comparisons of CBT with a wait list, the adjunctive use of drugs is common, and it is problematic to treat the effect size of such a combined treatment as a 'pure' CBT effect.

Comparisons of psychological and drug therapies exist for the three major anxiety disorders: panic disorder, generalized anxiety disorder (GAD), and social anxiety disorder (SAD). The studies are tabulated in Table 4.1.

PANIC DISORDER

SSRIs

Acute Studies

In direct randomized controlled comparisons of cognitive-behavioral or exposure therapy with psychopharmacological treatment, drugs were superior in two studies (Black et al. 1993; Bakker et al. 1999). In addition, an open study found larger effects with SSRI treatments (van Apeldoorn et al. 2008). No differences were found in one controlled study (Sharp et al. 1997); however, the statistical evaluation of this study was problematic and the study may also have been underpowered. In this study the authors say that CBT was superior to fluvoxamine; however, when adequate statistical methods are applied, CBT was not different from fluvoxamine (Mann-Whitney U test, $p = 0.17$, N.S.)

Three RCTs showed that the combination of SSRIs with CBT exposure therapy was superior to CBT alone (de Beurs et al. 1995; Oehrberg et al. 1995; Stein et al. 2000). Furthermore, a study using self-administered CBT, which may not be comparable with therapist-delivered treatment, found superiority of the combination treatment over CBT alone (Koszycki et al. 2011). In the study by Sharp et al. (1997), fluvoxamine combined with CBT was not superior to CBT plus placebo, although another study found that the combination of self-administered CBT and an SSRI (sertraline) was superior to the SSRI alone (Koszycki et al. 2011). Interestingly, fluvoxamine combined with CBT was not superior to either treatment alone in the study by Sharp et al. (1997).

In summary, there is limited evidence showing that SSRI treatment is superior to CBT or exposure, although two studies, which were methodologically problematic, did not show a difference. In the majority of studies, the combination of SSRIs and CBT was superior to CBT alone. Compared to SSRIs alone, the addition of CBT to an SSRI was not more effective, while the combination of self-administered CBT and an SSRI was superior to the SSRI alone.

Long-Term Effects

There was only one controlled study looking at long-term outcome of SSRI/CBT. Two years after completion of the de Beurs et al. (1995) study, a

Table 4.1. Panic disorder: comparisons of cognitive behavioral therapy (CBT) or exposure therapy with SSRIs, buspirone, and moclobemide. RCT, randomized controlled trial, =, treatments are equally effective on the main efficacy measures, > treatment is significantly superior. In brackets: patient numbers (included/evaluable patients)

Source	Efficacy (Post-treatment)	Daily dose/mg
RCTs		
SSRIs		
Bakker et al. 1999	Paroxetine (38/32) = clomipramine (39/32) > CBT (38/35) = placebo (39/32)	Paroxetine 20–60 Clomipramine 50–150
Black et al. 1993	Fluvoxamine (25/23) > CBT (25/20) = placebo (25/23)	Fluvoxamine 300
de Beurs et al. 1995	Fluvoxamine + exposure (24/19) > placebo + exposure (24/19) = panic management + exposure (24/20) = exposure (24/18)	Fluvoxamine 50–150
Koszycki et al. 2011	Sertraline (61/43) + self-administered CBT (sCBT) > sertraline (63/46) = placebo + sCBT (65/44) = placebo (62/43)	Sertraline 50–200
Oehrberg et al. 1995	Paroxetine + CBT(60/55) > placebo + CBT (60/52)	Paroxetine 20–60
Sharp et al. 1997	Fluvoxamine (?/29) = Fluvoxamine + CBT (?/29) = placebo + CBT (?/33) = CBT (?/30) > placebo (?/28)[1]	Fluvoxamine 150
Stein et al. 2000	CBT + paroxetine (16/15) > CBT + placebo (17/16)	Paroxetine 10–50
Moclobemide		
Loerch et al. 1999	Moclobemide + CBT (14/11) = placebo + CBT (14/13) > moclobemide + psychol. placebo (16/9) = placebo + psychol. placebo (11/9)	Moclobemide 300–600

Buspirone		
Cottraux et al. 1995	Buspirone + CBT (37/22) > placebo + CBT (40/27)	Buspirone 5–60
OPEN STUDIES		
van Apeldoorn et al. 2008	CBT + SSRI (49/37) = SSRI (48/27) > CBT (53/26)	5 different SSRIs

[1]In this study the authors say that CBT was superior to fluvoxamine; however, when adequate statistical methods are applied, CBT was not different from fluvoxamine (Mann-Whitney U test, p = 0.17, N.S.). Numbers of randomized patients were not given.

naturalistic follow-up study investigated the long-term efficacy of the treatments and found no difference between the original treatment groups (de Beurs *et al.* 1999). The effect in the fluvoxamine/exposure group was maintained, but was no longer superior, due to further improvements in the other treatment groups. There was a trend for patients in the fluvoxamine/exposure group to require less aftercare than those who received the other treatments. Nearly 50% of the patients who had received medication in the original trial were able to taper off fluvoxamine without a recurrence of symptoms.

In a 1-year follow-up of the open study by van Apeldoorn *et al.* (2008), no significant differences were found between the treatment groups (van Apeldoorn *et al.* 2010).

In summary, from these direct comparisons, there is no evidence that CBT has longer lasting effects than drug treatment, and further studies using larger sample sizes are required to investigate this issue.

Moclobemide

One study investigated the reversible selective monoamine oxidase A inhibitor moclobemide (Loerch *et al.* 1999). This drug cannot be considered as an adequate comparator to CBT, as it was not superior to placebo in panic disorder in a controlled study, which was not published (Buller 1994). The addition of moclobemide to CBT was not superior to a placebo/CBT combination and moclobemide plus a psychological placebo was not different from a combination of a pill placebo and psychological placebo. However, at 6-months follow-up, patients receiving moclobemide plus CBT in the acute treatment phase had the best outcome, followed by moclobemide plus psychological placebo and CBT plus pill placebo. These results were interpreted by the authors as a consequence of additional therapies that took place in the follow-up period.

Buspirone

Buspirone can enhance the effects of CBT in panic disorder (Cottraux *et al.* 1995). However, the drug is not a standard drug for panic disorder, as the results of controlled trials were disappointing. It was not superior to placebo (Sheehan *et al.* 1990; 1993) and less effective than imipramine (Sheehan *et al.* 1990), clorazepate (Schweizer and Rickels 1988), and alprazolam (Sheehan *et al.* 1993).

GENERALIZED ANXIETY DISORDER

Data on the advantages of combining drugs and psychological therapy are almost completely lacking for GAD. In particular, there are no comparisons

Table 4.2. Generalized anxiety disorder. Comparison of CBT and buspirone

Source	Efficacy (Post-treatment)	Daily dose/mg
Lader and Bond 1998	Buspirone + CBT (15/12) = buspirone + non-directive therapy (psychological placebo) (15/12) = placebo + CBT (15/12) = placebo + non-directive therapy (psychological placebo (15/12)	Buspirone up to 30

between standard drugs for GAD and psychotherapy. One study with four arms compared buspirone with CBT, placebo with CBT, buspirone plus a psychological placebo and a 'double placebo' (placebo pills with psychological placebo) (Table 4.2). All four treatments were found to be equally effective; however, the statistical power of this study may have been much too low to detect significant differences (Lader and Scotto 1998). Buspirone showed inconsistent results in other studies with patients with GAD (Bandelow et al. 2008). There are no follow-up comparisons of psychological and drug treatments for GAD.

(Table 4.3). In a placebo-controlled study, sertraline, exposure therapy, and their combination were compared (Blomhoff et al. 2001). Exposure therapy was not conducted by experienced behavioral therapists, but by CBT-trained general practitioners. Sertraline-treated patients improved significantly more than non-sertraline-treated patients. No significant difference was observed between exposure- and non-exposure-treated patients. Although the combination showed higher effect sizes than both treatment modalities alone, the difference was not statistically significant. In one study, patients received CBT, fluoxetine plus self-exposure, or placebo plus self-exposure. CBT was superior to the two other conditions, while fluoxetine showed no effect (Clark et al. 2003). Another study compared fluoxetine, cognitive-behavioral group therapy, placebo, and the combinations of CBT plus fluoxetine and CBT plus placebo. All treatments were superior to placebo, but did not differ between themselves (Davidson et al. 2004). In an open study, individual CBT was superior to group CBT and 'treatment as usual' with SSRIs (Mörtberg et al. 2007).

Moclobemide

Moclobemide is not an ideal comparison medication, as the drug showed inconsistent results in placebo-controlled studies and is therefore not

Table 4.3. Social anxiety disorder. Comparisons of CBT and SSRIs/moclobemide. In brackets: number of patients (included/evaluable patients)

Autoren	Efficacy (Post-Treatment)	Daily dose/mg
SSRIs		
RCTs		
Clark et al. 2003	CBT (20/20) > fluoxetine + self-exposure (20/20) = placebo + self-exposure (20/20)	fluoxetine 20–60
Davidson et al. 2004	CBT (60/48) = fluoxetine (57/13) = CBT + fluoxetine (59/42) = CBT + placebo > placebo (60/36)	fluoxetine 20–60
Blomhoff et al. 2001	sertraline (96/87) = sertraline + exposure (98/88) > exposure + placebo (98/91) = placebo (95/88)	sertraline 50–150
OPEN STUDY		
Mörtberg et al. 2007	individual CBT > group CBT = 'treatment as usual' with SSRIs	
Moclobemide		
Prasko et al. 2006	CBT + moclobemide (27/22) = CBT + placebo (27/24) > moclobemide (27/20)	moclobemide 600
Oosterbaan et al. 2001	CBT (28/24) > moclobemide (27/24) CBT = placebo (27/19)	moclobemide 300–600

regarded as a first-line medication for SAD (Bandelow et al. 2008). In a 6-month RCT, CBT plus pill placebo and the combination of moclobemide and CBT were both superior to moclobemide alone (Prasko et al. 2006). There was no psychological placebo control condition for CBT, but the efficacy was assessed by a rater who was blind to the treatment conditions. The combination of CBT and pharmacotherapy yielded the most rapid effect. In a comparison of CBT, moclobemide, and placebo, CBT was superior to moclobemide but not to a pill placebo. Moclobemide did not differentiate from placebo (Oosterbaan et al. 2001).

Follow-Up Studies

In a follow-up of the Blomhoff et al. study, patients were re-assessed after a treatment-free period of 28 and 52 weeks (Haug et al. 2003). The authors reported that exposure therapy alone yielded a further improvement during follow-up, whereas exposure plus sertraline and sertraline alone showed a tendency toward deterioration after the completion of treatment. However, exposure patients only reached the same degree of improvement after the treatment-free period that the sertraline patients already had during the acute study. Improvement was also shown in the placebo group. Thus, there was no evidence that the longer lasting effects in the exposure group were due to effects other than spontaneous remission (Bandelow and Haug 2004).

In the Prasko et al. (2006) study, the group previously treated with moclobemide had a significantly higher relapse rate than the groups treated with CBT alone or the combination after a 24-months follow-up period. In a 2-months follow-up of the open Oosterbaan et al. study, CBT was superior both to moclobemide and placebo, while moclobemide was not superior to placebo. At 15-months follow-up, all conditions were equal.

In summary, the data for comparisons of SSRIs and CBT for SAD are inconclusive, showing no clear advantage of one treatment modality over the other. There is no evidence that combination therapy is more effective than either monotherapies. In comparisons with the RIMA (reversible inhibitors of monoamine oxidase-A) moclobemide, CBT was superior and moclobemide was ineffective.

CONCLUSION

For panic disorder, available direct comparisons show a slight advantage of SSRIs over behavioral therapy. There is some evidence that the combination of both treatment modalities is superior to CBT alone, but only limited evidence that the combination is more effective than SSRIs alone. A meta-analysis of the available studies showed equal efficacy of CBT and SSRIs, and a clear advantage of combination therapies.

Moclobemide, a drug which is not approved for the treatment of panic disorder, was less effective than CBT in acute studies, but at follow-up, the combination of CBT and moclobemide was superior to both monotherapies.

For GAD, only inconclusive data exist. For SAD, we see a mixed picture, with SSRIs being less, similarly, or more effective than CBT. Follow-up studies with SAD patients did not show an advantage of CBT after the acute treatment period. For moclobemide, a drug which had shown inconsistent results in placebo-controlled studies, the results were generally worse than with CBT.

More treatment studies comparing CBT with first-line treatments for anxiety disorders, such as SSRIs, SNRIs, or pregabalin, should be performed – with large sample sizes that warrant enough power for a follow-up study. Until such studies are available, it seems rational to recommend combined treatment, as there is more evidence supporting than refuting such a strategy.

It has been argued that combined treatments are more expensive than monotherapies. However, because most SSRIs are now available as generic drugs, in most industrial countries, the costs of one CBT session equals the costs of 6 to 12 months of treatment with a generic SSRI. Therefore, the costs of combined treatment are mostly determined by the expenditures for CBT.

The choice between medications and CBT or a combination is also determined by a number of factors, particularly the patient's preference, treatment options at hand, adverse drug effects, onset of efficacy, comorbidity (e.g. with depression), economic considerations, time availability and commitment of the patient, accessibility of psychiatric and psychological treatment resources, and qualification and experience of the clinician. Unfortunately, in many regions of the world, the availability of CBT is often limited, and even in Western countries, CBT can only be started after a waiting period of some months. Therefore, under real world conditions, patients are offered drug therapy long before CBT can be started.

REFERENCES

Bakker, A., van Dyck, R., Spinhoven, P., and van Balkom, A. (1999). Paroxetine, clomipramine, and cognitive therapy in the treatment of panic disorder. *Journal of Clinical Psychiatry*, 60: 831–838.

Bandelow, B. and Haug, T. T. (2004). Sertraline and exposure therapy in social phobia (author's reply). *British Journal of Psychiatry*, 184: 271–272.

Bandelow, B., Zohar, J., Hollander, E., *et al*. (2008). World Federation of Societies of Biological Psychiatry (WFSBP) guidelines for the pharmacological treatment of anxiety, obsessive-compulsive and post-traumatic stress disorders – first revision. *World Journal of Biological Psychiatry* 9: 248–312.

Black, D. W., Wesner, R., Bowers, W., and Gabel, J. (1993). A comparison of fluvoxamine, cognitive therapy, and placebo in the treatment of panic disorder. *Archives of General Psychiatry*, 50: 44–50.

Blomhoff, S., Tangen Haug, T., Hellstrom, K. *et al.* (2001). Randomised controlled general practice trial of sertraline, exposure therapy and combined treatment in generalised social phobia. *British Journal of Psychiatry*, 179: 23–30.
Buller, R. (1994). Reversible inhibitors of monoamine oxidase A (RIMA) in anxiety disorders. Oral presentation on the 7th congress of the Association of European Psychiatrists (AEP); Copenhagen, 18–22 September, 1994.
Clark, D. M., Ehlers, A., McManus, F. *et al.* (2003). Cognitive therapy versus fluoxetine in generalized social phobia: a randomized placebo-controlled trial. *Journal of Consulting and Clinical Psychology*, 71: 1058–1067.
Cottraux, J., Note, I. D., Cungi, C. (1995). A controlled study of cognitive behaviour therapy with buspirone or placebo in panic disorder with agoraphobia. *British Journal of Psychiatry*, 167: 635–641.
Davidson, J. R., Foa, E. B., Huppert, J. D. *et al.* (2004). Fluoxetine, comprehensive cognitive behavioral therapy, and placebo in generalized social phobia. *Archives of General Psychiatry*, 61: 1005–1013.
de Beurs, E., van Balkom, A. J., Lange, A., Koele, P., and van Dyck, R. (1995). Treatment of panic disorder with agoraphobia: comparison of fluvoxamine, placebo, and psychological panic management combined with exposure and of exposure *in vivo* alone. *American Journal of Psychiatry*, 152: 683–691.
de Beurs, E., van Balkomm, A. J., Van Dyck, R., Lange, A. (1999). Long-term outcome of pharmacological and psychological treatment for panic disorder with agoraphobia: a 2-year naturalistic follow-up. *Acta Psychiatrica Scandinavica*, 99: 5 9–67.
Haby, M. M., Donnelly, M., Corry, J., and Vos, T. (2006). Cognitive behavioural therapy for depression, panic disorder and generalized anxiety disorder: a meta-regression of factors that may predict outcome. *Australia and New Zealand Journal of Psychiatry*, 40: 9–19.
Haug, T. T., Blomhoff, S., Hellstrom, K. *et al.* (2003). Exposure therapy and sertraline in social phobia: I-year follow-up of a randomised controlled trial. *British Journal of Psychiatry*, 182: 312–318.
Hofmann, S. G. and Smits, J. A. (2008). Cognitive-behavioral therapy for adult anxiety disorders: a meta-analysis of randomized placebo-controlled trials. *Journal of Clinical Psychiatry*, 69: 621–632.
Koszycki, D., Taljaard, M., Segal, Z., and Bradwejn, J. (2011). A randomized trial of sertraline, self-administered cognitive behavior therapy, and their combination for panic disorder. *Psychological Medicine*, 41: 373–383.
Lader, M. H. and Bond, A. J. (1998). Interaction of pharmacological and psychological treatments of anxiety. *British Journal of Psychiatry*. Supplement 42–48.
Lader, M., and Scotto, J. C. (1998). A multicentre double-blind comparison of hydroxyzine, buspirone and placebo in patients with generalized anxiety disorder. *Psychopharmacology (Berl.)*, 139: 402–406.
Loerch, B., Graf-Morgenstern, M., Hautzinger, M. *et al.* (1999). Randomised placebo-controlled trial of moclobemide, cognitive-behavioural therapy and their combination in panic disorder with agoraphobia. *British Journal of Psychiatry*, 174: 205–212.
Mörtberg, E., Clark, D. M., Sundin, O., and Aberg Wistedt, A. (2007). Intensive group cognitive treatment and individual cognitive therapy vs. treatment as usual in social phobia: a randomized controlled trial. *Acta Psychiatrica Scandinavica*, 115: 142–154.

Norton, P. J. and Price, E. C. (2007). A meta-analytic review of adult cognitive-behavioral treatment outcome across the anxiety disorders. *Journal of Nervous and Mental Disease*, 195: 521–531.

Nutt, D. J. and Sharpe, M. (2008). Uncritical positive regard? Issues in the efficacy and safety of psychotherapy. *Journal of Psychopharmacology*, 22: 3–6.

Oehrberg, S., Christiansen, P. E., Behnke, K. *et al.* (1995). Paroxetine in the treatment of panic disorder. A randomised, double-blind, placebo-controlled study. *British Journal of Psychiatry*, 167: 374–379.

Oosterbaan, D., van Balkom, A., Spinhoven, P., van Oppen, P., and van Dyck, R. (2001). Cognitive therapy versus moclobemide in social phobia: a controlled study. *Clinical Psychology and Psychotherapy*, 8: 263–873.

Prasko, J., Dockery, C., Horacek, J. *et al.* (2006). Moclobemide and cognitive behavioral therapy in the treatment of social phobia. A six-month controlled study and 24 months follow up. *Neuro Endocrinology Letters*, 27: 473–481.

Schweizer, E. and Rickels, K. (1988). Buspirone in the treatment of panic disorder: a controlled pilot comparison with clorazepate (letter). *Journal of Clinical Psychopharmacology*, 8: 303.

Sharp, D. M., Power, K. G., Simpson, R. J., Swanson, V., and Anstee, J. A. (1997). Global measures of outcome in a controlled comparison of pharmacological and psychological treatment of panic disorder and agoraphobia in primary care. *British Journal of General Practice*, 47: 150–155.

Sheehan, D. V., Raj, A. B., Sheehan, K. H., and Soto, S. (1990). Is buspirone effective for panic disorder? *Journal of Clinical Psychopharmacology*, 10: 3–11.

Sheehan, D. V., Raj, A. B., Harnett Sheehan, K., Soto, S., and Knapp, E. (1993). The relative efficacy of high-dose buspirone and alprazolam in the treatment of panic disorder: a double-blind placebo-controlled study. *Acta Psychiatrica Scandinavica*, 88: 1–11.

Stein, M. B., Norton, G., Walker, J. R., Chartier, M. J., and Graham, R. (2000). Do selective serotonin re-uptake inhibitors enhance the efficacy of very brief cognitive behavioral therapy for panic disorder? A pilot study. *Psychiatry Research*, 94: 191–200.

van Apeldoorn, F. J., van Hout, W. J., Mersch, P. P. *et al.* (2008). Is a combined therapy more effective than either CBT or SSRI alone? Results of a multicenter trial on panic disorder with or without agoraphobia. *Acta Psychiatrica Scandinavica*, 117: 260–270.

van Apeldoorn, F. J., Timmerman, M. E., Mersch, P. P. *et al.* (2010). A randomized trial of cognitive-behavioral therapy or selective serotonin reuptake inhibitor or both combined for panic disorder with or without agoraphobia: treatment results through 1-year follow-up. *Journal of Clinical Psychiatry*, 71: 574–586.

Chapter 5

D-CYCLOSERINE

Adam J. Guastella and Gail A. Alvares

Brain and Mind Research Institute, University of Sydney, Australia

INTRODUCTION

In an attempt to boost the efficacy of cognitive behavioral therapy (CBT), a novel strategy has emerged for the combination of pharmacotherapy and psychotherapy for treating anxiety disorders. This strategy is based on studies that have mapped some of the core pathways and neurotransmitters involved in fear extinction. These studies suggest that D-cycloserine (DCS), a partial agonist at the glycine recognition site of the glutamatergic *N*-methyl-D-aspartate receptor (NMDA-R), can facilitate extinction learning in animals and exposure therapy in humans. This chapter provides an overview of this literature.

BASIC LEARNING PROCESSES IN CBT

A critical component of CBT involves the patient learning to face their fears through exposure. In exposure therapy, patients are presented with feared images or stimuli in a prolonged or gradual manner. For example, an individual with spider phobia might be placed in a room with a spider in a glass box. Exposure therapy typically engages in hierarchical designs where patients learn mastery through anxiety reduction within each hierarchical step (e.g. standing 2 meters away from a spider; placing a hand in the glass box with a spider). Foa and Kozak's Emotion-Processing Theory (1986) has often been used as a theoretical model to explain

---

Psychobiological Approaches for Anxiety Disorders: Treatment Combination Strategies, First Edition.
Edited by Stefan G. Hofmann.
© 2012 John Wiley & Sons, Ltd. Published 2012 by John Wiley & Sons, Ltd.

the benefits of exposure therapy. They argue that three conditions are necessary for change in anxiety pathology to occur:

1) engagement with the fear structure, as evidenced by increases in physiological arousal;
2) reduction in physiological arousal, both during the exposure session (within session) and across multiple presentations of the fear structure (between sessions); and
3) incorporation of new information that is inconsistent with the fear structure (e.g. the observation that a spider does not attack unprovoked).

This process is essentially a learning procedure, occurring over time, with the end result being a gradual reduction in the anxiety response to the feared stimuli.

Experimental models testing the efficacy of exposure therapy are based on Pavlovian conditioning. This experimental model is simple and precise in application, making it amenable to scientific and neurobiological evaluation. In these designs, an initially neutral stimulus (the conditioned stimulus (CS), e.g. a light or tone) is repeatedly paired with a fear-inducing and aversive stimulus (the unconditioned stimulus (US), e.g. shock), resulting in the formation of a conditioned fear response (CR, e.g. freezing or startle) to the presentation of the CS and a corresponding fear memory (CS–US association). Due to these repeated pairings, the CS becomes associated with fear, and presentations of the CS alone will elicit the fear response. Repeated pairings of stimuli occur during the 'acquisition' phase of training.

Extinction of learned fear involves the repeated presentations of the CS in the absence of the US. This phase may be conducted immediately following acquisition or after a delay. In the extinction phase, animals gradually demonstrate a loss of fear expression to the CS. Following the extinction session, either immediately or after delay, the animal will be placed for a final 'test' phase. The fear response following the presentation of the CS alone provides an outcome for the success of previous extinction learning.

A number of theories have been put forward to explain the phenomenon of extinction (Myers and Davis 2007). Extinction does not appear to reflect an 'unlearning' mechanism in which previous CS–US associations are forgotten. For example, even though animals or humans no longer demonstrate fear in the face of the stimulus, they may experience a return of fear (ROF: Tansella *et al.* 2006) to the CS at a later point or in a different context (Guastella *et al.* 2007). If exposure erased the original association, then relapse should not occur. Instead, the process of extinction implies that the feared CS–US association has been overridden by the formation of a new association, reflecting a conditioned inhibition process that competes with the original fear memory (Myers and Davis 2007). Subsequent research has focused on methods to reduce the likelihood of ROF by enhancing extinction training (Rowe and Craske 1998).

DCS ENHANCES THE EXTINCTION OF FEAR

The last decade has witnessed huge advances in our understanding of the neurobiological mechanisms that underlie fear extinction. Evidence points to the central role of the amygdala in both the expression and acquisition of fear (Davis 2002). In particular, NMDA-R recognition sites play a crucial role in learning during extinction training. Stimulating or blocking NMDA-R recognition sites located in the basolateral nucleus of the amygdala (BLA) facilitates or blocks the extinction of fear, respectively. For example, NMDA antagonists, such as AP5, dose-dependently block extinction when injected into the BLA (Davis and Myers 2002). Furthermore, intra-amygdala infusions of DCS, an NMDA partial agonist that enhances glutamate function through NMDA-R activity (Hood et al. 1989), facilitates the extinction of learned fear (Walker et al. 2002). By contrast, DCS administered in the absence of extinction has no effect on fear responses to the CS during extinction, indicating a specific enhancing effect of DCS during extinction. Reviewed in more detail below, these pre-clinical studies suggest that glutamatergic synaptic plasticity in the amygdala critically enhances extinction learning.

DCS has a complicated modulatory role on NMDA-R function, both enhancing and reducing NMDA function, depending on surrounding glycine levels (Danysz and Parsons 1998). In medical settings, DCS is used primarily as a broad-spectrum antibiotic for tuberculosis (Seromycin). It is generally dosed between 250 to 500 mg twice-daily orally, with doses as high as 1000 mg per day in children. DCS peaks in blood within 45 minutes in fasting subjects, but is delayed for up to 3.5 hours with a high-fat meal (Tawanda 2006). In healthy male subjects, DCS is readily absorbed into the blood, with a half-life of 9 hours, and dose-dependently increases the amount of DCS available in plasma, with no corresponding neuroendocrine changes (Van Berckel et al. 1997). Concentrations of DCS are similar in both plasma and cerebrospinal fluid, implying it can cross the blood-brain barrier (D'Souza et al. 2000). To date, only a few minor adverse side effects have been noted in human clinical trials, with contra-indications including alcohol use, pregnancy, renal failure, epilepsy (due to risk of seizures), history of depression with suicidality, and some psychotropic medications. Neuropsychiatric symptoms that can occur with doses of 1 g per day include headache, somnolence, severe psychosis, seizures, and suicidal ideation, with a large alcohol intake increasing the risk of seizures (Tawanda 2006).

THE EFFECTS OF DCS ON FEAR EXTINCTION IN ANIMAL MODELS

DCS has been argued to elicit a number of central effects in the brain, mediated by NMDA-R activity. Some have suggested it may act as a general cognitive enhancer, with demonstrated effects on memory consolidation and retrieval processes (Monahan et al. 1989; Thompson et al. 1992). However, for the purposes of this review, we will specifically discuss evidence that DCS is involved in enhancing the neural processes surrounding fear extinction. Walker et al. (2002) reported the first evidence that DCS facilitates the extinction of learned fear. In a series of studies, the authors demonstrated that rats administered moderate to large doses of DCS prior to extinction training exhibited less fear, as measured by reduced fear-potentiated startle in response to a light CS, in comparison to rats given saline. This dose-dependent effect was specific to rats administered DCS prior to extinction and not to those rats given DCS without extinction training. This finding indicated that the effects were specific to extinction, and were not due to any general and non-context specific effect of the drug.

Subsequent research has specified important contexts and conditions under which optimal DCS effects on fear extinction can be observed. Ledgerwood et al. (2003) found that post-extinction administration of DCS facilitated extinction learning; DCS administered systematically or directly into the BLA after extinction reduced fear-induced freezing compared to rats given saline or rats given DCS with no extinction test. The results were interpreted by the authors to suggest that DCS facilitated the consolidation of new learning and memories acquired during extinction. The authors also demonstrated that by increasing the delay between extinction and DCS administration, effectiveness of DCS was also reduced, with effectiveness limited to administration less than 4 hours after extinction. More recently, Langton and Richardson (2010) demonstrated that DCS facilitates extinction when administered after extinction, even when there is a substantial delay after conditioning.

When an animal is stressed following an extinction procedure, reinstatement of fear may be observed; that is, the recovery of a learned fear response to the CS following presentation of the US. Ledgerwood et al. (2004) demonstrated that DCS reduces the ability of stress to disrupt extinction. Rats given DCS after extinction failed to show reinstatement of fear to the CS, and continued to express extinction, even when the CS was presented following stress. By contrast, saline-treated rats showed a return of fear to the CS, implying that DCS may decrease the likelihood of relapse following successful completion of fear extinction. Ledgerwood et al. (2005) also found that DCS-treated rats not only showed facilitated extinction, but demonstrated less fear to another CS previously paired with the US that had not been extinguished. Thus, it was argued that DCS might facilitate extinction of learned fear through a general devaluation of the US. Interestingly, two recent studies have indicated that DCS does not influence renewal effects (Woods and Bouton 2006; Bouton et al. 2008). Renewal is demonstrated with the return of fear when the CS becomes predictive of shock again in the original context in which it was conditioned (but not extinguished). Further research is required to clarify the reasons for these findings.

This pre-clinical animal work has also indicated a number of clinically important variables that seem to influence the impact of DCS on extinction training. Multiple administrations of DCS prior to the extinction training appears to reduces efficacy (Parnas et al. 2005), implying a potential tolerance of NMDA-R sites with chronic administration. Concurrent medication also seems to be an important factor, with long-term use of some antidepressants (specifically citalopram or imipramine) shown to modify NMDA-R function in mice (Popik et al. 2000). In addition, prior exposure to DCS or imipramine abolishes the effects of DCS on extinction (Werner-Seidler and Richardson 2007), suggesting a desensitization effect on NMDA-R functional activity with concurrent antidepressant use. Prior exposure to extinction procedures also reduces DCS efficacy on re-extinction training (Langton and Richardson 2008). Lastly, long-term DCS facilitation of extinction may only be observed when some extinction of fear can be observed within sessions (Weber et al. 2007), implying that DCS may only need to be administered after an effective exposure session in which levels of fear are reduced significantly.

CLINICAL APPLICATIONS OF DCS IN HUMANS

Post-Traumatic Stress Disorder

Post-traumatic stress disorder (PTSD) provides the closest human anxiety disorder to match pre-clinical conditioning models. The disorder itself is defined by the occurrence of an uncontrollable and life-threatening experience, which leaves the individual fearful and avoidant of cues that become associated with the traumatic event (APA 2000). However, there has been only one trial that has explored the effect of DCS on anxiety in PTSD. Conducted by Heresco-Levy et al. (2002), a total of 11 patients with PTSD were enrolled in a 12-week crossover study. Following an initial 2-week baseline, participants were assigned to receive DCS (25 mg) or placebo twice daily for 4 weeks. This was then followed by a 2-week washout, and a 4-week period of crossover drug administration. Assessments of PTSD symptoms, depression, anxiety, and neurocognition were taken before and after each phase of treatment. The results of this within-subject, crossover trial failed to show any benefits of DCS administration over placebo. Although the results failed to support the hypothesis that DCS improves therapeutic recovery in PTSD, concerns over the interpretation of findings have been raised (Richardson *et al.* 2004). Most notably, DCS administration in this study was independent of any combined psychological intervention, which accumulating evidence indicates is a critical factor for DCS efficacy.

Specific Phobias

The first human clinical treatment study to combine DCS administration with an exposure-based therapy was conducted by Ressler *et al.* (2004). In this study, a total of 28 individuals diagnosed with acrophobia (fear of heights) were randomized to receive either DCS (50 or 500 mg) or a placebo 1 hour prior to 2 sessions of virtual reality exposure-based therapy. Primary outcome measurements included subjective levels of fear within the virtual glass elevator, questionnaires assessing fear and anxiety, clinician ratings of improvement, and measures of skin conductance, with a 1-week and 3-month follow-up. This study demonstrated, for the first time, that DCS significantly enhanced outcomes from exposure therapy. Patients who received DCS exhibited reduced symptoms on all anxiety outcome measures compared to placebo, at both the 1-week and 3-month time-point. Furthermore, they demonstrated a greater number of self-exposures to real-world height environments. This landmark study was the first to extend the strong and growing literature of animal studies into human populations by demonstrating that DCS administration facilitated treatment outcome when combined with a simple exposure therapy treatment. However, an important caveat to these findings is that specific phobia is relatively easy to treat with exposure therapy in the community, and most individuals rarely seek treatment solely for specific phobia.

Social Anxiety Disorder

Social anxiety disorder (SAD) is characteristically defined by an excessive fear of evaluation, and subsequent avoidance of situations that result in perceived public scrutiny (APA 2000). Hofmann *et al.* (2006) recruited a total of 27 participants who were diagnosed with SAD and also reported a significant degree of public speaking anxiety. Following a single session of psycho-education, participants were randomized to receive either 50 mg of DCS or placebo 1 hour before 4 exposure-based therapy sessions in either a group or individual setting. Treatment consisted of increasingly difficult public speaking tasks and then watching video feedback of their own performance in front of the group, with homework practice assignments. Using measures of self-reported social anxiety symptoms, DCS significantly reduced social anxiety symptoms compared to placebo, with the greatest difference observed at a 1-month follow-up with moderate to high effect sizes.

We replicated these findings in what is currently the largest study of DCS in combination with exposure therapy to treat an anxiety disorder (Guastella *et al.* 2008). Fifty-six SAD patients were randomized to receive DCS (N = 28; 50 mg) or placebo (N = 28) 1 hour prior to each of 4 exposure-based therapy sessions in the same manner as Hofmann *et al.* (2006). At the conclusion of therapy, and at 1-month follow-up, participants who received DCS plus exposure therapy reported significantly fewer SAD symptoms compared to patients who received placebo plus exposure therapy. That is, DCS-administered patients reported fewer social fear and avoidance symptoms, fewer dysfunctional cognitions, and overall improved functioning in everyday life. Moderate effect sizes were found on most measures and near-significant effects indicated that fewer DCS-treated patients may have dropped out of treatment in comparison to placebo (3% versus 18%). We were also interested in how many exposure treatment sessions were required to show differences between DCS and placebo groups. A weekly social anxiety symptom tracking measure showed that differences between the DCS and placebo groups emerged following the third exposure plus DCS therapy session. Finally, this study showed a positive relationship between DCS enhancement of therapy outcomes and the amount of learning achieved between exposure therapy sessions. This study, therefore, provided indirect evidence that the greater the amount of learning achieved within exposure therapy sessions, the greater the effectiveness of DCS in combination with exposure therapy.

Obsessive-Compulsive Disorder

The characteristic features of obsessive-compulsive disorder (OCD) are recurrent obsessive thoughts, accompanied by intense anxiety, and a compulsive need for rituals, that cause substantial distress (APA 2000). The dominant psychological treatment for OCD is exposure and response prevention (ERP). Kushner *et al.* (2007) randomized patients diagnosed with OCD to 125 mg DCS or placebo 2 hours prior to a maximum of 10 exposure-based ERP sessions. Sessions were conducted twice weekly, with each participant identifying a personal hierarchy of obsession-related fears, rated on a scale from 1 (none) to 100 (maximum). Initial exposure sessions focused on items with lower ratings, with sessions progressing through the hierarchy until all ratings were reduced by 50%, or until the tenth session, whichever came first. Early assessments of clinical symptoms using this rating scale at session 4 indicated DCS administration was associated with clinical improvement, measured by greater reductions in subjective ratings of obsession-related distress within in-session exposure tasks. However, these early gains did not last; by the end of the trial and at the 3-month follow up, DCS was no longer associated with improved clinical outcome in comparison to placebo. Despite the apparent null findings, the study suggested that DCS may be associated with earlier improvements, compared to placebo, with the authors noting that patients receiving DCS demonstrated reduced dropout rates compared to those who received placebo.

Similarly, Wilhelm *et al.* (2008) conducted a trial of DCS versus placebo in combination with ERP for OCD. Participants received either 100 mg of DCS (n = 10) or placebo (n = 13) before 10 twice-weekly therapy sessions. Mirroring the findings from Kushner *et al.* (2007), participants given DCS exhibited mid-treatment clinical gains, with improved clinical severity of OCD symptoms, compared to placebo. However, these improvements disappeared by post-treatment and at 1-month follow-up assessments. Recently, these results were re-analyzed to determine the specific speeds of recovery in these participants (Chasson *et al.* 2010). The authors found that the effectiveness of DCS over placebo in response to ERP treatment was specific to the first 5 sessions. In fact, treatment response for participants given DCS was nearly 6 times faster in these first 5 sessions, and averaged to 2.3 times faster over the full 10 sessions. The authors argued that DCS does not necessarily improve the effects of ERP in reducing OCD symptoms generally, but instead initiates effectiveness of treatment earlier on in the course of treatment than placebo and ERP; thus DCS may exert a maximum utility in the first half of standard treatment, representing a potential ceiling effect for efficacy on neural systems underlying fear extinction.

Less promising findings were reported by Storch *et al.* (2007). The authors randomly assigned 24 adult participants with a diagnosis of OCD to 12 weekly sessions of ERP, with DCS (125 mg) or placebo administered 4 hours prior to each treatment session. Results showed that there were no group differences on any measure of treatment response, including OCD symptom ratings and independent clinician outcome ratings. There was also no impact of DCS on treatment responsiveness in the initial phases of treatment. However, there were two potential major differences between this study and that of previous DCS and exposure therapy studies. This study included an interval of 4 hours and it may be possible that the length of time between administration and the exposure session may have been too great. Furthermore, in this study, patients received drug administration before every treatment session. Given the potential confounds of repeated administration on DCS (Parnas *et al.* 2005) efficacy, it cannot be ruled out that too many doses of DCS were given for benefits to be observed.

Subsequent work by Storch *et al.* (2010) has indicated a potential efficacy of DCS for pediatric OCD. Youths diagnosed with OCD, aged between 8 and 17 years, were randomized to receive either DCS or placebo in conjunction with sessions 4 through 10 of 10 weekly CBT sessions, involving psycho-education, cognitive training, and ERP. As this study involved children, the authors implemented a weight-approximate dosage, each dose administered 1 hour before therapy. Thus, children weighing between 25 and 45 kg were assigned a 25 mg dose and children weighing between 45 and 90 kg a 50 mg dose. Overall, the authors found a significant reduction in obsessive symptoms, measured by a semi-structured child version of an obsessive symptoms scale, in participants administered DCS compared to placebo at post-treatment. In addition, significant reductions were observed for the DCS group compared to placebo in clinician rated symptoms using a semi-structured clinical interview. These treatment effects on two symptom severity indexes were found to be modest. This study provided the first evidence for the tolerability of DCS in a sample of youths, as well as demonstrating moderate effectiveness in reducing obsessive symptoms post-treatment. However, the authors did not evaluate whether gains were maintained after treatment cessation.

Panic Disorder and Agoraphobia

Panic disorder is defined by the presence of repeated panic attacks and an excessive fear about the consequences of a potential panic attack that may lead to an avoidance of associated situations (APA 2000). Unlike other anxiety disorders where feared cues may be observed, feared cues in panic disorder are internal, and exposure sessions involve interoceptive exposure tasks – that is, exposure to feared physical symptoms. Otto *et al.* (2010) administered 50 mg DCS or placebo prior to the last 3 of 5 sessions to 31 patients with panic disorder. The 5-session protocol included 3 sessions of intense interoceptive exposure with cognitive restructuring and *in vivo* exposure instructions. Baseline, post-treatment, and 1-month follow-up assessments were conducted, with the primary outcome a panic disorder scale measuring severity of symptoms, including frequency and distress of panic attacks, anticipatory anxiety, agoraphobic and interoceptive fear and avoidance, and impairment of work and social functioning. DCS patients showed a greater reduction in panic symptom severity at both post-treatment and follow-up time points. This effect was even maintained for patients who had previously failed to respond to other forms of pharmacotherapy.

Recently, Siegmund *et al.* (2011) examined the combination of DCS and CBT for panic disorder and agoraphobia. Participants were randomized to receive either 50 mg DCS or placebo before each of three exposure sessions. The CBT protocol consisted of 8 90-min group CBT sessions over a 1-month period with an additional 3 individual therapist-guided *in vivo* exposure sessions. Results indicated no significant differences between DCS and placebo groups on any of the clinical severity measures, at pre- or post-treatment, or 1- and 5-month follow-up. A closer look at the data indicated a trend for an augmenting effect of DCS over placebo immediately after treatment cessation on a measure of panic disorder and agoraphobia symptom severity. Splitting the sample into low and high symptom severity groups revealed a DCS facilitation effect on panic, agoraphobia, and anxiety symptoms in more severely symptomatic patients immediately post-treatment, with the placebo group catching up by 1-month follow-up. The study provided partial evidence for an initial facilitatory effect of DCS over placebo in more symptomatic patients at the acute phase of treatment response. However, the authors note that a potential floor effect may have been observed, as the placebo group exhibited a good treatment response with a 58% symptom reduction from baseline. However, the trend for an augmentation of DCS on panic symptoms early in treatment is in line with findings from the OCD field which suggests that the effects of DCS may only be observed with disorders that respond well to a limited number of exposure sessions.

IMPLICATIONS OF RESEARCH FOR CLINICAL PRACTICE

The evidence reviewed here largely supports the use of DCS as an adjunctive treatment to exposure-based treatments for specific phobia, SAD, panic disorder, and OCD. A meta-analysis of animal and human studies (Norberg *et al.* 2008) found an overall moderate to large effect size for a benefit of DCS over placebo. That is, DCS was found to enhance the extinction of fear, measured across the variety of study designs and outcome measures (Cohen's $d = 0.90$). Given that this effect size represents the additional benefit of DCS to exposure-based procedures, the effect size is particularly impressive. Furthermore, when studies have found benefits from DCS on exposure therapy outcomes, benefits appear to remain well beyond treatment cessation of both exposure therapy and DCS ($d = 0.47$). The strongest results in human populations to date have come from those with SAD. There is slightly mixed, but overall promising, evidence for DCS augmentation in OCD. Currently, no available evidence exists evaluating the combination of DCS and exposure therapy approaches for PTSD, and this gap in the literature will likely be filled in the near future. Evidence for the use of DCS to treat specific phobias is promising, notably acrophobia, when DCS is combined with specific and brief exposure treatments. Findings in the treatment of panic disorder are also supportive, although one study indicates that those with more severe forms of panic may obtain the most benefit.

DCS augmented therapy has a number of benefits over traditional approaches. Speeding treatment response to therapy allows for more efficient treatment, which is of benefit to the patient and the therapist.

DCS effects on learning may also enhance therapeutic response in aiding retention of learning in individuals who may not have otherwise responded to previously administered CBT (i.e. non-responders). This approach is likely to result in cost-effective outcomes and may also decrease attrition rates across services.

There are still a number of questions that remain to be answered. Issues around dosage, timing, and method of administration need to be resolved. Most studies have employed doses between 50 and 500 mg when used in combination with an exposure-based therapy, with 50 mg the most commonly chosen dose. Trials have also typically chosen to administer DCS 1 hour before exposure therapy, and trials that have chosen a greater interval of 4 hours or more have been criticized, given knowledge about when DCS is likely to peak following administration. Large-scale randomized controlled trials are now required to compare doses and timing of administration. As timing is of critical importance, we wonder whether faster delivery methods of DCS may be available that can more precisely target key receptors while clients are engaged in exposure therapy. Ideally, providing fast-acting DCS immediately during or after a successful exposure therapy would provide greatest flexibility for clinicians.

Norberg et al. (2008) reported that smaller effect sizes were observed in studies with increased number of DCS administrations and increased number of exposure sessions. In relation to this, four trials have provided full and comprehensive CBT packages in combination with DCS (Kushner et al. 2007; Storch et al. 2007; 2010; Wilhelm, et al. 2008). These studies have shown more inconsistent results. Three of these studies were in the context of OCD. Both Kushner et al. (2007) and Wilhelm et al. (2008) demonstrated significant group differences between DCS and placebo mid-way through treatment. As treatment progressed in these studies, the initial beneficial effect of DCS disappeared. Storch et al. (2007) also found a trend to indicate gains in the DCS group, compared to placebo, were greatest between session 4 and session 6. Finally, Siegmund et al. (2011) found that benefits were restricted to those with more severe forms of panic disorder. It remains unclear whether these inconsistencies in results, especially for the OCD studies, are caused by the use of more efficacious CBT treatment packages, the increased number of sessions, or because there are unique factors within the OCD population that may moderate the influence of DCS on response to ERP. Comprehensive CBT programs are widely used within mental health service settings, particularly by clinical psychologists, as the gold-standard treatment for anxiety disorders (McManus et al. 2008). A critical step in establishing treatment acceptability for DCS among clinical service providers is to demonstrate whether DCS augments best-practice CBT packages across multiple anxiety disorders.

There are a number of other variables, demonstrated in pre-clinical work, that appear to influence DCS effectiveness on extinction, and these require further evaluation in clinical studies. Factors such as antidepressant use, co-morbidity with substance misuse and other psychopathologies, and experience of past exposure therapy, need to be incorporated into large research trials to determine potential moderating influences. It is of particular concern that antidepressants appear to modulate NMDA-R function and DCS efficacy. A long history of antidepressant use, or even alcohol misuse, may result in reduced effectiveness of DCS with exposure-based therapies. Moreover, factors that might influence learning more generally, such as sleep, diet, and exercise, need to also be considered. These variables may vary dramatically across patient populations and could have important effects on the capacity of patients to learn, and receive any potential benefits, from DCS.

Of further importance is the evaluation of DCS use in service settings that dominate mental health practice in the community. Without research translating research findings into 'real world' mental health service settings, it is difficult to know whether DCS, combined with exposure therapy, will offer the desired benefits for mental health practice (Tansella *et al.* 2006). There are important differences between university-based randomized controlled trials (RCTs) and typical mental health services, which often make research outcomes difficult to translate (Tansella *et al.* 2006). For example, exposure therapy provided in university clinical trials may not represent the breadth or quantity of treatment provided in mental health services. Therapists in real world settings do not receive the same level of assistance as in RCTs and this could affect the purity and quality of the process-specific 'key' components of the intervention. We might suggest that therapists who provide patients with a more powerful exposure experience could produce improved outcomes from DCS in comparison to novice exposure therapists. Finally, potential challenges regarding the application of the intervention should be acknowledged. It is difficult to know whether the practical constraints of administering DCS 1 hour before therapy will be difficult for practitioners and clients to implement. The promising findings from pre-clinical work, suggesting post-extinction DCS administration may be just as efficacious in extinction learning, will need to be examined further in human populations as a potentially more practical solution to this challenge.

CONCLUSION

The use of DCS as a combinatorial treatment with exposure therapy represents an exciting approach to improve mental health treatments for anxiety. It provides one of the best examples of translational research leading to the development of a novel and innovative intervention for human clinical populations in the scientific literature. An antibiotic, traditionally used for over half a century to treat tuberculosis, has now become the focus of one of the most significant advances in the treatment of anxiety in the past decade. Pharmacotherapy has been used for the first time to enhance the learning process that underlies existing, best practice, exposure-based therapy. This is a truly synergistic approach to improving treatment outcomes. Based on the current data, DCS administration in combination with exposure therapy may have particular promise for settings where response rates for CBT-based interventions are low and where trained professionals who can provide more complex and time-consuming CBT packages are limited in number and capacity (Issakidis and Andrews 2002). The real potential of DCS is that, for a limited cost, it may substantially improve a simple treatment, exposure therapy, making an effective intervention more accessible and efficient. It also offers substantial potential to treat those patients who would otherwise remain non-responsive or relapse.

REFERENCES

APA (2000). *Diagnostic and Statistical Manual of Mental Disorders*. 4th edn. Text Revision. Washington DC: American Psychiatric Association.

Bouton, M. E., Vurbic, D., and Woods, A. M. (2008). D-cycloserine facilitates context-specific fear extinction learning. *Neurobiology of Learning and Memory*, 90(3): 504–510.

Chasson, G. S., Buhlmann, U., Tolin, D. F. *et al.* (2010). Need for speed: Evaluating slopes of OCD recovery in behavior therapy enhanced with D-cycloserine. *Behaviour Research and Therapy*, 48(7): 675–679.

Danysz, W. and Parsons, C. G. (1998). Glycine and N-methyl-D-aspartate receptors: physiological significance and possible therapeutic applications. *Pharmacological Reviews*, 50(4): 597–664.

Davis, M. (2002). Role of NMDA receptors and MAP kinase in the amygdala in extinction of fear: clinical implications for exposure therapy. *European Journal of Neuroscience*, 16(3): 395–398.

Davis, M. and Myers, K. M. (2002). The role of glutamate and gamma-aminobutyric acid in fear extinction: clinical implications for exposure therapy. *Biological Psychiatry*, 52(10): 998–1007.

D'Souza, D. C., Gil, R., Cassello, K. *et al.* (2000). IV glycine and oral D-cycloserine effects on plasma and CSF amino acids in healthy humans. *Biological Psychiatry*, 47(5): 450–462.

Foa, E. B. and Kozak, M. J. (1986). Emotional processing of fear: Exposure to corrective information. *Psychological Bulletin*, 99(1): 20–35.

Guastella, A. J., Lovibond, P. F., Dadds, M. R., Mitchell, P., and Richardson, R. (2007). A randomized controlled trial for the effect of D-Cycloserine on conditioning and extinction in humans. *Behaviour Research and Therapy*, 45(4): 663–672.

Guastella, A. J., Richardson, R., Lovibond, P. F. *et al.* (2008). A randomized controlled trial of D-cycloserine enhancement of exposure therapy for social anxiety disorder. *Biological Psychiatry*, 63(6): 544–549.

Heresco-Levy, U., Kremer, I., Javitt, D. C. et al. (2002). Pilot-controlled trial of D-cycloserine for the treatment of post-traumatic stress disorder. *The International Journal of Neuropsychopharmacology*, 5(4): 301–307.

Hofmann, S. G., Meuret, A. E., Smits, J. A. et al. (2006). Augmentation of exposure therapy for social anxiety disorder with D-Cycloserine. *Archives of General Psychiatry*, 63(3): 298–304.

Hood, W. F., Compton, R. P., and Monahan, J. B. (1989). D-cycloserine: a ligand for the N-methyl-*d*-aspartate coupled glycine receptor has partial agonist characteristics. *Neuroscience Letters*, 98(1): 91–95.

Issakidis, C. and Andrews, G. (2002). Service utilisation for anxiety in an Australian community sample. *Social Psychiatry and Psychiatric Epidemiology*, 37(4): 153–163.

Kushner, M. G., Kim, S. W., Donahue, C. et al. (2007). D-cycloserine augmented exposure therapy for obsessive-compulsive disorder. *Biological Psychiatry*, 62(8): 835–838.

Langton, J. M. and Richardson, R. (2008). D-cycloserine facilitates extinction the first time but not the second time: an examination of the role of NMDA across the course of repeated extinction sessions. *Neuropsychopharmacology*, 33(13): 3096–3102.

Langton, J. M. and Richardson, R. (2010). The effect of D-cycloserine on immediate vs. delayed extinction of learned fear. *Learning and Memory*, 17(11): 547–551.

Ledgerwood, L., Richardson, R., and Cranney, J. (2003). Effects of D-cycloserine on extinction of conditioned freezing. *Behavioral Neuroscience*, 117(2): 341–349.

Ledgerwood, L., Richardson, R., and Cranney, J. (2004). D-cycloserine and the facilitation of extinction of conditioned fear: consequences for reinstatement. *Behavioral Neuroscience*, 118(3): 505–513.

Ledgerwood, L., Richardson, R., and Cranney, J. (2005). D-cycloserine facilitates extinction of learned fear: effects on reacquisition and generalized extinction. *Biological Psychiatry*, 57(8): 841–847.

McManus, F., Grey, N., and Shafran, R. (2008). Cognitive therapy for anxiety disorders: Current status and future challenges. *Behavioural and Cognitive Psychotherapy*, 36(06): 695–704.

Monahan, J. B., Handelmann, G. E., Hood, W. F., and Cordi, A. A. (1989). D-cycloserine, a positive modulator of the N-methyl-D-aspartate receptor, enhances performance of learning tasks in rats. *Pharmacology Biochemistry and Behavior*, 34(3): 649–653.

Myers, K. M. and Davis, M. (2007). Mechanisms of fear extinction. *Molecular Psychiatry*, 12(2): 120–150.

Norberg, M. M., Krystal, J. H., and Tolin, D. F. (2008). A meta-analysis of D-cycloserine and the facilitation of fear extinction and exposure therapy. *Biological Psychiatry*, 63(12): 1118–1126.

Otto, M. W., Tolin, D. F., Simon, N. M. et al. (2010). Efficacy of D-cycloserine for enhancing response to cognitive-behavior therapy for panic disorder. *Biological Psychiatry*, 67(4): 365–370.

Parnas, A. S., Weber, M., and Richardson, R. (2005). Effects of multiple exposures to D-cycloserine on extinction of conditioned fear in rats. *Neurobiology of Learning and Memory*, 83(3): 224–231.

Popik, P., Wróbel, M., and Nowak, G. (2000). Chronic treatment with antidepressants affects glycine/NMDA receptor function: behavioral evidence. *Neuropharmacology*, 39(12): 2278–2287.

Ressler, K. J., Rothbaum, B. O., Tannenbaum, L. *et al.* (2004). Cognitive enhancers as adjuncts to psychotherapy: use of D-cycloserine in phobic individuals to facilitate extinction of fear. *Archives of General Psychiatry*, 61(11): 1136–1144.
Richardson, R., Ledgerwood, L., and Cranney, J. (2004). Facilitation of fear extinction by D-cycloserine: Theoretical and clinical implications. *Learning and Memory*, 11(5): 510–516.
Rowe, M. K. and Craske, M. G. (1998). Effects of an expanding-spaced vs massed exposure schedule on fear reduction and return of fear. *Behaviour Research and Therapy*, 36(7–8): 701–717.
Siegmund, A., Golfels, F., Finck, C. *et al.* (2011). D-Cycloserine does not improve but might slightly speed up the outcome of *in-vivo* exposure therapy in patients with severe agoraphobia and panic disorder in a randomized double blind clinical trial. *Journal of Psychiatric Research*, 45(8): 1042–1047.
Storch, E. A., Merlo, L. J., Bengtson, M. *et al.* (2007). D-cycloserine does not enhance exposure-response prevention therapy in obsessive-compulsive disorder. *International Clinical Psychopharmacology*, 22(4): 230–237.
Storch, E. A., Murphy, T. K., Goodman, W. K. *et al.* (2010). A preliminary study of D-cycloserine augmentation of cognitive-behavioral therapy in pediatric obsessive-compulsive disorder. *Biological Psychiatry*, 68(11): 1073–1076.
Tansella, M., Thornicroft, G., Barbui, C., Cipriani, A., and Saraceno, B. (2006). Seven criteria for improving effectiveness trials in psychiatry. *Psychological Medicine*, 36(5): 711–720.
Tawanda, G. (2006). Chemotherapy of tuberculosis, mycobacterium avium complex disease, and leprosy. In L. L. Brunton, B. A. Chabner, and B. C. Knollmann (eds), *Goodman and Gilman's The Pharmacological Basis of Therapeutics*, 12th edn. Accessed from http://www.accesspharmacy.com/content.aspx?aID=16678373.
Thompson, L. T., Moskal, J. R., and Disterhoft, J. F. (1992). Hippocampus-dependent learning facilitated by a monoclonal antibody or D-cycloserine. *Nature*, 359(6396): 638–641.
Van Berckel, B. N. M., Lipsch, C., Timp, S. *et al.* (1997). Behavioral and neuroendocrine effects of the partial NMDA agonist dcycloserine in healthy subjects. *Neuropsychopharmacology*, 16(5): 317–324.
Walker, D. L., Ressler, K. J., Lu, K. T., and Davis, M. (2002). Facilitation of conditioned fear extinction by systemic administration or intra-amygdala infusions of D-cycloserine as assessed with fear-potentiated startle in rats. *Journal of Neuroscience*, 22(6): 2343–2351.
Weber, M., Hart, J., and Richardson, R. (2007). Effects of D-cycloserine on extinction of learned fear to an olfactory cue. *Neurobiology of Learning and Memory*, 87(4): 476–482.
Werner-Seidler, A. and Richardson, R. (2007). Effects of D-cycloserine on extinction: consequences of prior exposure to imipramine. *Biological Psychiatry*, 62(10): 1195–1197.
Wilhelm, S., Buhlmann, U., Tolin, D. F. *et al.* (2008). Augmentation of behavior therapy with D-cycloserine for obsessive-compulsive disorder. *American Journal of Psychiatry*, 165(3): 335–341.
Woods, A. M. and Bouton, M. E. (2006). D-cycloserine facilitates extinction but does not eliminate renewal of the conditioned emotional response. *Behavioral Neuroscience*, 120(5): 1159–1162.

Chapter 6

YOHIMBINE HYDROCHLORIDE

Samantha G. Farris[1], Michelle L. Davis[2], Lindsey B. DeBoer[2], Jasper A. J. Smits[2] and Mark B. Powers[2]

[1] University of Houston, Department of Psychology, Houston, TX, USA
[2] Department of Psychology, Southern Methodist University, Dallas, TX, USA

INTRODUCTION

First-line treatments of choice for the anxiety disorders are the exposure-based therapies or cognitive behavioral therapy (CBT). In exposure-based treatment, patients gradually confront their feared stimuli until fear eventually declines (Emmelkamp et al. 1992; Heimberg and Becker 2002; Foa et al. 2006). There is a wealth of data supporting the efficacy and effectiveness of exposure-based treatments in reducing the symptoms of anxiety disorders (Gould et al. 1995; 1997; Hofmann and Smits 2008; Powers and Emmelkamp 2008; Powers et al. 2008; 2010; Smits et al. 2008; Wolitzky-Taylor et al. 2008). Despite these positive treatment effects, a substantial minority of patients do not respond to treatment, continue to suffer from residual symptoms, or discontinue treatment prematurely. For example, non-response rates in the anxiety disorders are high, including up to 42% in post-traumatic stress disorder (PTSD; Marks et al. 1998), 43% in generalized anxiety disorder (GAD; Borkovec et al. 2002), 14% in obsessive-compulsive disorder (OCD; Foa et al. 2005), 35% in social anxiety disorder (SAD; Davidson et al. 2004), and 33% in panic disorder (Barlow et al. 2000). In addition, approximately 20% of patients drop out during exposure-based treatment (Heimberg et al. 1998; 2003; Barlow et al. 2000). Furthermore, while exposure-based therapies are relatively short (e.g. 10–17 sessions lasting 45–90 minutes), their administration can be costly and require substantial effort due to the necessity of confronting fears in varied contexts. Together, these findings call for research on strategies that can enhance the efficacy and efficiency of CBT for anxiety disorders.

Psychobiological Approaches for Anxiety Disorders: Treatment Combination Strategies, First Edition. Edited by Stefan G. Hofmann.
© 2012 John Wiley & Sons, Ltd. Published 2012 by John Wiley & Sons, Ltd.

A recent advance in this area of work is the use of a class of medications (cognitive enhancers) to promote and enhance extinction learning, which is the proposed mechanism underlying the efficacy of exposure-based treatments. One relatively successful example is the use of D-cycloserine (DCS) to augment exposure-based treatment of the anxiety disorders (see Chapter 5 in this book for a review). More recently, yohimbine hydrochloride (YOH) has also shown to be a successful cognitive enhancer of fear extinction in both animals (Cain et al. 2004; Morris and Bouton 2007; Hefner et al. 2008; Mueller et al. 2009) and humans (Powers et al. 2009). In this chapter, we will present the current literature on YOH as a potential psychotherapeutic accelerant for exposure-based treatments for anxiety disorders. We briefly review its history, dosage, and safety considerations, present the neurological basis of fear learning and extinction, examine its current use in animal and human research, and discuss directions for future research.

BACKGROUND AND HISTORY OF YOHIMBINE

Yohimbine is derived from African yohimbe bark and has several uses. Herbal yohimbine extract is available over-the-counter and is often marketed as a dietary supplement for sexual dysfunction and as a fat metabolism enhancer during exercise (Galitzky et al. 1988; 1990; McCarty 2002). After manufacturers purified the substance called yohimbine hydrochloride (YOH) from the tree's bark, it was sold by prescription only in the United States for the treatment of erectile failure, and is commonly used to treat sexual side effects from SSRI medications (Ernst and Pittler 1998). YOH is an alpha 2-adrenoreceptor antagonist and was one of the approximately 4,000 drugs that were widely prescribed before the formation of the Food and Drug Administration (FDA) in 1938. Prior to 1938, drugs were regulated by the 1906 Pure Food and Drug Act, which only required that drugs meet strength and purity standards. After 1938, the FDA adopted a 'grandfathering' approval process allowing the continued prescription of existing drugs (including YOH). YOH popularity in treating sexual dysfunction has decreased as sildenafil (Viagra) and similar drugs were approved starting in the late 1990s. The enhancing effects of YOH on extinction learning have only recently been examined.

SAFETY AND TOLERABILITY OF YOHIMBINE HYDROCHLORIDE

YOH is compounded in 5.4 mg pills in the United States. Absorption half-time of YOH is 10 minutes and elimination half-life is 36 minutes (Owen et al. 1987). Side effects of YOH may include urinary retention, hyperglycemia, tachycardia, irritability, tremor, sweating, nausea, vomiting, dizziness, headache, flushing, nervousness, and hypertension. To date, no serious adverse events have been reported after taking YOH (Ernst and Pittler 1998), and there is no known lethal dose. There are reports of individuals taking as much as 100 times the normal daily dose with no long-term effects (Roth et al. 1984).

While YOH is technically a safe drug, it has been found to induce panic attacks when administered intravenously in doses of 30 mg among some individuals fearing bodily sensations, notably those with panic disorder and PTSD (Charney et al. 1984; 1987; Southwick et al. 1999). For example, in a study by Southwick et al. (1993), participants with PTSD were given an average of 33.2 mg of YOH intravenously after fasting for 10 hours. The majority of these participants (70%) experienced panic symptoms. It is important to note that the dosage delivered in this study was higher than the typical dose and delivered intravenously. Indeed, when administered orally, no such symptoms emerge. For example, Charney et al. (1982) administered 3 oral YOH (10 mg, 15 mg, and 20 mg) to healthy participants with no indications of increased anxiety. Also, when participants are fully informed of the bodily sensations associated with biological challenges, panic rates dramatically decrease. In the first human-based trial of YOH-enhanced exposure therapy, which involved 2 administrations of 10.8 mg over 2 weeks and information about the side effect profile of YOH, no patients withdrew due to side effects and there were no adverse events (Powers et al. 2009). In the second augmentation trial in humans with 5 administrations of 10.8 mg over 5 sessions, no participants withdrew due to side effects, which were similar to those reported in the placebo condition (Meyerbröker et al. in press). These findings are consistent with data from erectile failure trials with YOH. For example, one safety study reported that no participants withdrew due to adverse events and that side effects reported were similar to placebo (Vogt et al. 1997). Considering these findings, it appears thus far to be a safe and tolerable option for treatment augmentation, especially when the YOH dose is taken orally (for slower absorption). In addition, in the event that fasting increases panic reactions, food consumption before medication administration may be considered.

FEAR CONDITIONING AND EXTINCTION LEARNING

When a neutral stimulus is paired with an aversive event (the unconditioned stimulus (US)), an unconditioned response is elicited (e.g. freezing, increased heart rate, increase respiration, vigilance, or startle (McAllister and McAllister 1971)). In fear conditioning, the previously neutral stimulus becomes a conditioned stimulus (CS) and can evoke fear (the conditioned response (CR)), even in the absence of the initial aversive US. These behavioral responses characterize anxiety pathology.

Extinction learning occurs when, after repeated presentation of the feared CS in the absence of the US, the association between the CS and US is changed. There is currently debate over this alteration process. One theory is that the CS–US association is simply 'unlearned' (Rescorla and Wagner 1972). Another theory posits that 'new learning' suppresses stimulation previously caused by the CS–US association (Rescorla and Heth 1975; Bouton 2004; McNally 2007). A third theory suggests that non-associative mechanisms, such as habituation, may play a role in extinction (McSweeney and Swindell 2002). Emerging evidence suggests that extinction may proceed through multiple mechanisms (Myers and Davis 2007).

Exposure-based therapies are procedurally akin to fear extinction paradigms and have demonstrated success in modulating emotional memory. Strategies that improve cognitive processing of disconfirming, corrective evidence, such as physiological feedback (Telch *et al*. 2000), or disconfirmation of expected threat (Grayson *et al*. 1982; 1986; Kamphuis and Telch 2000; Sloan and Telch 2002), have been shown to enhance fear reduction. Therefore, exposure therapy can be conceptualized as a form of extinction learning.

While the specific biological mechanisms of conditioning and extinction learning are still unclear, physiological studies have implicated the amygdala and the hippocampus as areas of the brain involved in fear conditioning (Davis 2002; Anderson and Insel 2006). For example, Indovina *et al*. (2011) found that high trait anxiety patients (i.e. those with deficits in adaptive fear responses) had higher amygdala functioning in response to conditioned fear, whereas low trait anxiety patients had a lower frequency of response in the central prefrontal cortex. Furthermore, in a contextual fear-conditioning paradigm (Alvarez *et al*. 2008), participants were repeatedly exposed to two virtual reality contexts, one with an accompanying shock and one without. Using functioning imaging (fMRI) studies, participants in the conditioned context with the accompanying shock showed greater activation of the right anterior hippocampus and bilateral amygdala compared to participants in the virtual reality context without shock. These findings are consistent with animal models implicating the amygdala and hippocampus in contextual fear conditioning (Rudy *et al*. 2004).

Activity in both the amygdala and hippocampus has also been linked to extinction learning. Animal studies have shown a correlation between amygdala activation and early extinction (Phelps *et al*. 2004). Animal studies investigating the role of the hippocampus in extinction learning found that inhibition of the dorsal hippocampus (via muscimol, a GABA receptor agonist) prior to extinction training in rats decreased both the rate (Corcoran *et al*. 2005) and the contextual expression of extinction (Corcoran and Maren 2001). These findings suggest that increased activity in the amygdala and hippocampus is associated with the acceleration and enhancement of extinction learning.

The adrenergic system is also associated with fear in several different ways, including being linked with the fight or flight response (Cain et al. 2004). Also, norepinephrine is released in the amygdala post-exposure to aversive stimuli (Tanaka et al. 2000). Pharmacological agents such as YOH have been found to accelerate and consolidate extinction learning via stimulation of the noradrenergic system (by enhancing adrenergic activity). This enhancement may occur through several processes, including memory recall consolidation, promoting memory formation, and modulating extinction learning (Cain et al. 2004).

YOHIMBINE AND EMOTIONAL LEARNING

Research with both animal and human subjects has demonstrated that stimulation of the noradrenergic pathways enhances emotional memory consolidation, while inhibition of these pathways impairs it (Cahill et al. 1994; O'Carroll et al. 1999; McGaugh 2000; Southwick et al. 2002; Berlau and McGaugh 2006; Roozendaal et al. 2006). For example, O'Carroll et al. (1999) orally administered 20 mg YOH, 50 mg metoprolol (a noradrenaline blocker), or placebo to healthy human subjects 90 minutes before viewing an emotionally activating story about an accident. As predicted, the YOH group recalled significantly more slides, and the metoprolol group recalled significantly less, in comparison to the placebo group. This effect was significant only for the most emotional part of the story, suggesting that the memory-enhancing effects of YOH are specific to emotional material or experiences. These results suggest that using a pharmacological agent such as YOH to activate the noradrenergic system (i.e. to increase sympathetic nervous system activity) may improve emotional learning.

Other studies have found somewhat conflicting results, which seem to primarily stem from methodological differences or misunderstandings. For example, van Stegeren et al. (2010) did not find enhancements in memory for emotional stimuli among subjects who had received 20 mg of YOH. After YOH or placebo administration, these subjects viewed neutral and emotional pictures while brain activity was monitored with fMRI. The null findings may have resulted from the fMRI procedure increasing sympathetic arousal (i.e. elevations in endogenous noradrenaline levels) in all subjects, thereby decreasing the size of the noradrenergic differences between groups and enhancing emotional memory to some extent in all subjects.

Southwick et al. (2002) found evidence for the effect of post-learning adrenergic modulation on memory for emotional material. Using the same experimental paradigm as O'Carroll et al. (1999), they examined the effect of YOH on memory for an emotional story, as well as levels of plasma methoxy-4-hyrdroxyphenylglycol (MHPG). MHPG is the principal norepinephrine metabolite in the brain, and increased levels of MHPG found in the blood are indicative of recent sympathetic nervous system activity. Although the experimental manipulation (i.e. intravenous administration of YOH versus placebo) was not effective and there were no significant group differences in MHPG or memory of the story, participants in the YOH group who did respond to YOH with increases in MHPG demonstrated significantly better memory of the story than the YOH non-responders. Furthermore, there was a significant correlation between peak change of MHPG and memory in the sample as a whole, suggesting that the mechanism through which YOH is believed to operate on emotional learning (i.e. activation of the noradrenergic system) is indeed related to memory of emotional experiences. The finding that YOH did not directly enhance memory (due to the manipulation failure) is inconsistent with other studies and could have resulted from administering the YOH after instead of before the emotional story.

YOH's arousing and anxiogenic effects (Bremner et al. 1996) may also contribute to its enhancement of emotional memory consolidation. Extinction learning tends to be more effective when emotional arousal corresponds to the arousal experienced when the fear memory was first learned (Foa and Kozak 1986). Indeed, Vasa et al. (2009) found that compared to YOH + hydrocortisone and placebo groups, participants administered YOH reported more panic symptoms and demonstrated less attention bias to threat (i.e. angry faces in the dot probe task). They also found that panic symptoms were inversely related to attention bias to threat, suggesting that the increase in physiological arousal and anxiety produced by YOH may diminish threat bias. This decrease in attention bias could be another mechanism through which YOH may facilitate emotional learning in exposure therapy for anxiety.

YOHIMBINE IN ANIMAL STUDIES OF EXTINCTION

To date, four animal studies of YOH-augmented extinction have been conducted (Cain et al. 2004; Morris and Bouton 2007; Hefner et al. 2008; Mueller et al. 2009), demonstrating the value of YOH in factilitating extinction learning. Cain et al. (2004) investigated the administration of YOH (5 mg/kg) in comparison to propranolol (10 mg/kg) by presenting a CS to mice, using either a massed (20 min long) or spaced trial. YOH facilitated extinction of cue and contextual CSs during both massed trials and spaced trials. Propranolol increased fear of the CS. The authors suggest that activation of the norepinephrine system enhances fear extinction in mice. Overall, YOH reduced the average number of trials needed for extinction from 30 to only 5 (Figure 6.1).

Similarly, Hefner et al. (2008) examined YOH using the same type of mice and found no differential effect with extensive extinction (50 trials), but did find an effect when testing YOH on a different strain of mice that were

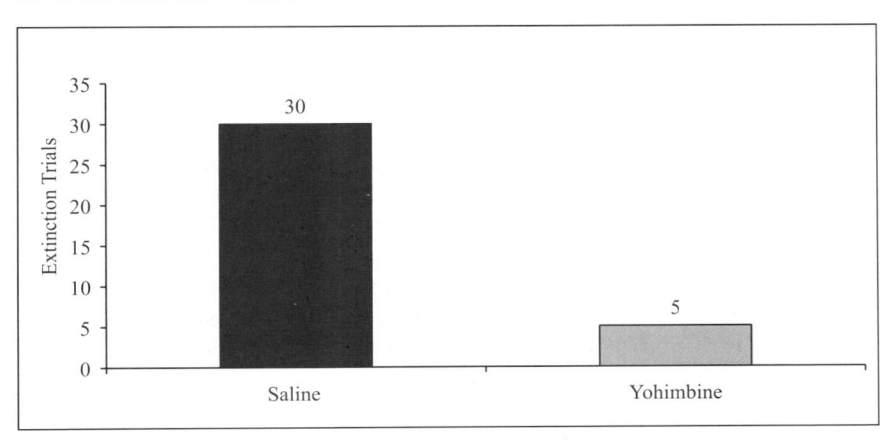

Figure 6.1. Average number of extinction trials to extinguish fear responding in conditioned mice by drug condition (Cain *et al.* 2004).

extinction resistant. When compared to the effects of DCS (an NMDA partial agonist) in the extinction resistant mice, no extinction effect was found. This suggests that yohimbine may confer a distinct advantage over DCS in extinction resistant subjects.

Examination of YOH's effect on contextual extinction learning in rats has revealed similar results (Morris and Bouton 2007). YOH (1.0 mg/kg) was administered to Wistar rats and was found to decrease freezing after extinction training. YOH did not eliminate the original conditioned fear learning, as freezing response returned when the fear stimulus was presented in a different context from extinction training. The fourth study (Mueller *et al.* 2009) examined Sprague-Dawley rats, and found contradictary results. YOH (1.0, 2.0, or 5.0 mg/kg) was administered prior to extinction training and was found to decrease freezing during extinction training. However, once drug free, the rats treated with YOH showed no differences in freezing response compared to control rats. The authors concluded that while YOH is capable of enhancing extinction responses, these gains may not be sustained. It is important to note that the strain of rat, Sprague-Dawley, is not known to be extinction-resistant, which may reconcile inconsistent results from previous studies (Hefner *et al.* 2008). Thus, YOH may best be applied in the treatment of extinction resistant individuals who may be most likely to suffer from persistent anxiety disorders.

YOHIMBINE AUGMENTATION OF EXPOSURE TREATMENT IN HUMANS

There have been few studies that have extended YOH animal findings to human research, though the results have thus far been promising. First,

YOH augmented exposure-based CBT was examined in adults with claustrophobic fears (Powers et al. 2009). Participants (n = 24) reporting concerns with closed spaces were randomized to take either YOH (10.8 mg) or a placebo 1 hour prior to a 60-minute *in vivo* exposure session. The *in vivo* exposure consisted of sitting in a closed, dark chamber measuring approximately 6 ft (height) by 3 ft (width) by 2 ft (depth). A second identical exposure session was conducted 1 week after the initial session. Participants rated their subjective units of distress every 10 minutes during the *in vivo* exposure. Assessment of claustrophobic fears was conducted at baseline, immediately after session 2, and at 1 week post-treatment. Assessments included self-report measures of severity of claustrophobia concerns and a behavioral approach task (BAT). The BAT assessed how long a participant would sit in the chamber (2-min uninformed ceiling) and their peak reported fear rating (0–100 scale).

Results revealed similar reductions in distress and fear ratings in both groups post-treatment, but superior gains were made by the YOH group at follow-up in claustrophobia severity (ES = .18), concerns (ES = .23), and peak fears during BAT (ES = .35). Figure 6.2 shows that YOH enhanced the exposure-based treatment, particularly at the follow-up assessment on subjective fear ratings during the behavioral assessments.

Figure 6.3 shows that YOH also significantly enhanced reductions in scores on the Claustrophobia Questionnaire.

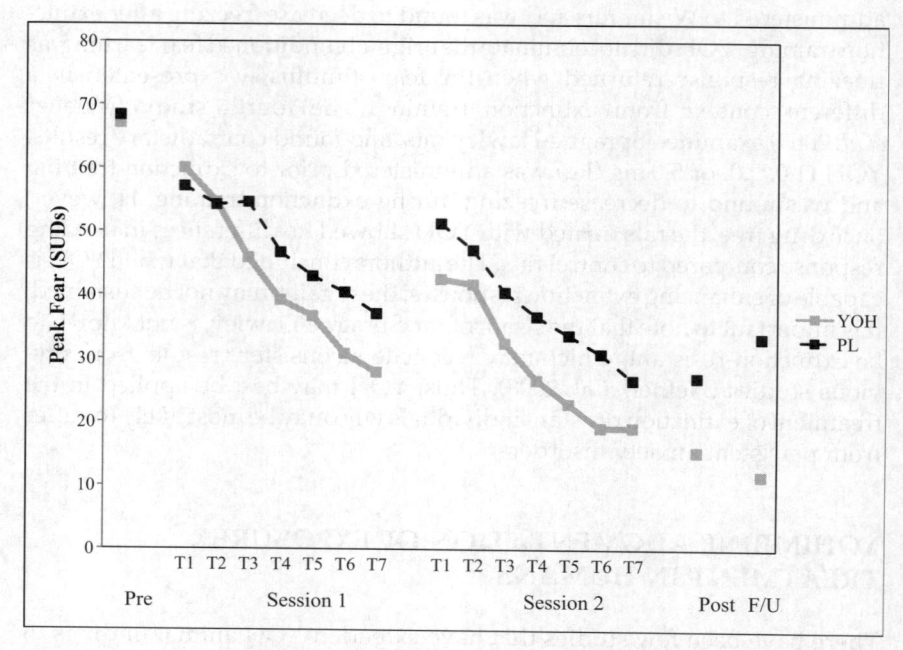

Figure 6.2. Fear ratings during assessments and treatment.

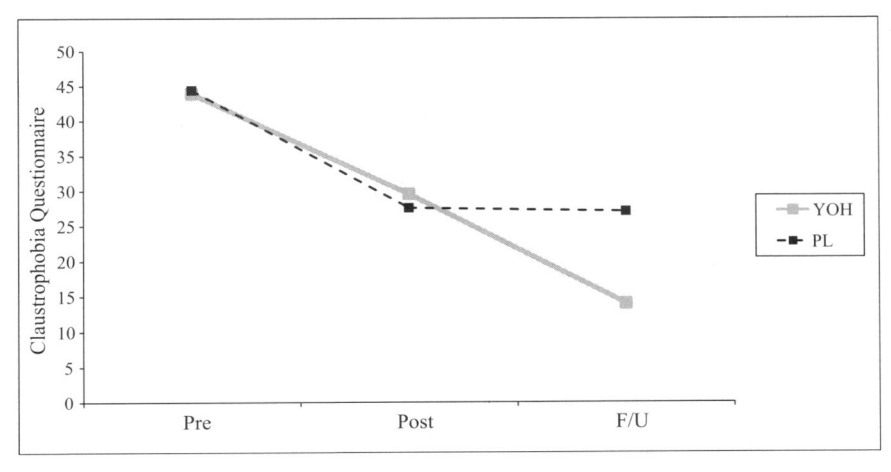

Figure 6.3. Claustrophobia symptoms at pre-treatment, post-treatment, and 1-week follow-up.

This pilot study was the first to examine effects of YOH given prior to exposure in humans. YOH was well tolerated and none of the participants reported increased arousal symptoms. However, it is important to note that participants with high anxiety sensitivity were not included in this sample. Another important consideration, as noted by Holmes and Quirk (2010), is that YOH may not be ideal for use in anxiety disorders because gains may be context-specific and reactivation of fear may occur after leaving the treatment site. Whether YOH is appropriate for specific disorders warrants further investigation.

Next, YOH was used in conjunction with virtual reality treatment for adults (n = 67) with a fear of flying (Meyerbröker et al., 2012). Participants were randomized to receive either 10.8 mg of YOH or a placebo 1 hour prior to treatment sessions. Participants received five virtual reality treatment sessions. Results revealed no difference in peak anxiety within sessions, flight anxiety situations, or modality between the YOH and placebo groups (Figure 6.4).

A relative strength of this study was the addition of a manipulation check. More specifically, salivary alpha amylase analysers confirmed that yohimbine significantly ellevated norepinephrine relative to placebo (van Stegeren et al. 2006). It is important to note that no follow-up assessment was conducted in this study. The previous trial (Powers et al. 2009) only found the superiority of the YOH condition at follow-up. Thus, YOH may only confer significant benefits over longer periods of time. Also, it is possible that the virtual reality treatment was more robust than any medication effect, or that in comparison to claustrophobic fears, fear of flying is more complicated, and/or less context-specific.

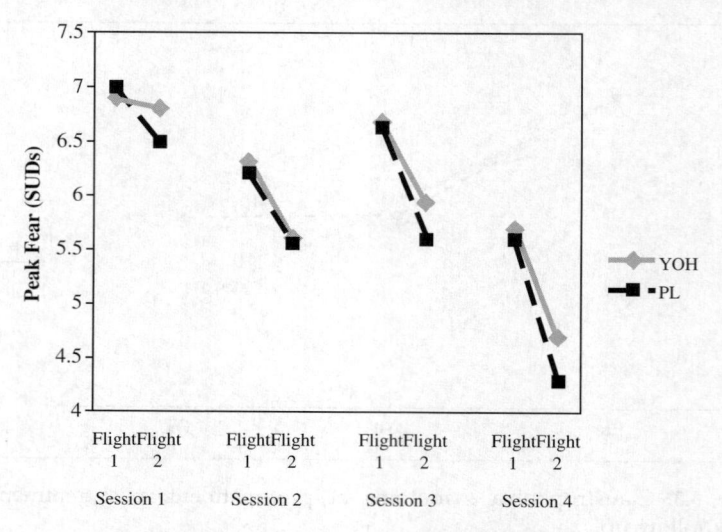

Figure 6.4. Fear ratings during treatment.

CONCLUSION

In summary, studies to date suggest that YOH may enhance exposure-based treatment of anxiety disorders (see Holmes and Quirk 2010, for a review). However, the facilitative effects may only be evident over time (at follow-up assessments) or among those with extinction deficits (Table 6.1).

Future studies have been proposed examining the potential augmentation properties of YOH in other anxiety disorders where extinction deficits are common. One such study includes a shortened treatment protocol for PTSD, including six sessions of imaginal exposure augmented with YOH or placebo. Investigators expect that YOH groups will achieve superior gains in comparison to placebo groups receiving the traditional full course of prolonged exposure for PTSD. With shorter treatment, lower dropout rates are expected, which would allow more patients to obtain the full benefit of treatment. With faster symptom reduction, patients would be more encouraged and promptly rewarded, promoting protocol adherence and better treatment retention. Shorter treatments could be more easily disseminated and more cost effective, effectively increasing the number of patients that could receive treatment.

However, further investigation of YOH is still necessary. For example, it appears that the learning enhancement seen with YOH augmentation may be contextually dependent (Alvarez *et al.* 2008; Powers *et al.* 2009), a consideration in need of further investigation. Genetic factors should also be the focus of further research, as evidenced by YOH's differential effect across varying strains of rodents (Mueller *et al.* 2009). In summary, the

Table 6.1. Summary of pre-clinical and clinical Yohimbine HCL augmentation studies

Study	Sample	Design	Dose	Side Effects	Findings
Cain et al. 2004	Mice (male, C57/bl6)	Fear extinction with partial, extensive, and spaced training; ABB contextual design	5 mg/kg; s.c.	None reported	YOH > PL Facilitated fear extinction
Morris and Bouton 2007	Rats (female, Wistar)	Fear extinction with extensive training; ABB, ABCC, ABA, and ACC contextual designs	0.1 mg/kg; s.c.	None reported	YOH > PL Did not eliminate original conditioned fear learning (freezing response returned in different context)
Hefner et al. 2008	Mice (male, 129/SvImJ)	Fear extinction with extensive training but impaired learning; ABB contextual design	5 mg/kg; s.c.	None reported	YOH > DCS > PL Conferred advantage over DCS in extinction-resistant mice
Mueller et al. 2009	Rats (male, Sprague-Dawley)	Fear extinction with partial training, AAA and ABB contextual designs	1, 2, and 5 mg/kg; i.p.	None reported	YOH > PL Facilitated fear extinction, but did not sustain gains

(*Continued*)

Table 6.1 (Continued)

Study	Sample	Design	Dose	Side Effects	Findings
Powers et al. 2009	Humans (n = 24), claustrophobic	Randomized placebo-controlled trial of YOH augmented exposure-based CBT	10.8 mg, p.o.	None: Equal to PL	YOH > PL Enhanced exposure-based treatment, most notably at follow-up assessment
Meyerbröker et al. 2012	Humans (n = 67), aviatophobic	Randomized placebo-controlled trial of YOH-augmented virtual reality treatment	10.8 mg, p.o.	None: Equal to PL	YOH = PL Did not confer an advantage over placebo, but no follow-up

Notes: s.c. = subcutaneous injection, i.p. = intraperitoneal injection, p.o. = administered orally; PL refers to a non-active drug initial research on YOH as an enhancer of fear extinction is promising, though underdeveloped. Future research is necessary to determine YOH's full augmentation potential.

REFERENCES

Alvarez, R. P., Biggs, A., Chen, G., Pine, D. S., and Grillion, C. (2008). Contextual rear conditioning in humans: Cortical-hippocampal and amygdala contributions. *The Journal of Neuroscience*, 28(24): 6211–6219.

Anderson, K. C. and Insel, T. R. (2006). The promise of extinction research for the prevention and treatment of anxiety disorders. *Biological Psychiatry*, 60(4): 319–321.

Barlow, D. H., Gorman, J. M., Shear, M., and Woods, S. W. (2000). Cognitive-behavioral therapy, imipramine, or their combination for panic disorder. *Journal of the American Medical Association*, 283(19): 2529.

Berlau, D. J., and McGaugh, J. L. (2006). Enhancement of extinction memory consolidation: The role of the noradrenergic and GABAergic systems within basolateral amygdala. *Neurobiology of Learning and Emotion*, 86(2): 123–132.

Borkovec, T. D., Newman, M. G., Pincus, A. L., and Lytle, R. (2002). A component analysis of cognitive-behavioral therapy for generalized anxiety disorder and the role of interpersonal problems. *Journal of Consulting and Clinical Psychology*, 70: 288–298.

Bouton, M. E. (2004). Context and behavioral processes in extinction. *Learning and Memory*, 11(5): 485–494.

Bremner, J. D., Krystal, J. H., Southwick, S. M., and Charney, D. S. (1996). Noradrenergic mechanisms in stress and anxiety: II. Clinical studies. *Synapse*, 23: 39–51.

Cahill, L., Prins, B., Weber, M., and McGaugh, J. L. (1994). Beta-adrenergic activation and memory for emotional events. *Nature*, 371(6499): 702–704.

Cain, C. K., Blouin, A. M., and Barad, M. (2004). Adrenergic transmission facilitates extinction of conditional fear in mice. *Learning and Memory*, 11(2): 179–87.

Charney, D. S., Heninger, G. R., and Sternberg, D. E. (1982). Assessment of alpha-2 adrenergic autoreceptor function in humans: Effects of oral yohimbine. *Life Sciences*, 30: 2033–2041.

Charney, D. S., Heninger, G. R., and Breier, A. (1984). Noradrenergic function in panic anxiety. Effects of yohimbine in healthy subjects and patients with agoraphobia and panic disorder. *Archives of General Psychiatry*, 41(8): 751–763.

Charney, D. S., Woods, S. W., Goodman, W. K., and Heninger, G. R. (1987). Neurobiological mechanisms of panic anxiety: Biochemical and behavioral correlates of yohimbine-induced panic attacks. *The American Journal of Psychiatry*, 144(8): 1030–1036.

Corcoran, K. A., and Maren, S. (2001). Hippocampal inactivation disrupts contextual retrieval of fear memory after extinction. *Journal of Neuroscience*, 21(5), 1720–1726.

Corcoran, K. A., Desmond, T. J., Frey, K. A., and Maren, S. (2005). Hippocampal inactivation disrupts the acquisition and contextual encoding of fear extinction. *Journal of Neuroscience*, 25(39): 8978–8987.

Davidson, J. R., Foa, E. B., Huppert, J. D. et al. (2004). Fluoxetine, comprehensive cognitive behavioral therapy, and placebo in generalized social phobia. *Archives of General Psychiatry*, 61: 1005–1013.

Davis, M. (2002). Role of NMDA receptors and MAP kinase in the amygdala in extinction of fear: Clinical implications for exposure therapy. *European Journal of Neuroscience*, 16(3): 395–398.

Emmelkamp, P. M. G., Bouman, T. K., and Scholing, A. (1992). *Anxiety Disorders: A Practioner's Guide*. Chichester, UK: John Wiley & Sons, Ltd.

Ernst, E. and Pittler, M. H. (1998). Yohimbine for erectile dysfunction: A systematic review and meta-analysis of randomized clinical trials. *Journal of Urology*, 159(2): 433–436.

Foa, E. B. and Kozak, M. J. (1986). Emotional processing of fear: Exposure to corrective information. *Psychological Bulletin*, 99: 20–35.

Foa, E. B., Liebowitz, M. R., Kozak, M. J. et al. (2005). Randomized, placebo-controlled trial of exposure and ritual prevention, clomipramine, and their combination in the treatment of obsessive-compulsive disorder. *American Journal of Psychiatry*, 162(1): 151–161.

Foa, E. B., Huppert, J. D., and Cahill, S. P. (2006) Emotional processing theory: An update. In B. O. Rothbaum. ed. *Pathological anxiety: Emotional Processing in Etiology and Treatment*. New York, Guilford: 3–24.

Galitzky, J., Taouis, M., Berlan, M., Riviere, D., Garrigues, M., and Lafontan, M. (1988) Alpha-2-antagonist compounds and lipid mobilization: evidence for a lipid mobilizing effect of oral yohimbine in healthy male volunteers. *European Journal of Clinical Investigation*, 18(6): 587–594.

Galitzky, J., Riviere, D., Tran, M. A., Montastruc, J. L., and Berlan, M. (1990). Pharmacodynamic effects of chronic yohimbine treatment in healthy volunteers. *European Journal of Clinical Pharmacology*, 39(5): 447–451.

Gould, R. A., Otto, M. W., and Pollack, M. H. (1995). A meta-analysis of treatment outcome for panic disorder. *Clinical Psychology Review*, 15(8): 819–844.

Gould, R. A., Otto, M. W., Pollack, M. H., and Yap, L. (1997). Cognitive behavioral and pharmacological treatment of generalized anxiety disorder: A preliminary meta-analysis. *Behavior Therapy*, 28(2): 285–305.

Grayson, J. B., Foa, E. B., and Steketee, G. (1982). Habituation during exposure treatment: Distraction vs. attention-focusing. *Behavior Research and Therapy*, 20(4): 323–328.

Grayson, J. B., Foa, E. B., and Stekette, G. S. (1986). Exposure *in vivo* of obsessive-compulsives under distracting and attention-focusing conditions: Replication and extension. *Behavior Research and Therapy*, 24(4): 475–479.

Hefner, K., Whittle, N., Juhasz, J. et al. (2008). Impaired fear extinction learning and cortico-amygdala circuit abnormalities in a common genetic mouse strain. *Journal of Neuroscience*, 28(32): 8074–8085.

Heimberg, R. G., and Becker, R. E. (2002). *Cognitive-Behavioral Group Therapy for Social Phobia: Basic Mechanisms and Clinical Strategies*. New York: Guilford.

Heimberg, R. G., Liebowitz, M. R., Hope, D. A. et al. (1998). Cognitive behavior group therapy vs. phenelzine therapy for social phobia. *Archives of General Psychiatry*, 55: 1133–1141.

Hembree, E. A., Foa, E. B., Dorfan, N. M., Street, G. P., Kowalski, J., and Tu, X. (2003). Do patients drop out prematurely from exposure therapy for PTSD? *Journal of Traumatic Stress*, 16: 555–562.

Hofmann, S. G. and Smits, J. A. (2008). Cognitive-behavioral therapy for adult anxiety disorders: A meta-analysis of randomized placebo-controlled trials. *Journal of Clinical Psychiatry*, 69: 621–632.

Holmes, A. and Quirk, G. J. (2010). Pharmacological facilitation of fear extinction and the search for adjunct treatments for anxiety disorders – the case of yohimbe. *Trends in Pharmacological Science*, 31(1): 2–7.

Indovina, I., Robbins, T. W., Núñez-Elizalde, A. O., Dunn, B. D., and Bishop, S. J. (2011). Fear-conditioning mechanisms associated with trait vulnerability to anxiety in humans. *Neuron*, 69(3): 563–571.

Kamphuis, J. H. and Telch, M. J. (2000). Effects of distraction and guided threat reappraisal on fear reduction during exposure-based treatments for specific fears. *Behavior Research and Therapy*, 38(12): 1163–1181.

Marks, I., Lovell, H., Noshirvani, M., Livanou, M., and Thrasher, S. (1998). Treatment of posttraumatic stress disorder by exposure and/or cognitive restructuring: A controlled study. *Archives of General Psychiatry*, 55(4): 317–325.

McAllister, W. R., and McAllister, D. E. (1971). Behavioral measurement of conditioned fear. In F. R. Brush, ed *Aversive Conditioning and Learning*. New York: Academic Press.

McCarty, M. F. (2002). Pre-exercise administration of yohimbine may enhance the efficacy of exercise training as a fat loss strategy by boosting lipolysis. *Medical Hypotheses*, 58(6): 491–495.

McGaugh, J. L. (2000). Memory – A century of consolidation. *Science*, 287(5451): 248–251.

McNally, R. J. (2007). Mechanisms of exposure therapy: How neuroscience can improve psychological treatments for anxiety disorders. *Clinical Psychology Review*, 27: 750–759.

McSweeney, F. K. and Swindell, S. (2002). Common processes may contribute to extinction and habituation. *Journal of General Psychology*, 129: 364–400.

Meyerbröker, K., Powers, M. B., van Stegeren, A., and Emmelkamp, P. M. G. (2012). Does yohimbine hydrochloride facilitate fear extinction in virtual reality treatment of fear of flying? A randomized placebo-controlled Trial. *Psychotherapy and Psychosomatics*, 81, 29–37.

Morris, R. W. and Bouton, M. E. (2007). The effect of yohimbine on the extinction of conditioned fear: A role for context. *Behavioral Neuroscience*, 121(3): 501–514.

Mueller, D., Olivera-Figueroa, L. A., Pine, D. S., and Quirk, G. J. (2009). The effects of yohimbine and amphetamine on fear expression and extinction in rats. *Psychopharmacology*, 204(4): 599–606.

Myers, K. M. and Davis, M. (2007). Mechanisms of fear extinction. *Molecular Psychiatry*, 12: 120–150.

O'Carroll, R. E., Drysdale, E., Cahill, L., Shajahan, P., and Ebmeier, K. P. (1999). Stimulation of the noradrenergic system enhances and blockade reduces memory for emotional material in man. *Psychological Medicine*, 25(5): 1083–1088.

Owen, J., Nakatsu, S., Fenemore, J., Condra, M., Surridge, D., and Morales, A. (1987). The pharmacokinetics of yohimbine in man. *European Journal of Clinical Pharmacology*, 32(6): 577–582.

Phelps, E. A., Delgado, M. R., Nearing, K. I., and LeDoux, J. E. (2004). Extinction learning in humans: Role of the amygdala and vmPFC. *Neuron*, 43: 897–905.

Powers, M. B. and Emmelkamp, P. M. G. (2008). Virtual reality exposure therapy for anxiety disorders: A meta-analysis. *Journal of Anxiety Disorders*, 22: 561–569.

Powers, M. B., Sigmarsson, S. R., and Emmelkamp, P. M. G. (2008). A meta-analytic review of psychological treatments for social anxiety disorder. *International Journal of Cognitive Therapy*, 12: 94–113.

Powers, M. B., Smits, J. A. J., Otto, M. W., Sanders, C., and Emmelkamp, P. M. G. (2009). Facilitation of fear extinction in phobic participants with a novel cognitive enhancer: a randomized placebo controlled trial of yohimbine augmentation. *Journal of Anxiety Disorders*, 23(3): 350–356.

Powers, M. B., Halpern, J. M., Ferenschak, M. P., Gillihan, S. J., and Foa, E. B. (2010). A meta-analytic review of prolonged exposure for posttraumatic stress disorder. *Clinical Psychology Review*, 30(6): 635–641.

Rescorla, R. A. and Wagner, A. R. (1972). A theory of Pavlovian conditioning: Variations in the effectiveness of reinforcement and nonreinforcement. In A. H. Black, and W. F. Prokasy (eds), *Classical Conditioning II: Current Research and Theory*. New York: Appleton-Century-Crofts.

Rescorla, R. A. and Heth, C. D. (1975). Reinstatement of fear to an extinguished conditioned stimulus. *Journal of Experimental Psychology: Animal Behavior Processes*, 1: 88–96.

Roozendaal, B., Okuda, S., Van Der Zee, E. A., and McGaugh, J. L. (2006). Glucocorticoid enhancement of memory requires arousal-induced noradrenergic activation in the basolateral amygdala. *Proceedings of the National Academy of Sciences in the United States of America*, 103(17): 6741–6746.

Roth, L., Daunderer, M., Korman, K. (1984). *Giftpflanzen – Planzengifte: Vorkommen, Wirkung, Therapie*. Munich: Ecomed.

Rudy, J. W., Huff, N. C., and Matus-Amat, P. (2004). Understanding contextual fear conditioning: Insights from a two-process model. *Neuroscience and Biobehavioral Reviews*, 28: 675–685.

Sloan, T. and Telch, M. J. (2002). The effects of safety-seeking behavior and guided threat reappraisal on fear reduction during exposure: an experimental investigation. *Behavior Research and Therapy*, 40(3): 235–251.

Smits, J. A., Berry, A. C., Tart, C. D., and Powers, M. B. (2008). The efficacy of cognitive- behavioral interventions for reducing anxiety sensitivity: A meta-analytic review. *Behaviour Research and Therapy*, 46(9): 1047–1054.

Southwick, S. M., Krystal, J. H., Morgan, C. A. *et al*. (1993). Abnormal noradrenergic function in posttraumatic stress disorder. *Archives of General Psychiatry*, 50(4): 266–274.

Southwick, S. M., Morgan, C. A., Charney, D. S., and High, J. R. (1999) Yohimbine use in a natural setting: Effects on posttraumatic stress disorder. *Biological Psychiatry*, 46(3): 442–444.

Southwick, S. M., Davis, M., Horner, B. *et al*. (2002). Relationship of enhanced norepinephrine activity during memory consolidation to enhanced long-term memory in humans. *American Journal of Psychiatry*, 159(8): 1420–1422.

Tanaka, M., Yoshida, M., Emoto, H., and Ishii, H. (2000). Noradrenaline systems in the hypothalamus, amygdala and locus coeruleus are involved in the provocation of anxiety: Basic studies. *European Journal of Pharmacology*, 405: 397–406.

Telch, M. J., Valentiner, D. P., Ilai, D., Petruzzi, D., and Hehmsoth, M. (2000). The facilitative effects of heart-rate feedback in the emotional processing of claustrophobic fear. *Behavior Research and Therapy*, 38(4): 373–87.

van Stegeren, A. H., Rohleder, N., Everaerd, W., and Wolf, O. T. (2006). Salivary alpha amylase as marker for adrenergic activity during stress: Effect of beta-blockade. *Psychoneuroendocrinology*, 31: 137–141.

van Stegeren, A. H., Roozendaal, B., Kindt, M., Wolf, O. T., and Joëls, M. (2010). Interacting noradrenergic and corticosteroid systems shift human brain activation patterns during encoding. *Neurobiology of Learning and Memory*, 93(1): 56–65.

Vasa, R. A., Pine, D. S., Masten, C. L. et al. (2009). Effects of yohimbine and hydrocortisone on panic symptoms, autonomic responses, and attention to threat in healthy adults. *Psychopharmacology*, 204(3): 445–455.

Vogt, H. J., Brandl, P., Kockott, G. et al. (1997). Double-blind, placebo-controlled safety and efficacy trial with yohimbine hydrochloride in the treatment of nonorganic erectile dysfunction. *International Journal of Impotence Research*, 9: 155–161.

Wolitzky-Taylor, K. B., Horowitz, J. D., Powers, M. B., and Telch, M. J. (2008). Psychological approaches in the treatment of specific phobias: A meta-analysis. *Clinical Psychology Review*, 28(6): 1021–1037.

Chapter 7

CORTISOL

Leila Maria Soravia[1] and Dominique J. -F. de Quervain[2]

[1] Department of Psychiatric Neurophysiology, University Hospital of Psychiatry, University of Berne, Berne, Switzerland
[2] Division of Cognitive Neuroscience, Faculty of Medicine, University of Basel, Basel, Switzerland

INTRODUCTION

Stress activates the hypothalamus-pituitary-adrenal axis, which results in the release of glucocorticoid hormones (cortisol in humans, corticosterone in rodents) from the adrenal cortex. It has long been recognized that glucocorticoids readily enter the brain and affect cognition. Early reports on both enhancing and impairing properties of glucocorticoids on memory (Bohus and Lissak 1968; Flood *et al.* 1978; Beckwith *et al.* 1986; Luine *et al.* 1993; Arbel *et al.* 1994) have indicated that these hormones have complex effects on cognitive functions. More recent studies investigating glucocorticoid effects on distinct memory phases, and studies discerning acute from chronic effects helped to disentangle the multifaceted actions of these stress hormones. For example, acute elevations of glucocorticoids are known to enhance the consolidation of memory of new information, but to impair the retrieval of already stored information (Roozendaal and McGaugh 1996b; De Quervain *et al.* 1998; 2000; Roozendaal 2000). Conditions with chronically elevated glucocorticoid levels are usually associated with impaired cognitive performance and these deficits are thought to result from a cumulative and long-lasting burden on hippocampal function and morphology (Sapolsky 2000; McEwen 2001). However, recently it became clear that memory deficits observed under such chronic conditions can also result, at least in part, from acute and reversible glucocorticoid actions on memory retrieval processes (Coluccia *et al.* 2008).

In this chapter, we will summarize and discuss how glucocorticoids affect memory consolidation, retrieval, and working memory and that

Psychobiological Approaches for Anxiety Disorders: Treatment Combination Strategies, First Edition.
Edited by Stefan G. Hofmann.
© 2012 John Wiley & Sons, Ltd. Published 2012 by John Wiley & Sons, Ltd.

these stress hormones specifically modulate memory of emotionally arousing experiences. Furthermore, because emotional memory plays a crucial role in the pathogenesis and symptomatology of anxiety disorders, such as post-traumatic stress disorder (PTSD) or phobias, we will discuss to what extent the basic findings on glucocorticoid effects on emotional memory might have on clinical implications.

CORTISOL AND THE REGULATION OF MEMORY

A large body of studies in animals and humans demonstrates that glucocorticoids have multifaceted effects on memory, depending on which memory phase is affected by the hormone. Memory consolidation and the retrieval of already stored experiences, as well as working-memory processes, are of special interest regarding the understanding of fear memory in anxiety disorders. Therefore, a short overview of these memory processes and the effects of cortisol on these processes will follow.

Memory Consolidation

Memory consolidation is the process by which a fragile short-term memory trace is transferred into a stable long-term memory. However, not all information is equally well transferred into long-term storage. In fact, it is well recognized that especially emotionally arousing experiences are well remembered, even after decades (McGaugh *et al.* 2003). Successful memory consolidation depends on *de-novo* protein synthesis and on long-term changes in synaptic plasticity (Kandel 2001). There is extensive evidence that glucocorticoids, along with other components of the stress response, are critically involved in regulating memory consolidation of emotionally arousing experiences (McGaugh and Roozendaal 2002). Blockade of glucocorticoid production with the synthesis inhibitor metyrapone impairs memory consolidation in both animals and humans (Roozendaal *et al.* 1996b; Maheu *et al.* 2004) and prevents stress- or epinephrine-induced memory enhancement (Roozendaal *et al.* 1996b; Liu *et al.* 1999). Acute systemic administration of glucocorticoids dose-dependently enhances long-term memory consolidation when given either before or immediately after training in emotionally arousing learning tasks (Flood *et al.* 1978; Sandi and Rose 1994; Roozendaal and McGaugh 1996a; Roozendaal *et al.* 1999; Buchanan and Lovallo 2001; Cordero *et al.* 2002; Abercrombie *et al.* 2003). Such glucocorticoid effects on memory consolidation follow an inverted U-shape dose–response relationship: Moderate doses enhance memory, whereas higher doses are typically less effective or may even impair memory consolidation (Roozendaal *et al.* 1999).

Glucocorticoids also play a role in the consolidation of memory of extinction training in emotionally arousing learning tasks. Extinction occurs when conditioned responding to a stimulus decreases when the reinforcer is omitted (Quirk and Mueller 2008). Like other forms of learning, extinction acquisition is followed by a consolidation phase and it has been found that the administration of glucocorticoids facilitates the consolidation of extinction memory, whereas a suppression of glucocorticoid function impairs such extinction processes (Bohus and Lissak 1968; Barrett and Gonzalez-Lima 2004; Cai et al. 2006; Yang et al. 2006). Glucocorticoids have been shown to enhance memory consolidation and synaptic plasticity by influencing a wide variety of cellular functions, including cell signaling, ion channel properties, as well as cell structure (Karst et al. 2002; Revest et al. 2005; Bisaz et al. 2009). Furthermore, growing evidence indicates that acute glucocorticoid effects on memory consolidation depend on emotional arousal-induced activation of noradrenergic transmission within the amygdala and on interactions of the amygdala with other brain regions, such as the hippocampus and neocortical regions (Roozendaal et al. 2008; de Quervain et al. 2009).

Memory Retrieval

In contrast to the memory consolidation process, during which new information is stabilized in the memory, memory retrieval refers to the process of recollecting previously stored information. In the first study investigating the specific effects of stress and glucocorticoids on memory retrieval (de Quervain et al. 1998), we reported that 30 min after exposure to foot shock stress, rats had impaired retrieval of spatial memory (i.e. memory for the location of a platform in a water-maze task), which they had acquired 24 h earlier. Interestingly, memory performance was not impaired when rats were tested either 2 min or 4 h after the foot shock. These time-dependent effects on retrieval processes corresponded to the circulating corticosterone levels at the time of testing, which suggested that the retrieval impairment was directly related to increased adrenocortical function. In support of this idea, we found that suppression of corticosterone synthesis with metyrapone blocked the stress-induced retention impairment. In addition, systemic corticosterone administered to nonstressed rats 30 min before retention testing induced dose-dependent retention impairment. Further control experiments indicated that glucocorticoids did not affect spatial navigation, motivation, or motor performance. Then we translated these findings to healthy humans and found that a single administration of cortisone (at a dose resulting in high physiological levels) impaired the recall of words learned 24 h earlier (de Quervain et al. 2000). Several further studies from different laboratories have indicated that glucocorticoids impair the retrieval of hippocampus-dependent memory in rats (spatial or contextual memory) and humans (declarative memory) (Wolf et al. 2001; de Quervain et al. 2003; Roozendaal et al. 2003; 2004; Buss et al. 2004; Domes et al. 2004; Rashidy-Pour et al. 2004; Het et al. 2005; Kuhlmann et al. 2005a;b Buchanan et al. 2006; Sajadi *et al.* 2007; Coluccia *et al.* 2008; Wolf 2008). Furthermore, recent evidence indicates that emotionally arousing information is especially sensitive to the impairing effects of glucocorticoids (de Quervain *et al.* 2009). Thus, the mechanisms of acute glucocorticoid effects on memory retrieval are highly comparable to those seen in studies investigating memory consolidation, in that the effects depend on emotional arousal. Moreover, comparable to the glucocorticoid effects on memory consolidation, the amygdala interacts with the hippocampus in mediating glucocorticoid effects on the retrieval of hippocampus-dependent memory (Roozendaal *et al.* 2008; de Quervain *et al.* 2009).

Working Memory

Working memory is a dynamic process whereby information is updated continuously, providing a temporary storage of information (Baddeley 1992; Jones 2002). Several studies in animals and humans show that stress and glucocorticoids impair working memory performance (Baddeley 1992; Lupien *et al.* 1999; Roozendaal *et al.* 2004). Like glucocorticoid effects on memory consolidation and retrieval, these hormones interact with noradrenergic mechanisms in inducing working memory impairment (Roozendaal *et al.* 2004).

In summary, extensive evidence indicates that glucocorticoids enhance memory consolidation but impair memory retrieval and working memory (Figure 7.1).

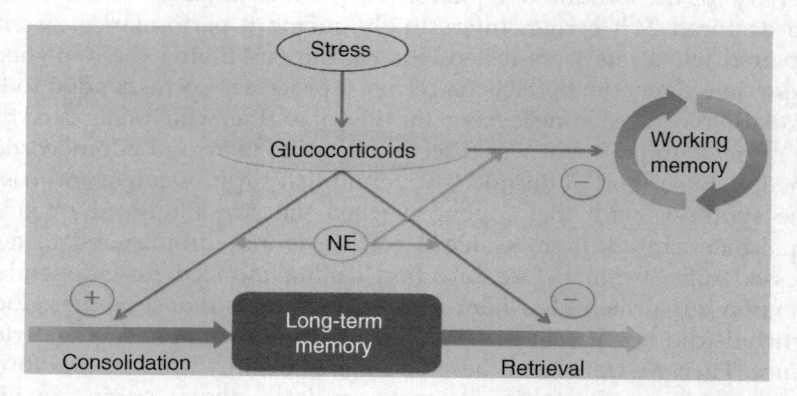

Figure 7.1. Effects of stress and glucocorticoids on memory functions. Whereas glucocorticoids enhance memory consolidation, they impair memory retrieval and working memory. All these hormone effects depend on emotional arousal-induced activation of noradrenergic transmission. NE, norepinephrine. Reprinted from *Frontiers in Neuroendocrinology*, 30 (3), de Quervain, D. J. F., Aerni, A., Schelling, G., & Roozendaal, B., Glucocorticoids and the regulation of memory in health and disease, 358–370. Copyright (2009), with permission from Elsevier.

Whereas enhanced memory for emotionally arousing events in most cases has a clear adaptive value, in certain circumstances extremely aversive experiences can also lead to highly emotional, traumatic or fearful memories, which contribute to the development and symptoms of anxiety disorders. Therefore, understanding the basic modulatory actions of glucocorticoids on different aspects of cognition may have important implications for understanding and, possibly, treating anxiety disorders (de Quervain et al. 2009).

THE IMPACT OF FEAR MEMORIES IN ANXIETY DISORDERS

Anxiety disorders are characterized by persistent and excessive fear, cued by the anticipation or presence of a specific object or situation (APA 1994; Barlow and Liebowitz 1995). The exposure or even the anticipation of the phobic stimulus almost invariably provokes the retrieval of associated fear memories, which themselves activate the HPA-axis and cause a fear response (Foa and Kozak 1986; Cuthberg 2003; de Quervain 2008). Furthermore, phobic individuals tend to construct highly negative images of a phobic situation, which substantially contribute to anticipatory anxiety as well as negative post-event processing. Such images are usually associated with explicit fearful memories of past phobic experiences, which reinforce negative beliefs and may strengthen the phobic response (Rapee and Heimberg 1997; Fehm and Margraf 2002). Furthermore, the confrontation with a fearful situation provokes the retrieval of fear memories, which results in a fear response, in the (re)consolidation of fear memories and, finally, in a strengthening of the fear memory trace (Sara 2000). The retrieval and (re)consolidation of fearful memories therefore seem to play a crucial role in the symptomatology and maintenance of anxiety disorders (Figure 7.2a). Consequently, novel treatment strategies targeting these memory processes might be promising approaches.

ENHANCING EXPOSURE THERAPY EFFECTS WITH CORTISOL

Exposure techniques are a core element of CBT, and have been highly influenced by the emotional processing theory of Foa and Kozak (1986). Based on this theory, there are two conditions necessary to modify fear memories:

1) the activation of the fear structure;
2) corrective or alternative experience with the phobic stimulus that is incompatible with the old fear structure (no psychological or physiological fear response in the presence of a phobic stimulus).

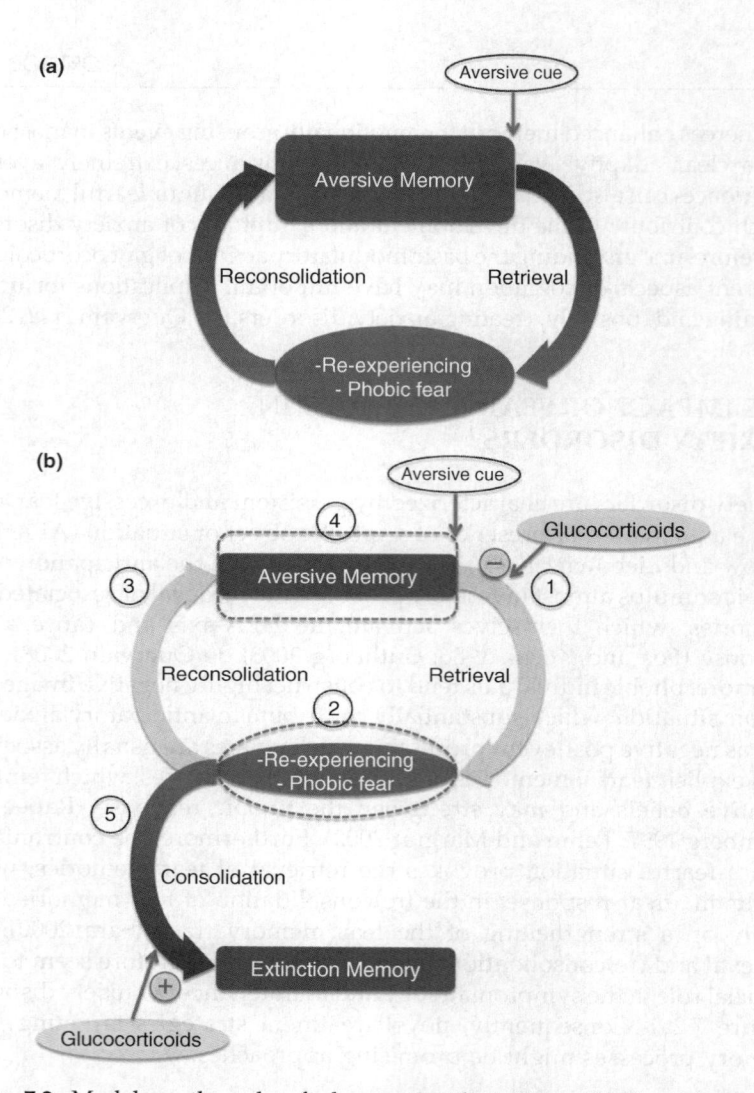

Figure 7.2. Model on the role of glucocorticoids in the reduction of aversive memory. a) Excessive retrieval of aversive memories causes re-experiencing symptoms in PTSD and phobic fear in phobia. Reconsolidation of such aversive experiences further cements the aversive memory trace. b) Glucocorticoid-induced reduction of the aversive memory trace. By inhibiting memory retrieval, glucocorticoids partly interrupt this vicious cycle of retrieving (1), re-experiencing (2) and reconsolidating (3) aversive memories, which leads to a weakening of the aversive memory trace (4). Furthermore, because the aversive cue is no longer followed by the usual aversive memory retrieval and related clinical symptoms, the cue becomes associated with a non-aversive experience, which is stored as extinction memory (5). Based on the findings of animal studies, glucocorticoids are likely to enhance long-term consolidation of extinction memory. Reprinted from *Frontiers in Neuroendocrinology*, 30 (3), de Quervain, D. J. F., Aerni, A., Schelling, G., & Roozendaal, B., Glucocorticoids and the regulation of memory in health and disease, 358–370. Copyright (2009), with permission from Elsevier.

However, the level of psychological or physiological fear during exposure does not seem to be a good predictor for the reconstruction of fear memory. It is rather the reduction of expected harmfulness or aversive valence of the feared stimulus that supports the creation of new non-fear associations (Bentz et al. 2010).

During exposure sessions, the patients experience a decline in psychological and physiological fear that is comparable to the continuous decrease in conditioned response in successive extinction trials (Bentz et al. 2010). Accordingly, exposure therapy can be compared to extinction training. Extinction training does not stand for unlearning of conditioned responses, but rather additional learning (Bentz et al. 2010). Therefore, after successful extinction training, a fear memory trace is not erased but rather an alternative set of non-fear memory association are created (Bouton 2002). These additional non-fear structures compete with the original fear memory associations when triggered. Based on this assumption, exposure therapy should be combined with a substance that facilitates the extinction of conditioned fear and enhances the consolidation of the new experiences.

As previously outlined, glucocorticoids are crucially involved in memory processes such as memory retrieval and consolidation. Based on this knowledge, effects of cortisol treatment in patients with chronic PTSD (Aerni et al. 2004) and patients suffering from social phobia or spider phobia (Soravia et al. 2006) and specific phobia for heights (de Quervain et al. 2011) have been investigated. In a double-blind placebo-controlled design, a small number of patients with chronic PTSD were treated with low-dose cortisol daily over 1 month. The administration of 10 mg cortisol over 1 month does not cause major side effects nor does it suppress the endogenous production of the hormone (Cleare et al. 1999). During the 1 month cortisol treatment, the patients reported a significant reduction of the intensity of reliving the traumatic event, the physiological distress, as well as the frequency of nightmares. The results show that the low-dose administration of glucocorticoids reduced the core symptoms of PTSD, while it did not cause any side effects or treatment-related disturbances of everyday memory.

In studies with phobic patients, the acute effect of glucocorticoid administration during the confrontation with a phobic stimulus has been investigated (Soravia et al. 2006). In a double-blind placebo-controlled study, patients with social phobia received orally either cortisone (25 mg) or placebo 1 hour before a socio-evaluative stress-test (Trier Social Stress Test: TSST). The results showed that the exogenous elevation of the cortisol level before the confrontation with a phobic stimulus significantly reduced self-reported fear during anticipation-, exposure-, and recovery phase. Furthermore, the stress-induced release of cortisol in placebo-treated patients correlated negatively with the fear ratings; the more stress hormones they released, the less subjective fear they reported.

This suggests that the release of the stress hormone cortisol in a phobic situation buffers fear symptoms. Comparable results were shown in the study with spider phobic patients, where the repeated oral administration of hydrocortisone (10 mg), but not placebo, 1 hour before exposure to spider photographs caused a progressive reduction of stimulus-induced fear. This effect was maintained, even in further exposure to the stimulus 2 days after the last cortisol administration. This maintaining effect suggests that cortisol also facilitates the extinction of phobic fear. It is important to note, that in both phobia studies, the administration of glucocorticoids did not cause any side effects, nor did it affect phobia-unrelated anxiety, mood, wakefulness, or calmness, suggesting that this hormone reduced phobia-specific fear.

A further study investigated if the administration of cortisol might be useful in enhancing exposure therapy (de Quervain *et al.* 2011). In this randomized, double-blind, placebo-controlled study, 40 patients with specific phobia for heights were treated with 3 sessions of exposure therapy. One hour before exposure, patients received either cortisol (20 mg) or placebo. The results show that patients who received cortisol in combination with exposure showed significantly less phobic fear symptoms at post-treatment and at 1-month follow-up compared to the placebo group. The findings of this study indicate that the administration of cortisol can enhance extinction-based psychotherapy.

POSSIBLE UNDERLYING MECHANISMS FOR GLUCOCORTICOID-INDUCED FEAR REDUCTION

There is extensive evidence that the activation of the medial temporal lobe is associated with successful memory retrieval (Squire 1992; Cabeza and Nyberg 2000). A study in patients suffering from PTSD demonstrated that the medial temporal lobe is activated by viewing masked traumatic images (Sakamoto *et al.* 2005). Furthermore, a PET study in patients with social phobia reported that after successful psycho- or pharmacotherapy, the medial temporal lobe is less activated during a public speaking task (Furmark *et al.* 2002). Further studies investigating the acute administration of glucocorticoids in the brain showed that high cortisol levels reduce cerebral blood flow in the medial temporal lobe during memory retrieval (de Quervain *et al.* 2003; Oei *et al.* 2007). In summary, the results indicate that the medial temporal lobe is involved in mediating the inhibitory effects of glucocorticoids on memory processes – especially on the retrieval of aversive memory.

As described above, the retrieval of fear or traumatic memories plays an important role in the pathogenesis and maintenance of anxiety disorders. One of the major symptoms in PTSD is the excessive retrieval of traumatic experiences, triggered by trauma cues or even spontaneously. Retrieval of traumatic memories leads to reliving and re-experiencing the traumatic event. Unfortunately, this results in a (re)consolidation of the aversive experience and, thereby, further cements the aversive memory trace. This process is likely to contribute to the persistence and maintenance of the disorder (Bentz et al. 2010). In phobias we see a comparable picture; a phobic situation provokes the retrieval of associated fear memories that trigger a fear response. Here again, the re-experiencing of fear reinforces the aversive memory trace and thereby adds to the persistence of the anxiety disorder (Figure 7.2a). As elucidated in Figure 7.2b, glucocorticoids might weaken aversive memory traces by inhibiting memory retrieval, which results in reduced symptoms. In particular, an aversive cue is no longer followed by the usual full-blown aversive memory retrieval and related symptoms but instead becomes associated with a less aversive experience, which is stored as extinction memory. In addition to the inhibitory effects on memory retrieval, we know that glucocorticoids enhance memory consolidation (Roozendaal 2000; Buchanan et al. 2001). Therefore, the consolidation of a corrective experience (extinction memory) during the exposure to phobic stimulus is enhanced, thus having double benefits from elevated glucocorticoid levels during the confrontation with a phobic stimulus. First they inhibit the retrieval of fear memories resulting in a reduced fear response. Second, they enhance the long-term consolidation of corrective experiences, which further promotes the extinction of the aversive memory trace. This idea is in line with recent findings in animals, indicating that glucocorticoids enhance the extinction of fear memory (Barrett and Gonzalez-Lima 2004; Cai et al. 2006).

CONCLUSION

Because emotionally aversive memories play an important role in the development and symptomatology of anxiety disorders, we aimed to translate the basic findings on the effects of glucocorticoids on emotional memory in animals and healthy humans to clinical conditions. Specifically, the findings, which indicated that glucocorticoids reduce memory retrieval and enhance extinction of emotional memories, led us to hypothesize that these stress hormones might be useful in the treatment of anxiety disorders. Clinical studies and studies of animal models of acquired fear indicate that glucocorticoid treatment indeed reduces the retrieval of aversive memories and enhances extinction processes. These dual actions of glucocorticoids seem to be especially suited for the treatment of acquired fear. By inhibiting memory retrieval, glucocorticoids may partly interrupt the vicious cycle of spontaneous retrieving, re-experiencing and (re)consolidating aversive memories. Furthermore, by enhancing extinction processes, glucocorticoids facilitate the storage of corrective experiences. Therefore, the combination of glucocorticoids with exposure techniques in cognitive-behavioral therapy seems to be a promising approach, as recently demonstrated (de Quervain *et al*. 2011; Sandi 2011).

More research is needed to investigate the efficacy of the combination of glucocorticoids and psychotherapy for the treatment of anxiety disorders. Furthermore, future studies are needed to address the questions of optimal dosage and application, and to investigate the synergistic or antagonistic potential of a combined application of cortisol with other drugs. However, these first findings support the assumption that especially the combination of glucocorticoids and exposure techniques seem to be a promising new approach for the treatment of anxiety disorders.

ACKNOWLEDGEMENTS

The authors and publisher gratefully acknowledge the permission to reproduce the copyright material (i.e. text extracts and two figures from de Quervain *et al*. 2009, *Frontiers in Neuroendocrinology*, Elsevier Inc.) in this book.

REFERENCES

Abercrombie, H. C., Kalin, N. H., Thurow, M. E., Rosenkranz, M. A., and Davidson, R. J. (2003). Cortisol variation in humans affects memory for emotionally laden and neutral information. *Behavioral Neuroscience*, 117(3): 505–516.

Aerni, A., Traber, R. *et al*. (2004). Low-dose cortisol for symptoms of posttraumatic stress disorder. *American Journal of Psychiatry*, 161(8): 1488–1490.

APA (1994). *Diagnostic and statistical manual of mental disorders*, 4th edn. Washington, DC: American Psychiatric Association.

Arbel, I., Kadar, T., Silbermann, M., and Levy, A. (1994). The effects of long-term corticosterone administration on hippocampal morphology and cognitive performance of middle-aged rats. *Brain Research*, 657(1–2): 227–235.

Baddeley, A. (1992). Working memory. *Science*, 255(5044): 556–559.

Barlow, D. H. and Liebowitz, M. R. (1995). Specific and social phobias. In H. L. Kaplanand B. J. Sadock, eds. *Comprehensive Textbook of Psychiatry*, vol. VI., New York, Williams and Wilkins: 1204–1218.

Barrett, D. and Gonzalez-Lima, F. (2004). Behavioral effects of metyrapone on Pavlovian extinction. *Neuroscience Letters*, 371(2–3): 91–96.

Beckwith, B. E., Petros, T. V., Scaglione, C., and Nelson, J. (1986). Dose-dependent effects of hydrocortisone on memory in human males. *Physiological Behavior*, 36(2): 283–286.

Bentz, D., Michael, T., de Quervain, D. J. F., and Wilhelm, F. H. (2010). Enhancing exposure therapy for anxiety disorders with glucocorticoids: From basic mechanisms of emotional learning to clinical applications. *Journal of Anxiety Disorders*, 24(2): 223–230.

Bisaz, R., Conboy, L., and Sandi, C. (2009). Learning under stress: a role for the neural cell adhesion molecule NCAM. *Neurobiology of Learning and Memory*, 91(4): 333–242.

Bohus, B. and Lissak, K. (1968). Adrenocortical hormones and avoidance behaviour of rats. *International Journal of Neuropharmacology*, 7(4): 301–306.

Bouton, M. E. (2002). Context, ambiguity, and unlearning: Sources of relapse after behavioral extinction. *Biological Psychiatry*, 52: 976–986.

Buchanan, T. W. and Lovallo, W. R. (2001). Enhanced memory for emotional material following stress-level cortisol treatment in humans. *Psychoneuroendocrinology*, 26(3): 307–317.

Buchanan, T. W., Brechtel, A., Sollers, J. J., and Lovallo, W. R. (2001). Exogenous cortisol exerts effects on the startle reflex independent of emotional modulation. *Pharmacology Biochemistry and Behavior*, 68(2): 203–210.

Buchanan, T. W., Tranel, D., and Adolphs, R. (2006). Impaired memory retrieval correlates with individual differences in cortisol response but not autonomic response. *Learning and Memory*, 13(3): 382–387.

Buss, C., Wolf, O. T., Witt, J., and Hellhammer, D. H. (2004). Autobiographic memory impairment following acute cortisol administration. *Psychoneuroendocrinology*, 29(8): 1093–1096.

Cabeza, R. and Nyberg, L. (2000). Imaging cognition II: An empirical review of 275 PET and fMRI studies. *Journal of Cognitive Neuroscience* 12: 1–47.

Cai, W. -H., Blundell, J., Han, J., Greene, R. W., and Powell, C. M. (2006). Post-reactivation Glucocorticoids Impair Recall of Established Fear Memory. *Journal of Neuroscience*, 26(37): 9560–9566.

Cleare, A. J., Heap, E. *et al.* (1999). Low-dose hydrocortisone in chronic fatigue syndrome: a randomized crossover trial. *Lancet*, 353: 455–458.

Coluccia, D., Wolf, O. T., Kollias, S., Roozendaal, B., Forster, A., and De Quervain, D. J. (2008). Glucocorticoid therapy-induced memory deficits: acute versus chronic effects. *Journal of Neuroscience*, 28(13): 3474–3478.

Cordero, M. I., Kruyt, N. D., Merino, J. J., and Sandi, C. (2002). Glucocorticoid involvement in memory formation in a rat model for traumatic memory. *Stress*, 5(1): 73–79.

Cuthbert, B. N., Lang, P. J. *et al.* (2003). The psychophysiology of anxiety disorder: Fear memory imagery. *Psychophysiology*, 40(3): 407–422.

de Quervain, D. J., Roozendaal, B., and McGaugh, J. L. (1998). Stress and glucocorticoids impair retrieval of long-term spatial memory. *Nature*, 394(6695): 787–790.

de Quervain, D. J., Roozendaal, B., Nitsch, R. M., McGaugh, J. L., and Hock, C. (2000a). Acute cortisone administration impairs retrieval of long-term declarative memory in humans. *Nature Reviews Neuroscience*, 3(4): 313–314.

de Quervain, D. J. F., Roozendaal, B., Müller-Spahn, F., McGaugh, J. L., and Hock, C. (2000b). Cortisol impairs free recall of long-term declarative memory in healthy human subjects. *Psychoneuroendocrinology*, 25 (Supplement 1): S51–S51.

de Quervain, D. J. -F., Henke, K., Aerni, A. *et al.* (2003). Glucocorticoid-induced impairment of declarative memory retrieval is associated with reduced blood flow in the medial temporal lobe. *European Journal of Neuroscience*, 17: 1296–1302.

de Quervain, D. J. F. and Margraf, J. (2008). Glucocorticoids for the treatment of post-traumatic stress disorder and phobias: a novel therapeutic approach. *European Journal of Pharmacology*, 583(2–3): 365–371.

de Quervain, D. J. F., Aerni, A., Schelling, G., and Roozendaal, B. (2009). Glucocorticoids and the regulation of memory in health and disease. *Frontiers in Neuroendocrinology*, 30(3): 358–370.

de Quervain, D. J. -F., Bentz, D., Michael, T. et al. (2011). Glucocorticoids enhance extinction-based psychotherapy. *Proceedings of the National Academy of Sciences*, 108(16): 6621–6625.

Domes, G., Heinrichs, M., Rimmele, U., Reichwald, U., and Hautzinger, M. (2004). Acute stress impairs recognition for positive words association with stress-induced cortisol secretion. *Stress*, 7(3): 173–181.

Fehm, L. and Margraf, J. (2002). Thought suppression: specificity in agoraphobia versus broad impairment in social phobia? *Behavior Research and Therapy*, 40: 57–66.

Flood, J. F., Vidal, D., Bennett, E. L., Orme, A. E., Vasquez, S., and Jarvik, M. E. (1978). Memory facilitating and anti-amnesic effects of corticosteroids. *Pharmacological Biochemical Behavior*, 8(1): 81–87.

Foa, E. B. and Kozak, M. J. (1986). Emotional Processing of Fear: Exposure to Corrective Information. *Psychological Bulletin*, 99(1): 20–35.

Furmark, T., Tillfors, M., Marteinsdottir, I. et al. (2002). Common changes in cerebral blood flow in patients with social phobia treated with citalopram or cognitive-behavioral therapy. *Archives of General Psychiatry*, 59: 425–433.

Het, S., Ramlow, G., and Wolf, O. T. (2005). A meta-analytic review of the effects of acute cortisol administration on human memory. *Psychoneuroendocrinology*, 30 (8): 771–784.

Jones, M. W. (2002). A comparative review of rodent prefrontal cortex and working memory. *Curren. Molecular Medicine*, 2: 639–647.

Kandel, E. R. (2001). The molecular biology of memory storage: a dialogue between genes and synapses. *Science*, 294(5544): 1030–1038.

Karst, H., Nair, S., Velzing, E. et al. (2002). Glucocorticoids alter calcium conductances and calcium channel subunit expression in basolateral amygdala neurons. *European Journal of Neuroscience*, 16(6): 1083–1089.

Kuhlmann, S., Kirschbaum, C., and Wolf, O. T. (2005a). Effects of oral cortisol treatment in healthy young women on memory retrieval of negative and neutral words. *Neurobiology of Learning and Memory*, 83(2): 158–162.

Kuhlmann, S., Piel, M., and Wolf, O. T. (2005b). Impaired memory retrieval after psychosocial stress in healthy young men. *Journal of Neuroscience*, 25(11): 2977–2982.

Liu, L., Tsuji, M., Takeda, H., Takada, K., and Matsumiya, T. (1999). Adrenocortical suppression blocks the enhancement of memory storage produced by exposure to psychological stress in rats. *Brain Research*, 821(1): 134–140.

Luine, V. N., Spencer, R. L., and McEwen, B. S. (1993). Effects of chronic corticosterone ingestion on spatial memory performance and hippocampal serotonergic function. *Brain Research*, 616(1–2): 65–70.

Lupien, S. J., Gillin, C. J., and Hauger, R. L. (1999). Working memory is more sensitive than declarative memory to the acute effects of corticosteroids: a dose-response study in humans. *Behavioral Neuroscience*, 113: 420–430.

Maheu, F. S., Joober, R., Beaulieu, S., and Lupien, S. J. (2004). Differential effects of adrenergic and corticosteroid hormonal systems on human short- and long-term declarative memory for emotionally arousing material. *Behavioral Neuroscience*, 118(2): 420–428.

McEwen, B. S. (2001). Plasticity of the hippocampus: adaptation to chronic stress and allostatic load. *Annals of the New York Academy of Science*, 933: 265–277.

McGaugh, J. L. and Roozendaal, B. (2002). Role of adrenal stress hormones in forming lasting memories in the brain. *Current Opinions in Neurobiology*, 12(2): 205–210.

McGaugh, J. L. (2003). *Memory and Emotion: The Making of Lasting Memory*. New York: (Columbia Unversity Press), Weidenfeld and Nicolson.
Oei, N. Y. L., Elzinga, B. M. et al. (2007). Glucocorticoids decrease hippocampal and prefrontal activation during declarative memory retrieval in young men. *Brain Imaging and Behavior*, 1: 31–41.
Quirk, G. J. and Mueller, D. (2008). Neural mechanisms of extinction learning and retrieval. *Neuropsychopharmacology*, 33(1): 56–72.
Rapee, R. M. and Heimberg, R. G. (1997). A cognitive-behavioral model of anxiety in social phobia. *Behaviour Research and Therapy*, 35: 741–756.
Rashidy-Pour, A., Sadeghi, H., Taherain, A. A., Vafaei, A. A., and Fathollahi, Y. (2004). The effects of acute restraint stress and dexamethasone on retrieval of long-term memory in rats: an interaction with opiate system. *Behavioral Brain Research*, 154(1): 193–198.
Revest, J. M., Di Blasi, F., Kitchener, P. et al. (2005). The MAPK pathway and Egr-1 mediate stress-related behavioral effects of glucocorticoids. *Nat. Neuroscience*, 8 (5): 664–672.
Roozendaal, B. (2000). 1999 Curt P. Richter award. Glucocorticoids and the regulation of memory consolidation. *Psychoneuroendocrinology*, 25(3): 213–238.
Roozendaal, B. and McGaugh, J. L. (1996a). Amygdaloid nuclei lesions differentially affect glucocorticoid-induced memory enhancement in an inhibitory avoidance task. *Neurobiology of Learning andMemory*, 65(1): 1–8.
Roozendaal, B. and McGaugh, J. L. (1996b). The memory-modulatory effects of glucocorticoids depend on an intact stria terminalis. *Brain Research*, 709(2): 243–250.
Roozendaal, B., Bohus, B., and McGaugh, J. L. (1996a). Dose-dependent suppression of adrenocortical activity with metyrapone: effects on emotion and memory. *Psychoneuroendocrinology*, 21(8): 681–693.
Roozendaal, B., Carmi, O., and McGaugh, J. L. (1996b). Adrenocortical suppression blocks the memory-enhancing effects of amphetamine and epinephrine. *Proceedings of the National Academy of Science, USA*, 93(4): 1429–1433.
Roozendaal, B., Williams, C. L., and McGaugh, J. L. (1999). Glucocorticoid receptor activation in the rat nucleus of the solitary tract facilitates memory consolidation: involvement of the basolateral amygdala. *European Journal of Neuroscience*, 11(4): 1317–1323.
Roozendaal, B., Griffith, Q. K., Buranday, J., De Quervain, D. J., and McGaugh, J. L. (2003). The hippocampus mediates glucocorticoid-induced impairment of spatial memory retrieval: dependence on the basolateral amygdala. *Proceedings of the National Academy of Science, USA*, 100(3): 1328–1333.
Roozendaal, B., Hahn, E. L., Nathan, S. V., De Quervain, D. J., and McGaugh, J. L. (2004a). Glucocorticoid effects on memory retrieval require concurrent noradrenergic activity in the hippocampus and basolateral amygdala. *Journal of Neuroscience*, 24(37): 8161–8169.
Roozendaal, B., McReynolds, J. R., and McGaugh, J. L. (2004b). The basolateral amygdala interacts with the medial prefrontal cortex in regulating glucocorticoid effects on working memory impairment. *Journal of Neuroscience*, 24(6): 1385–1392.
Roozendaal, B., Barsegyan, A., and Lee, S. (2008). Adrenal stress hormones, amygdala activation, and memory for emotionally arousing experiences. *Progress in Brain Research*, 167: 79–97.

Sajadi, A. A., Samaei, S. A., and Rashidy-Pour, A. (2007). Blocking effects of intrahippocampal naltrexone microinjections on glucocorticoid-induced impairment of spatial memory retrieval in rats. *Neuropharmacology*, 52(2): 347–354.

Sakamoto, H., Fukuda, R., Okuaki, T. *et al.* (2005). Parahippocampal activation evoked by masked traumatic images in posttraumatic stress disorder: A functional MRI study. *NeuroImage*, 26(3): 813–821.

Sandi, C. (2011). Glucocorticoids act on glutamatergic pathways to affect memory processes. *Trends in Neurosciences*, 34(4): 165–176.

Sandi, C. and Rose, S. P. (1994). Corticosterone enhances long-term retention in one-day-old chicks trained in a weak passive avoidance learning paradigm. *Brain Research*, 647(1): 106–112.

Sapolsky, R. M. (2000). Glucocorticoids and hippocampal atrophy in neuropsychiatric disorders. *Archives of General Psychiatry*, 57(10): 925–935.

Sara, S. J. (2000). Retrieval and reconsolidation: Toward a neurobiology of remembering. *Learning and Memory*, 7: 73-84.

Soravia, L. M., Heinrichs, M., Aerni, A. *et al.* (2006). *Proceedings of the National Academy of Sciences of the United States of America*, 130: 5585–5590.

Squire, L. R. (1992). Memory and the hippocampus: a synthesis from findings with rats, monkeys, and humans. *Psychological Review*, 99: 1995–1231.

Wolf, O. T. (2008). The influence of stress hormones on emotional memory: relevance for psychopathology. *Acta Psycholog (Amst.)*, 127(3): 513–531.

Wolf, O. T., Convit, A., McHugh, P. F. *et al.* (2001). Cortisol differentially affects memory in young and elderly men. *Behavioral Neuroscience*, 115(5): 1002–1011.

Yang, Y. L., Chao, P. K., and Lu, K. T. (2006). Systemic and intra-amygdala administration of glucocorticoid agonist and antagonist modulate extinction of conditioned fear. *Neuropsychopharmacology*, 31(5): 912–924.

Chapter 8

OXYTOCIN

Markus Heinrichs, Frances S. Chen, and Gregor Domes

Department of Psychology, University of Freiburg, Freiburg, Germany

INTRODUCTION

The neuropeptide oxytocin (OXT) plays an important role in the regulation of complex social cognition and behavior (Heinrichs *et al.* 2009; Meyer-Lindenberg *et al.* 2011), including social approach, social recognition (Winslow and Insel 2004), and attachment (Insel and Young 2001). Recent studies on clinical populations suggest that impaired functioning of the OXT system may contribute to mental disorders associated with social deficits, such as social anxiety disorder (SAD), autism, and borderline personality disorder (BPD). OXT, especially in combination with psychotherapy, is emerging as a promising component of novel treatment approaches for these and other mental disorders characterized by social dysfunction.

NEUROPHYSIOLOGICAL BASES OF OXYTOCIN

OXT is synthesized in magnocellular neurons in the paraventricular and supraoptic nuclei of the hypothalamus. It is processed along the axonal projections to the posterior lobe of the pituitary, where it is stored in secretory vesicles and released into peripheral circulation. In addition to the release from axonal terminals, there is also dendritic release into the extracellular space, resulting not only in local action but also in diffusion through the brain to reach distant targets (Ludwig and Leng 2006). Furthermore, smaller parvocellular neurons in the paraventricular nucleus, which also produce OXT, project directly to other regions in the brain. Within the brain, OXT travels via axonal projection from parvocellular

---

Psychobiological Approaches for Anxiety Disorders: Treatment Combination Strategies, First Edition. Edited by Stefan G. Hofmann.
© 2012 John Wiley & Sons, Ltd. Published 2012 by John Wiley & Sons, Ltd.

neurons of the hypothalamus to different brain regions including the amygdala, hippocampus, striatum, suprachiasmatic nucleus, bed nucleus of stria terminalis, and brainstem, where it acts as a neuromodulator or neurotransmitter, influencing neurotransmission in these areas. For example, OXT modulates neural populations in the central amygdala (Huber *et al.* 2005; Viviani *et al.* 2011). However, the distribution of OXT in the brain is not yet fully understood. For an overview of studies on endogenous levels of OXT and human behavior, see Heinrichs *et al.* (2009). For an overview of the neurogenetic mechanisms of the OXT system including neuro-imaging studies, see Meyer-Lindenberg *et al.* (2011).

OXYTOCIN AND HUMAN SOCIAL BEHAVIOR

The discovery that neuropeptide availability in the human brain can be experimentally manipulated via the relatively non-invasive method of intranasal administration has opened up an exciting new avenue for research (Born *et al.* 2002; Heinrichs and Domes 2008). In recent years, this method in combination with established behavioral and neuro-imaging paradigms has greatly advanced our understanding of OXT actions in the human brain as well as effects of OXT on human social interaction. In addition, inter-individual variation in social neuropeptide signaling has been productively studied using genetic methodologies. This work has recently acquired a translational dimension focused on therapeutic applications. The goal of this chapter is to assess the role of the OXT system on human social behavior from a translational viewpoint.

METHODOLOGICAL ISSUES

A number of different methods have been employed to study the relationship between OXT and behavior. First, peripheral levels of OXT can be readily measured through the plasma, and correlations between peripheral levels of OXT and behavior have been reported in several studies. For instance, high levels of plasma OXT have been associated with trust and trustworthiness (Zak *et al.* 2005), and with the experience of receiving support and physical contact from a partner (Grewen *et al.* 2005); it has also been found to predict lower levels of anxiety in patients with depression (Scantamburlo *et al.* 2007). In addition, schizophrenia (Goldman *et al.* 2008; Keri *et al.* 2008), depression (Cyranowski *et al.* 2008), and autism spectrum disorders (ASD) (Green *et al.* 2001) have all been associated with generally attenuated levels of plasma OXT relative to levels observed in healthy samples. However, contrasting results have also been reported, with high levels of plasma OXT also associated with relationship stress in women (Taylor *et al.* 2006). Furthermore, the relationship between peripheral neuropeptide levels and central nervous system (CNS) availability of these neuropeptides remains unclear (Landgraf and Neumann 2004; Horvat-Gordon *et al.* 2005; Anderson 2006; Carter *et al.* 2007). Although OXT has both peripheral and central functions, peripheral and central release are not necessarily associated; therefore, the interpretation of peripheral neuropeptide levels in psychological terms remains highly controversial. Further investigation of this issue will be necessary to resolve this debate and should represent a research priority given its implications for future translational research.

As CNS neuropeptide function is more directly relevant for behavioral effects or psychopathology than peripheral levels (Heinrichs and Domes 2008), an alternative approach to studying OXT effects involves the measurement of neuropeptides from cerebrospinal fluid (CSF). The level of neuropeptides in CSF has been shown to more directly reflect their immediate availability in the brain (Born *et al.* 2002). Unfortunately, the invasiveness of this method limits its use in routine human research. Therefore, most recent studies investigating the central actions of neuropeptides in humans have oriented on the strategy of delivering peptides intranasally, a method that provides a direct pathway to the brain (Born *et al.* 2002; Heinrichs *et al.* 2009).

Natural inter-individual variations in the OXT system and their implications for human social behavior have been studied using molecular genetic methods. One single nucleotide polymorphism (SNP) located in the third intron of the OXT receptor gene (*OXTR*), rs53576 (G/A), has been associated in a number of studies with socio-emotional functioning; specifically, the A allele has been linked to reduced maternal sensitivity to child behavior (Bakermans-Kranenburg and van Ijzendoorn 2008), lower empathy (Rodrigues *et al.* 2009), and in men, reduced positive affect (Lucht *et al.* 2009). The A allele has also been associated with a larger startle response (Rodrigues *et al.* 2009), reduced amygdala activation during emotional face processing (Tost *et al.* 2010), and increased risk for autism (Wu *et al.* 2005), though a handful of null or contrasting effects have also been reported (Costa *et al.* 2009; Tansey *et al.* 2010; Bradley *et al.* 2011).

SOCIAL STRESS AND ANXIETY

A suite of behavioral and physiological responses is typically triggered in response to a stressful social interaction, with the endocrine component of this response including hypothalamus-pituitary-adrenal (HPA) axis activation and the secretion of CRH, ACTH, and cortisol. A number of studies suggest that OXT dampens this endocrine response to stress. Breastfeeding women – in whom endogenous secretion of OXT is naturally increased – show muted cortisol responses to psychosocial stressors (Altemus *et al.* 1995; Heinrichs *et al.* 2001). Similarly, healthy males randomly assigned to receive social support along with OXT during preparation for the 'Trier Social Stress Test' (TSST) (Kirschbaum *et al.* 1993) showed the lowest cortisol response to the TSST, whereas subjects who received no social support and placebo showed the highest response (Heinrichs et al. 2003) (Figure 8.1). Notably, lower levels of subjective stress (lower anxiety and higher calmness) were also reported during the stress test by the group receiving social support and OXT. The stress-buffering effect of OXT appears to be robust and has been replicated in other recent studies (de Oliveira et al. 2011; Quirin et al. 2011). Complementary inter-individual differences have been linked to the variation in the OXT receptor gene; individuals homozygous for the A allele of *OXTR* rs53576 and for whom explicit social-support seeking behavior is culturally normative in one study reported being less likely to seek social support (Kim et al. 2010) and in another study did not profit physiologically or psychologically from social support to the same degree as carriers of the G allele (Chen et al, in press).

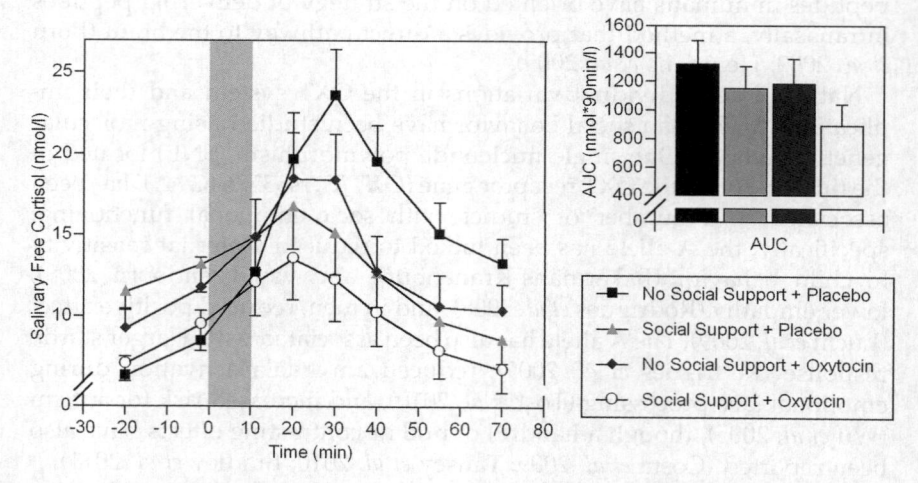

Figure 8.1. Mean salivary free cortisol concentrations (± SEM) during psychosocial stress exposure (TSST). Participants were randomly assigned to receive intranasal oxytocin (24 IU) or placebo and either no social support or social support from their best friend before stress. The shaded area indicates the period of the stress tasks (public speaking followed by mental arithmetic in front of a panel of evaluators). The areas under the individual response curves (AUC) represent cumulative cortisol release (calculated by aggregating data from 8 saliva sampling points) throughout the session. Significant interaction effects on cortisol were observed (social support by time effect, $p < .001$; social support by oxytocin by time effect, $p < .01$). Reprinted from *Biological Psychiatry*, 54 (12), Markus Heinrichs, Thomas Baumgartner, Clemens Kirschbaum and Ulrike Ehlert, Social support and oxytocin interact to suppress cortisol and subjective responses to psychosocial stress, 1389–1398. Copyright (2003), with permission from the Society of Biological Psychiatry.

OXT administration reduced plasma cortisol levels and increased positive communication in both men and women during a couple conflict (Ditzen et al. 2009), providing evidence that central OXT facilitates human pair bonding in a manner parallel to that observed in prior animal studies (Young and Wang 2004). OXT also enhanced secure interpretations of ambiguous attachment-related scenarios in men with an insecure attachment pattern (Buchheim et al. 2009). As secure attachment in humans is associated with lower stress reactivity and a better ability to interact socially (Ditzen et al. 2008), understanding the role of OXT in attachment may have clinical implications for several mental and developmental disorders associated with stress and impaired social behavior.

Taken together, these results imply that OXT enhances the buffering effect of positive social interactions on stress responsiveness; however, the underlying biological and developmental mechanisms of this effect have not yet been fully delineated (Gamer and Buchel 2011; Norman et al. 2011). It is likely that the baseline sensitivity of the CNS to OXT is influenced by significant events occurring early in life. Early parental separation stress, for example, has been shown to reduce the suppressing effect of OXT on cortisol levels (Meinlschmidt and Heim 2007). Future research in this domain is expected to have direct translational relevance for SAD, which is characterized by heightened stress reactivity in a range of social situations. The implications of research in this area are also likely to extend beyond SAD, as stress also increases risk for many psychiatric disorders (Selten and Cantor-Graae 2005), whereas positive social interactions decrease it.

EMOTION RECOGNITION

OXT also has been found to play a role in the recognition and processing of subtle social signals encoded in facial expressions. This finding has potential clinical implications for autism, SAD, BPD, and schizophrenia, in which impairments and biases in this core social ability are common (Winton et al. 1995; Celani et al. 1999; Kohler et al. 2003; Domes et al. 2009). In one study, intranasal OXT administration improved the performance of healthy men on difficult stimuli in the 'Reading the Mind in the Eyes' test (Domes et al. 2007), which was developed to assess the social cognitive abilities of adults with ASD (Baron-Cohen et al. 2001). Specifically, participants receiving OXT were more accurate than those receiving placebo in determining other individuals' emotional or mental states based on photos of those individuals' eyes (Figure 8.2).

OXT may also have a role in individual differences in emotion recognition accuracy (Bartz et al. 2010). In a task that measured 'empathic accuracy' (the match between a participant's ratings of emotional states displayed by another individual in a film clip, and the displayed individual's own ratings of what he or she was actually feeling), intranasal OXT

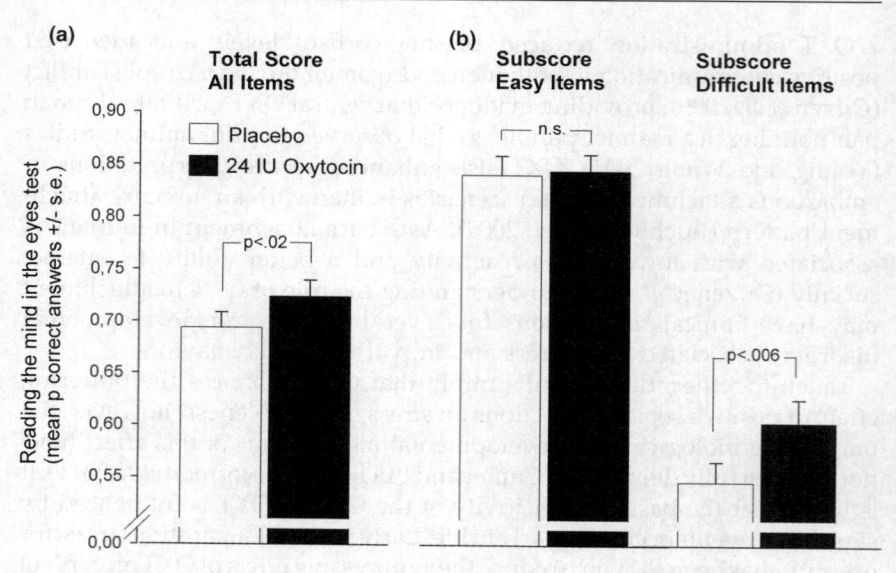

Figure 8.2. (a) Oxytocin improved performance in the Reading the Mind in the Eyes Test (RMET) compared to placebo. (b) Performance in the RMET as a function of item difficulty: oxytocin improved performance on the difficult items and not on the easy items. Reprinted from *Biological Psychiatry*, 61 (6), Gregor Domes, Markus Heinrichs, Andre Michel, Christoph Berger, Sabine C. Herpetz, Oxytocin Improves "Mind-Reading" in Humans, 731–733. Copyright (2007), with permission from the Society of Biological Psychiatry.

(compared to placebo) improved empathic accuracy only in individuals with high levels of autistic traits, who presumably have low baseline empathic abilities. These results are in line with research suggesting that empathic abilities are associated with genetic variation of the OXT system marked by *OXTR* rs53576 (Rodrigues *et al.* 2009).

Other studies have investigated whether OXT selectively improves the recognition of specific emotions, with mixed results. Some studies have demonstrated that OXT specifically enhances processing of positive facial expressions (Di Simplicio *et al.* 2009; Marsh *et al.* 2010) or specifically decreases aversion to angry faces (Evans *et al.* 2010). Another recent study showed enhanced emotion recognition for both happy and angry faces at very short presentation durations of 17 to 83 milliseconds, suggesting that at least during the early stages of visual processing, OXT promotes recognition of a range of emotional expressions (Schulze *et al.* 2011). Other studies have reported improved recognition only of fearful faces after OXT administration (Fischer-Shofty *et al.* 2010), or no effect on emotion recognition in a visual search task (Guastella *et al.* 2009). Further research will be necessary to reconcile these findings.

To date, four studies have examined the effects of OXT on patterns of visual attention to neutral and emotional faces, which is generally assumed to play a crucial role in the recognition of facial emotions (Adolphs 2002). With one exception (Domes *et al.* 2010), these studies have reported increased gazing time on the eye region compared to other parts of the face (Guastella *et al.* 2008; Andari *et al.* 2010; Gamer *et al.* 2010). Though these results suggest that improved facial emotion recognition after OXT treatment might be due at least in part to increased eye gaze, this hypothesis has not yet been explicitly tested. As several mental disorders involving social deficits including autism, SAD, and BPD have been linked to impaired or biased processing of emotional expressions as well as reduced or atypical gaze to the eye region (Klin *et al.* 2002; Horley *et al.* 2003), a more complete understanding of the conditions under which OXT can enhance emotion recognition and eye gaze will likely have translational implications for the treatment of these disorders.

In comparison to studies investigating the effects of OXT on emotion recognition (generally theorized to represent a cognitive facet of empathy), research on OXT effects on emotional empathy, i.e. the vicarious feeling of an emotion, have been relatively rare to date (Singer *et al.* 2008; Hurlemann *et al.* 2010). Recent studies have begun to address this issue, with one study reporting positive effects of intranasal OXT on emotional empathy but not cognitive empathy (Hurlemann *et al.* 2010) and another reporting positive effects of OXT on 'compassion-focused imagery' (Rockliff *et al.* 2011).

SOCIAL COGNITION AND MEMORY

Although early studies on the cognitive effects of OXT suggested an impairment of general semantic memory under OXT (Fehm-Wolfsdorf *et al.* 1984), more recent studies suggest that OXT selectively modulates social memory. One study in healthy males showed that intranasal OXT selectively reduced implicit memory of socially relevant (and not neutral) words (Heinrichs *et al.* 2004). In another recent study, intranasal OXT selectively improved recognition memory for faces but not for non-social stimuli (Rimmele *et al.* 2009). Whether and how OXT administration influences memory for specific emotions remains unclear; existing studies have documented different effects depending on the timing of OXT administration. One study, in which OXT was administered after a learning task, showed improved memory after both a 30-minute and 1-day delay specifically for faces that had displayed angry or neutral (and not happy) expressions during the learning task (Savaskan *et al.* 2008), although there was no effect of OXT on explicit memory for which specific facial expressions had been associated with specific identities. However, in a different study, intranasal OXT administered before a learning task enhanced memory for happy faces over angry and neutral faces (Guastella *et al.* 2008).

PROSOCIAL BEHAVIOR

In animal research, OXT has been shown to promote social approach behavior and to reduce the typical tendency to avoid proximity with unfamiliar others. In humans, trust of others is often considered an indicator of psychological readiness for social approach. In the first study to investigate the role of OXT in interpersonal trust (Kosfeld et al. 2005), participants' willingness to take social risks (in a trust game) versus nonsocial risks (in a lottery game) was assessed. Participants who had received OXT showed greater trust relative to the placebo group (Figure 8.3), a result that has been replicated in follow-up studies (Mikolajczak et al. 2010a; b). Notably, OXT increased participants' willingness to take risks only when the interaction involved a social component.

A subsequent study investigated the effects of OXT on social behavior following a breach of trust (Baumgartner et al. 2008). After several rounds of a trust game, participants were informed that their social partners had made selfish decisions that were disadvantageous to the participant (i.e. betrayed the participant's trust). Whereas participants who had received placebo adjusted their behavior in subsequent rounds of the trust game, participants who had received intranasal OXT continued to make decisions indicative of sustained trust, despite the betrayal that had just occurred. Another experiment using the 'cyberball' paradigm (a virtual ball-tossing game designed to manipulate feelings of social inclusion or exclusion) showed that OXT increased the desire for future social interactions following an experience of inclusion but did not provide a buffer against the negative feelings associated with blunt social ostracism (Alvares et al. 2010).

In addition to promoting trusting behavior, OXT has also been shown to promote generosity (Zak et al. 2007), increase perceived trustworthiness and attractiveness in facial expressions (Theodoridou et al. 2009), and also positively affect the responsivity of fathers toward their toddlers, thereby possibly promoting positive interactions (Naber et al. 2010). However, it has also been reported that OXT administration enhances envy and gloating in a social game (Shamay-Tsoory et al. 2009). Prior social information, such as brief prior face-to-face contact with a social partner (Declerck et al. 2010), seems to enhance the effects of OXT on cooperative or prosocial behavior. The social context appears to be a critical modulator of OXT effects on social interaction, with other recent studies supporting the hypothesis that OXT specifically promotes in-group but not out-group trust and cooperation (De Dreu et al. 2010; 2011; Chen et al. 2011).

The overall picture that emerges from the existing literature is that OXT enhances the motivation to engage in social interactions, enhances the ability to decode and recall key social cues such as facial expressions of emotion, and promotes trusting behavior, cooperation, and willingness to

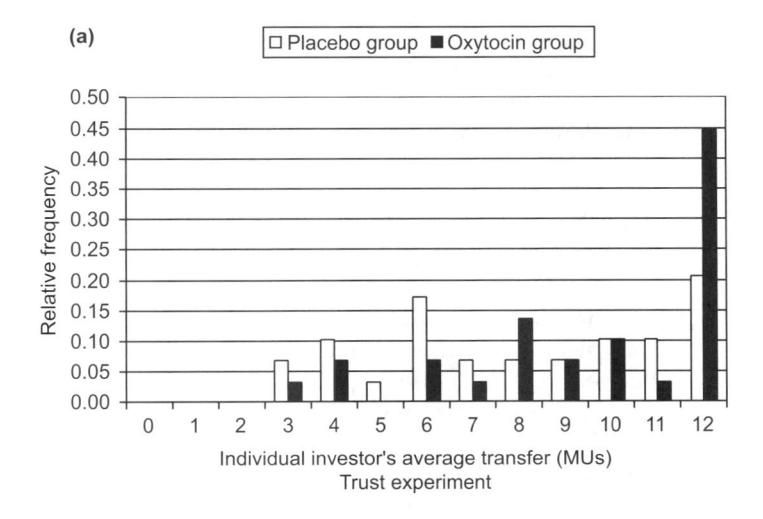

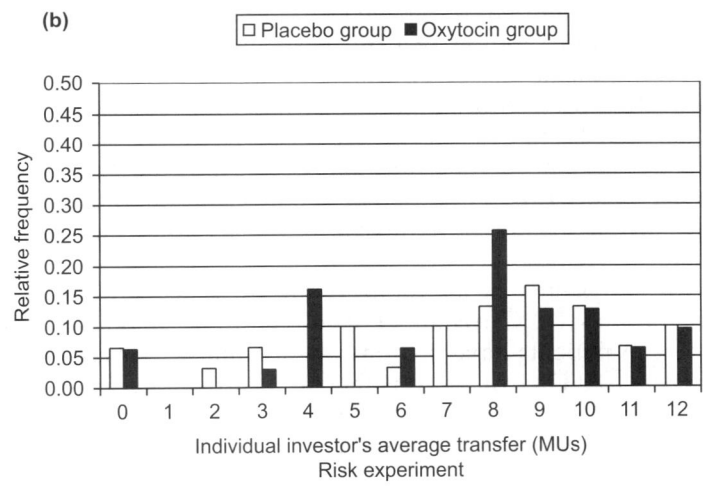

Figure 8.3. Transfers in the trust and risk experiments. Each observation represents the average transfer amount (in monetary units, MU) per investor across four transfer decisions. (a) Relative frequency of investors' average transfers in the oxytocin (filled bars) and placebo (open bars) groups in the trust experiment: subjects given oxytocin showed significantly higher transfer levels. (b) Relative frequency of investors' average transfers in the oxytocin (filled bars) and placebo (open bars) groups in the risk experiment: subjects in the oxytocin and the placebo group show statistically identical transfer levels. Kosfeld, M., Heinrichs, M., Zak, P. J., Fischbacher, U., & Fehr, E. (2005). Oxytocin increases trust in humans. *Nature*, 435(7042), 673–676, with permission from © 2005 Nature Publishing Group.

take social risks. The few studies that have directly investigated the specificity of these effects, through the inclusion of both social and non-social stimuli, suggest that the effects are more pronounced for social stimuli (Keri and Benedek 2009; Norman *et al.* 2010).

COMBINING OXYTOCIN AND PSYCHOTHERAPY FOR THE TREATMENT OF 'SOCIAL DISORDERS'

Taken together, the effects of OXT administration on social behavior, links between atypical levels of endogenous OXT and mental disorders, associations between *OXTR* polymorphisms and social behavior, and associations between *OXTR* polymorphisms and risk for mental disorders characterized by severe social deficits, are strongly suggestive of OXT's potential therapeutic value for such disorders. For an overview of studies on endogenous levels of OXT in different mental disorders, see a recent review (Heinrichs *et al.* 2009). Unfortunately, the method of intravenous administration of OXT has only limited applicability in clinical settings, as only a small fraction of intravenously administered neuropeptides pass through the blood–brain barrier (Kang and Park 2000). Furthermore, intravenous infusion could potentially have side effects due to actions on hormone systems. Intranasal administration, and the more direct pathway to the human brain afforded by this method, currently shows the most promise as a clinical intervention methodology (Heinrichs *et al.* 2009).

Though no systematic, randomized control trials on the therapeutic effects of intranasal OXT treatment have been completed to date, preclinical studies in patients have demonstrated promising results of a single dose of intranasal OXT on various mental disorders. Larger-scale neuropharmacological studies on clinical samples that systematically manipulate neuropeptide availability in the CNS will be necessary to assess in detail the therapeutic value of OXT. In the following section, we survey the state of the field and review recent advances made using OXT as part of a therapeutic program for several psychopathological states (see the ClinicalTrials website: http://clinicaltrials.gov).

Social Anxiety Disorder

SAD is characterized by a fear of negative evaluation by others and extreme anxiety and discomfort before, during, and after exposure to social settings. SAD is the third most common mental health disorder in the USA after depression and alcoholism (Kessler *et al.* 1994), and thus represents an issue of major public health significance. In one study, OXT was administered intranasally to patients with SAD who also participated in 5 weekly sessions of brief exposure intervention (Guastella et al. 2009b). OXT administration improved speech performance over the course of the exposure sessions. However, possibly due to the low frequency of sessions, a more generalized overall improvement in treatment outcome was not observed. In another study (Labuschagne et al. 2010), SAD patients and healthy controls performed an emotional face matching task involving pictures of fearful, angry, and happy faces after OXT and placebo administration. In the placebo condition, both groups showed bilateral amygdala activation to all emotional faces, but patients with SAD showed a hyperactive amygdala response to fearful faces relative to the control group. While OXT administration did not change amygdala reactivity to emotional faces in the control group, it dampened amygdala reactivity to fearful faces in the SAD group (Labuschagne et al. 2010). These findings – in line with other studies suggesting that the effects of OXT depend on the baseline functioning of the individual (Bartz et al. 2010) – suggest that OXT has a specific effect on fear-related amygdala activity particularly when the amygdala is hyperactive as in SAD.

Autism Spectrum Disorder

ASD is a neurodevelopmental disorder characterized by speech and communication deficits, repetitive or compulsive behaviors in combination with restricted interests, and severe impairments in social functioning. In a recent study (Guastella et al. 2010), adolescent males (aged 12 to 19) with ASD were treated with intranasal OXT or placebo. OXT administration improved performance on the 'Reading the Mind in the Eyes' Task (Baron-Cohen et al. 2001), suggesting that early treatment with intranasal OXT has the potential to improve social functioning in adolescents with ASD. In another study (Andari et al. 2010) involving individuals with ASD, intranasal OXT increased social interactions and feelings of trust in a simulated ball game ('cyberball') that involved interactions with fictitious partners. In addition, OXT administration increased ASD patients' gazing time toward the eye region of facial photos. Intravenous infusion of OXT has also been shown to induce subtle behavioral and psychological effects in individuals with ASD, including enhanced understanding of emotional speech and decreased repetitive behaviors (Bartz and Hollander 2008), although it should be noted that only a small fraction of intravenously administered OXT infusion is thought to pass the blood–brain barrier. These studies, as a whole, suggest that OXT has therapeutic potential for the core deficits associated with ASD, by enhancing emotion recognition, reducing repetitive behaviors, and improving responsiveness to others and social behavior.

Borderline Personality Disorder

BPD is characterized by emotional instability, impulsivity, identity diffusion, and dysfunctional social relationships. Perceived rejection and loss often trigger angry outbursts or impulsive, suicidal, or self-injurious behavior, suggesting disruptions to the normal functioning of the attachment and affiliative systems (Stanley and Siever 2010).

Although the suite of symptoms that characterizes BPD points to OXT treatment as a particularly promising intervention option, investigation in this area has so far been limited. A recent pilot study suggests that OXT attenuates stress reactivity in BPD patients during the TSST (Simeon

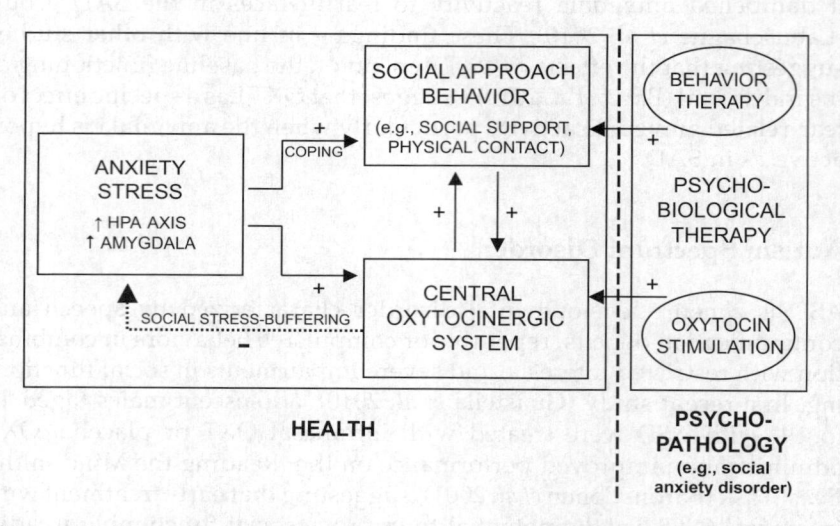

Figure 8.4. Integrative translational model of the interactions of the oxytocin system, social approach behavior, and social stress in humans. *Left side*: Social stress and social anxiety stimulate the amygdala–cingulate circuit and the hypothalamic–pituitary–adrenal (HPA) axis. In healthy individuals, stress and anxiety encourage social approach behavior as a coping strategy. They also stimulates oxytocin release, which further promotes social approach behavior. Furthermore, positive social interaction (e.g. physical contact) is itself associated with OXT release and therefore promotes continued social approach behavior. OXT reduces amygdala and HPA axis reactivity to social stressors, and as such serves as an important mediator of the anxiolytic and stress-protective effects of positive social interaction ('social buffering'). *Right side*: Patients with mental and developmental disorders characterized by severe deficits in social interactions (e.g. autism, SAD, BPD) may benefit from novel 'psychobiological therapy' approaches wherein psychotherapy is combined with administration of OXT or OXT receptor agonists. Reprinted from *Progress in Brain Research*, 170, Markus Heinrichs and Gregor Domes, Neuropeptides and social behavior: effects of oxytocin and vasopressin in humans, 337–350. Copyright (2008), with permission from Elsevier.

et al. 2011). In another initial study, OXT administration decreased cooperative responses within the context of a social dilemma game; however, these effects were observed in mixed-sex sample of 14 adult (4 male) BPD patients (Bartz *et al.* 2010) and therefore warrant replication. Several clinical trials involving larger sample sizes are indeed currently being conducted to examine the therapeutic value of OXT for patients with BPD (see clinicaltrials.gov).

Schizophrenia

Schizophrenia is a chronic brain disorder characterized by severely disorganized thought patterns, hallucinations and delusions, and disrupted, often flat, affect. Altered plasma OXT levels have been documented in schizophrenia patients (Heinrichs *et al.* 2009). In animal models of schizophrenia, systematic OXT administration has been observed to have antipsychotic-like effects, including reversed prepulse inhibition deficits induced by amphetamine or the phencyclidine analogue MK 801 (Feifel and Reza 1999). In one study (Feifel *et al.* 2010), schizophrenia patients received intranasal OXT (40 IU twice a day) or placebo for 3 weeks in addition to antipsychotics. OXT reduced positive and negative symptoms of schizophrenia compared with placebo. In another study, either 10 or 20 IU of intranasal OXT was administered to schizophrenia patients (Goldman *et al.* 2011) and subsequent effects on emotion recognition (often impaired in schizophrenia) were measured. Although performance fell in patients administered 10 IU of OXT, emotion recognition improved following administration of 20 IU of OXT in polydipsic relative to non-polydipsic patients.

CONCLUSION

Intranasal administration of OXT improves social cognition, emotion recognition, secure attachment, and empathy (Heinrichs *et al.* 2004; Domes *et al.* 2007; Guastella *et al.* 2008; Buchheim *et al.* 2009; Ditzen *et al.* 2009; Rimmele *et al.* 2009), reduces physiological and psychological stress responses (Heinrichs *et al.* 2003), mediates stress-protective consequences of social support ('social buffering') (Heinrichs *et al.* 2003), and attenuates amygdala reactivity to social stimuli (Kirsch *et al.* 2005; Domes *et al.* 2007; Baumgartner *et al.* 2008; Gamer *et al.* 2010) in healthy humans (Figure 8.4). For those with pathologies in these domains, pharmacological intervention in the OXT system represents a promising new angle for treatment. Administration of OXT or selective and longer-acting *OXTR* agonists such as carbetocin, especially in combination with interaction-based psychotherapy, may represent an effective treatment option for mental disorders characterized by extreme difficulties in social interactions and/or disrupted attachment relationships, such as SAD, ASD, BPD, and schizophrenia (Meyer-Lindenberg et al. 2011). Initial results of experimental neuropeptide administration in these patient groups have been encouraging, especially as these 'social disorders' are notoriously difficult to treat or (as in the case of ASD) currently cannot be effectively treated at all.

Several clinical trials are currently being carried out (see list of projects in clinicaltrials.gov) to develop and evaluate new clinically relevant approaches for neuropeptide administration. Intranasal OXT treatment in particular is expected to enhance patients' willingness to interact socially (e.g. in cognitive-behavioral group therapy) as well as to confront feared social situations outside of therapy sessions. Figure 8.4 depicts an integrative model of the relationships among the human central OXT system, social anxiety and stress, and social approach behavior. In this model, translational success is contingent upon systematic inquiry into 'propsychotherapeutic' neuropharmacology designed to support and enhance psychotherapeutic interventions rather than to serve in isolation as an alternative route to a cure. We therefore propose the term 'psychobiological therapy' for this novel integrative approach (Figure 8.4).

The model also highlights priorities for further research. For instance, more research is required to clarify the relationship between peripheral and central OXT, as well as the mechanisms by which OXT, receptor agonists, and antagonists reach the brain following different forms of administration. More detailed knowledge about these mechanisms would foster the development of optimal strategies to manipulate neuropeptide availability or to use them as potential markers of beneficial treatment. The development on non-peptidergic drugs (Decaux et al. 2008) acting on these receptors represents another significant goal. In addition, the development of specific radioactive labeling of neuropeptides in positron emission tomography would help to clarify the precise location of OXT receptors in the human brain. In combination with *in vitro* studies identifying OXT binding sites in the human brain (Loup et al. 1991) as well as fMRI studies identifying brain areas responsive to OXT administration (Heinrichs and Domes 2008; Meyer-Lindenberg 2008), positron emission tomography with OXT would provide much-needed, detailed information about brain circuits involved in social information processing. As the neuro-anatomical distribution and sensitivity of OXT receptors is likely to be influenced by variations in the regulatory regions of their respective genes, further studies on how specific genetic variants influence behavioral and brain response to OXT administration will be crucial for decoding individual differences in the functioning of the social brain and to tailor new treatment strategies sensitive to individual differences. Overall, the tremendous growth in this research field offers not only a promising new path for exploring the neuroendocrinology of the social brain, but also a translational perspective for developing novel treatment strategies for social disorders.

REFERENCES

Adolphs, R. (2002). Recognizing emotion from facial expressions: psychological and neurological mechanisms. *Behavioral Cognitive Neuroscience Review*, 1(1): 21–62.

Altemus, M., Deuster, P. A., Galliven, E., Carter, C. S., and Gold, P. W. (1995). Suppression of hypothalmic-pituitary-adrenal axis responses to stress in lactating women. *Journal of Clinical Endocrinology and Metabolism*, 80(10): 2954–2959.

Alvares, G. A., Hickie, I. B., and Guastella, A. J. (2010). Acute effects of intranasal oxytocin on subjective and behavioral responses to social rejection. *Experiments in Clinical Psychopharmacology*, 18(4): 316–321.

Andari, E., Duhamel, J. R., Zalla, T., Herbrecht, E., Leboyer, M., and Sirigu, A. (2010). Promoting social behavior with oxytocin in high-functioning autism spectrum disorders. *Proceedings of the National Academy of Science, USA*, 107(9): 4389–4394.

Anderson, G. M. (2006). Report of altered urinary oxytocin and AVP excretion in neglected orphans should be reconsidered. *Journal of Autism and Developmental Disorders*, 36(6): 829–830.

Bakermans-Kranenburg, M. J. and van Ijzendoorn, M. H. (2008). Oxytocin receptor (*OXTR*) and serotonin transporter (5-HTT) genes associated with observed parenting. *Social Cognitive and Affective Neuroscience*, 3(2): 128–134.

Baron-Cohen, S., Wheelwright, S., Hill, J., Raste, Y., and Plumb, I. (2001). The 'Reading the Mind in the Eyes' test revised version: a study with normal adults, and adults with Asperger syndrome or high-functioning autism. *Journal of Child Psychology and Psychiatry*, 42(2): 241–251.

Bartz, J. A. and Hollander, E. (2008). Oxytocin and experimental therapeutics in autism spectrum disorders. *Progress in Brain Research*, 170: 451–462.

Bartz, J. A., Simeon, D., Hamilton, H. et al. (2010a). Oxytocin can hinder trust and cooperation in borderline personality disorder. *Soc Cogn Affect Neurosci*, doi: 10.1093/scan/nsq085.

Bartz, J. A., Zaki, J., Bolger, N. et al. (2010b). Oxytocin selectively improves empathic accuracy. *Psychological Science*, 21(10): 1426–1428.

Baumgartner, T., Heinrichs, M., Vonlanthen, A., Fischbacher, U., and Fehr, E. (2008). Oxytocin shapes the neural circuitry of trust and trust adaptation in humans. *Neuron*, 58(4): 639–650.

Born, J., Lange, T., Kern, W., McGregor, G. P., Bickel, U., and Fehm, H. L. (2002). Sniffing neuropeptides: a transnasal approach to the human brain. *Nature Reviews Neuroscience*, 5(6): 514–516.

Bradley, B., Westin, D., Mercer, K. et al. (2011). Association between childhood maltreatment and adult emotional dysregulation in a low-income, urban, African-American sample: moderation by oxytocin receptor gene. *Development and Psychopathology*, 23(2): 439–452.

Buchheim, A., Heinrichs, M., George, C. et al. (2009). Oxytocin enhances the experience of attachment security. *Psychoneuroendocrinology*, 34(9): 1417–1422.

Carter, C. S., Pournajafi-Nazarloo, H., Kramer, K. M. et al. (2007). Oxytocin: behavioral associations and potential as a salivary biomarker. *Annals of the New York Academy of Science*, 1098: 312–322.

Celani, G., Battacchi, W., and Arcidiacono, L. (1999). The understanding of the emotional meaning of facial expressions in people with autism. *Journal of Autism and Developmental Disorders*, 29(1): 57–66.

Chen, F. S., Kumsta, R., and Heinrichs, M. (2011). Oxytocin and intergroup relations: Goodwill is not a fixed pie. *Proeedings of the National Academy of Scienmce, USA*, 108(13): E45.

Chen, F. S., Kumsta, R., von Dawans, B., Monakhov, M., Ebstein, R. P., and Heinrichs, M. (in press). An oxytocin receptor gene (*OXTR*) polymorphism and social support interact to reduce physiological and psychological responses to stress. Proceedings of the National Academy of Sciences, USA.

Costa, B., Pini, S., Gabelloni, P., Abelli, M. et al. (2009) Oxytocin receptor polymorphisms and adult attachment style in patients with depression. *Psychoneuroendocrinology*, 34(10): 1506–1514.

Cyranowski, J. M., Hofkens, T. L., Frank, E., Seltman, H., Cai, H. M., and Amico, J. A. (2008). Evidence of dysregulated peripheral oxytocin release among depressed women. *Psychosomatic Medicine*, 70(9): 967–975.

Decaux, G., Soupart, A., and Vassart, G. (2008). Non-peptide arginine-vasopressin antagonists: the vaptans. *Lancet*, 371(9624): 1624–1632.

Declerck, C. H., Boone, C., and Kiyonari, T. (2010). Oxytocin and cooperation under conditions of uncertainty: the modulating role of incentives and social information. *Hormones and Behavior*, 57(3): 368–374.

De Dreu, C. K., Greer, L. L., Handgraaf, M. J. et al. (2010). The neuropeptide oxytocin regulates parochial altruism in intergroup conflict among humans. *Science*, 328 (5984): 1408–1411.

De Dreu, C. K., Greer, L. L., Van Kleef, G. A., Shalvi, S., and Handgraaf, M. J. (2011). Oxytocin promotes human ethnocentrism. *Proceedings of the National Academy of Science, USA*, 108 (4): 1262–1266.

de Oliveira, D. C., Zuardi, A. W., Graeff, F. G., Queiroz, R. H., and Crippa, J. A. (2011). Anxiolytic-like effect of oxytocin in the simulated public speaking test. *J Psychopharmacol, doi: 10.1177/0269881111400642*.

Di Simplicio, M., Massey-Chase, R., Cowen, P., and Harmer, C. (2009). Oxytocin enhances processing of positive versus negative emotional information in healthy male volunteers. *Journal of Psychopharmacology*, 23(3): 241–248.

Ditzen, B., Schmidt, S., Strauss, B., Nater, U. M., Ehlert, U., and Heinrichs, M. (2008). Adult attachment and social support interact to reduce psychological but not cortisol responses to stress. *Journal of Psychosomatic Research*, 64(5): 479–486.

Ditzen, B., Schaer, M., Gabriel, B., Bodenmann, G., Ehlert, U., and Heinrichs, M. (2009). Intranasal oxytocin increases positive communication and reduces cortisol levels during couple conflict. *Biololgical Psychiatry*, 65(9): 728–731.

Domes, G., Heinrichs, M., Glascher, J., Buchel, C., Braus, D. F., and Herpertz, S. C. (2007a). Oxytocin attenuates amygdala responses to emotional faces regardless of valence. *Biological Psychiatry*, 62(10): 1187–1190.

Domes, G., Heinrichs, M., Michel, A., Berger, C., and Herpertz, S. C. (2007b). Oxytocin improves 'mind-reading' in humans. *Biological Psychiatry*, 61(6): 731–733.

Domes, G., Schulze, L., and Herpertz, S. C. (2009). Emotion recognition in borderline personality disorder – a review of the literature. *Journal of Personality Disorders*, 23(1): 6–19.

Domes, G., Lischke, A., Berger, C. et al. (2010). Effects of intranasal oxytocin on emotional face processing in women. *Psychoneuroendocrinology*, 35(1): 83–93.

Evans, S., Shergill, S. S., and Averbeck, B. B. (2010). Oxytocin decreases aversion to angry faces in an associative learning task. *Neuropsychopharmacology*, 35(13): 2502–2509.

Fehm-Wolfsdorf, G., Born, J., Voigt, K. H., and Fehm, H. L. (1984). Human memory and neurohypophyseal hormones: opposite effects of vasopressin and oxytocin. *Psychoneuroendocrinology*, 9(3): 285–292.

Feifel, D. and Reza, T. (1999). Oxytocin modulates psychotomimetic-induced deficits in sensorimotor gating. *Psychopharmacology (Berl.)*, 141(1): 93–98.

Feifel, D., Macdonald, K., Nguyen, A. et al. (2010). Adjunctive intranasal oxytocin reduces symptoms in schizophrenia patients. *Biological Psychiatry*, 68(7): 678–680.

Fischer-Shofty, M., Shamay-Tsoory, S. G., Harari, H., and Levkovitz, Y. (2010). The effect of intranasal administration of oxytocin on fear recognition. *Neuropsychologia*, 48(1): 179–184.

Gamer, M. and Buchel, C. (2011). Oxytocin specifically enhances valence-dependent parasympathetic responses. *Psychoneuroendocrinology*, doi: 10.1016/j.psyneuen.2011.05.007.

Gamer, M., Zurowski, B., and Buchel, C. (2010). Different amygdala subregions mediate valence-related and attentional effects of oxytocin in humans. *Proceedings of the National Academy of Sciences, USA*, 107(20): 9400–9405.

Goldman, M., Marlow-O'Connor, M., Torres, I., and Carter, C. S. (2008). Diminished plasma oxytocin in schizophrenic patients with neuroendocrine dysfunction and emotional deficits. *Schizophrenia Research*, 98(1–3): 247–255.

Goldman, M., Gomes, A. M., Carter, C. S., and Lee, R. (2011). Divergent effects of two different doses of intranasal oxytocin on facial affect discrimination in schizophrenic patients with and without polydipsia. *Psychopharmacology (Berl.)*, 216(1): 101–110.

Green, L., Fein, D., Modahl, C., Feinstein, C., Waterhouse, L., and Morris, M. (2001). Oxytocin and autistic disorder: alterations in peptide forms. *Biolpogical Psychiatry*, 50(8): 609–613.

Grewen, K. M., Girdler, S. S., Amico, J., and Light, K. C. (2005). Effects of partner support on resting oxytocin, cortisol, norepinephrine, and blood pressure before and after warm partner contact. *Psychosomatic Medicine*, 67(4): 531–538.

Guastella, A. J., Mitchell, P. B., and Dadds, M. R. (2008a). Oxytocin increases gaze to the eye region of human faces. *Biological Psychiatry*, 63(1): 3–5.

Guastella, A. J., Mitchell, P. B., and Mathews, F. (2008b). Oxytocin enhances the encoding of positive social memories in humans. *Biological Psychiatry*, 64(3): 256–258.

Guastella, A. J., Carson, D. S., Dadds, M. R., Mitchell, P. B., and Cox, R. E. (2009a). Does oxytocin influence the early detection of angry and happy faces? *Psychoneuroendocrinology*, 34(2): 220–225.

Guastella, A. J., Howard, A. L., Dadds, M. R., Mitchell, P., and Carson, D. S. (2009b). A randomized controlled trial of intranasal oxytocin as an adjunct to exposure therapy for social anxiety disorder. *Psychoneuroendocrinology*, 34(6): 917–923.

Guastella, A. J., Einfeld, S. L., Gray, K. M. et al. (2010). Intranasal oxytocin improves emotion recognition for youth with autism spectrum disorders. *Biological Psychiatry*, 67(7): 692–694.

Heinrichs, M. and Domes, G. (2008). Neuropeptides and social behavior: effects of oxytocin and vasopressin in humans. *Progress in Brain Research*, 170: 337–350.

Heinrichs, M., Meinlschmidt, G., Neumann, I. *et al.* (2001). Effects of suckling on hypothalamic-pituitary-adrenal axis responses to psychosocial stress in postpartum lactating women. *Journal of Clinical Endocrinology and Metabolism*, 86(10): 4798–4804.

Heinrichs, M., Baumgartner, T., Kirschbaum, C., and Ehlert, U. (2003). Social support and oxytocin interact to suppress cortisol and subjective responses to psychosocial stress. *Biological Psychiatry*, 54(12): 1389–1398.

Heinrichs, M., Meinlschmidt, G., Wippich, W., Ehlert, U., and Hellhammer, D. H. (2004). Selective amnesic effects of oxytocin on human memory. *Physiological Behavior*, 83(1): 31–38.

Heinrichs, M., von Dawans, B., and Domes, G. (2009). Oxytocin, vasopressin, and human social behavior. *Frontiers in Neuroendocrinology*, 30(4): 548–557.

Horley, K., Williams, L.M., Gonsalvez, C., and Gordon, E. (2003). Social phobics do not see eye to eye: a visual scanpath study of emotional expression processing. *Anxiety Disorders*, 17: 33–44.

Horvat-Gordon, M., Granger, D. A., Schwartz, E. B., Nelson, V. J., and Kivlighan, K. T. (2005). Oxytocin is not a valid biomarker when measured in saliva by immunoassay. *Physiological Behavior*, 84(3): 445–448.

Huber, D., Veinante, P., and Stoop, R. (2005). Vasopressin and oxytocin excite distinct neuronal populations in the central amygdala. *Science*, 308(5719): 245–248.

Hurlemann, R., Patin, A., Onur, O. A. *et al.* (2010). Oxytocin enhances amygdala-dependent, socially reinforced learning and emotional empathy in humans. *Journal of Neuroscience*, 30(14): 4999–5007.

Insel, T. R. and Young, L. J. (2001). The neurobiology of attachment. *Nature Reviews Neuroscience*, 2(2): 129–136.

Kang, Y. S. and Park, J. H. (2000). Brain uptake and the analgesic effect of oxytocin – its usefulness as an analgesic agent. *Archives of Pharmacological Research*, 23(4): 391–395.

Keri, S. and Benedek, G. (2009). Oxytocin enhances the perception of biological motion in humans. *Cognitive Affective Behavioral Neuroscience*, 9(3): 237–241.

Keri, S., Kiss, I., and Kelemen, O. (2009). Sharing secrets: Oxytocin and trust in schizophrenia. *Social Neuroscience*, 4(4): 287–293.

Kessler, R. C., McGonagle, K. A., Zhao, S. *et al.* (1994). Lifetime and 12-month prevalence of DSM-III-R psychiatric disorders in the United States. Results from the National Comorbidity Survey. *Archives of General Psychiatry*, 51(1): 8–19.

Kim, H. S., Sherman, D. K., Sasaki, J. Y. *et al.* (2010). Culture, distress, and oxytocin receptor polymorphism (*OXTR*) interact to influence emotional support seeking. *Proceedings of the National Academy of Sciences,USA*, 107(36): 15717–15721.

Kirsch, P., Esslinger, C., Chen, Q. *et al.* (2005). Oxytocin modulates neural circuitry for social cognition and fear in humans. *Journal of Neuroscience*, 25(49): 11489–11493.

Kirschbaum, C., Pirke, K. M., and Hellhammer, D. H. (1993). The 'Trier Social Stress Test' – a tool for investigating psychobiological stress responses in a laboratory setting. *Neuropsychobiology*, 28(1–2): 76–81.

Klin, A., Jones, W., Schultz, R., Volkmar, F., and Cohen, D. (2002). Visual fixation patterns during viewing of naturalistic social situations as predictors of social competence in individuals with autism. *Archives of General Psychiatry*, 59(9): 809–816.

Kohler, C. G., Turner, T. H., Bilker, W. B. (2003). Facial emotion recognition in schizophrenia: intensity effects and error pattern. *American Journal of Psychiatry*, 160(10): 1768–1774.

Kosfeld, M., Heinrichs, M., Zak, P. J., Fischbacher, U., and Fehr, E. (2005). Oxytocin increases trust in humans. *Nature*, 435(7042): 673–676, with permission from 2005 Nature Publishing Group.

Labuschagne, I., Phan, K. L., Wood, A. *et al.* (2010). Oxytocin attenuates amygdala reactivity to fear in generalized social anxiety disorder. *Neuropsychopharmacology*, 35(12): 2403–2413.

Landgraf, R. and Neumann, I. D. (2004). Vasopressin and oxytocin release within the brain: a dynamic concept of multiple and variable modes of neuropeptide communication. *Frontiers in Neuroendocrinol*, 25(3–4): 150–176.

Loup, F., Tribollet, E., Dubois-Dauphin, M., and Dreifuss, J. J. (1991). Localization of high-affinity binding sites for oxytocin and vasopressin in the human brain. An autoradiographic study. *Brain Research*, 555(2): 220–232.

Lucht, M. J., Barnow, S., Sonnenfeld, C. *et al.* (2009). Associations between the oxytocin receptor gene (*OXTR*) and affect, loneliness and intelligence in normal subjects. *Progress in Neuropsychopharmacology and Biological Psychiatry*, 33(5): 860–866.

Ludwig, M. and Leng, G. (2006). Dendritic peptide release and peptide-dependent behaviors. *Nature Reviews Neuroscience*, 7(2): 126–136.

Marsh, A. A., Yu, H. H., Pine, D. S., and Blair, R. J. (2010). Oxytocin improves specific recognition of positive facial expressions. *Psychopharmacology (Berl.)*, 209(3): 225–232.

Meinlschmidt, G. and Heim, C. (2007). Sensitivity to intranasal oxytocin in adult men with early parental separation. *Biological Psychiatry*, 61(9): 1109–1111.

Meyer-Lindenberg, A. (2008). Impact of prosocial neuropeptides on human brain function. *Progress in Brain Research*, 170: 463–470.

Meyer-Lindenberg, A., Domes, G., Kirsch, P., and Heinrichs, M. (2011). Oxytocin and Vasopressin in the human brain: social neuropeptides for translational medicine. *Nature Reviews Neuroscience*, 12: 524–538.

Mikolajczak, M., Gross, J. J., Lane, A., Corneille, O., de Timary, P., and Luminet, O. (2010a). Oxytocin makes people trusting, not gullible. *Psychological Science*, 21(8): 1072–1074.

Mikolajczak, M., Pinon, N., Lane, A., de Timary, P., and Luminet, O. (2010b). Oxytocin not only increases trust when money is at stake, but also when confidential information is in the balance. *Biological Psychology*, 85(1): 182–184.

Naber, F., van Ijzendoorn, M. H., Deschamps, P., van Engeland, H., and Bakermans-Kranenburg, M. J. (2010). Intranasal oxytocin increases fathers' observed responsiveness during play with their children: a double-blind within-subject experiment. *Psychoneuroendocrinology*, 35(10): 1583–1586.

Norman, G. J., Cacioppo, J. T., Morris, J. S. *et al.* (2010). Selective influences of oxytocin on the evaluative processing of social stimuli. *Journal of Psychopharmacology*, doi: 10.1177/0269881110367452.

Norman, G. J., Cacioppo, J. T., Morris, J. S., Malarkey, W. B., Berntson, G. G., and Devries, A. C. (2011). Oxytocin increases autonomic cardiac control: moderation by loneliness. *Biological Psychology*, 86(3): 174–180.

Quirin, M., Kuhl, J., and Dusing, R. (2011). Oxytocin buffers cortisol responses to stress in individuals with impaired emotion regulation abilities. *Psychoneuroendocrinology*, 36(6): 898–904.

Rimmele, U., Hediger, K., Heinrichs, M., and Klaver, P. (2009). Oxytocin makes a face in memory familiar. *Journal of Neuroscience*, 29(1): 38–42.

Rockliff, H., Karl, A., McEwan, K., Gilbert, J., Matos, M., and Gilbert, P. (2011). Effects of intranasal oxytocin on 'compassion focused imagery.' *Emotion*, doi: *10.1037/a0023861*.

Rodrigues, S., Saslow, L., Garcia, N., John, O., and Keltner, D. (2009). Oxytocin receptor genetic variation relates to empathy and stress reactivity in humans. *Proceedings of the National Academy of Sciences, USA*, 106(50): 21437–31441.

Savaskan, E., Ehrhardt, R., Schulz, A., Walter, M., and Schachinger, H. (2008). Post-learning intranasal oxytocin modulates human memory for facial identity. *Psychoneuroendocrinology*, 33(3): 368–374.

Scantamburlo, G., Hansenne, M., Fuchs, S. *et al.* (2007). Plasma oxytocin levels and anxiety in patients with major depression. *Psychoneuroendocrinology*, 32(4): 407–410.

Schulze, L., Lischke, A., Greif, J., Herpertz, S. C., Heinrichs, M., and Domes, G. (2011). Oxytocin increases recognition of masked emotional faces. *Psychoneuroendocrinology*, 36(9): 1378–1382.

Selten, J. P., and Cantor-Graae, E. (2005). Social defeat: risk factor for schizophrenia? *British Journal of Psychiatry*, 187: 101–102.

Shamay-Tsoory, S. G., Fischer, M., Dvash, J., Harari, H., Perach-Bloom, N., and Levkovitz, Y. (2009). Intranasal administration of oxytocin increases envy and schadenfreude (gloating). *Biological Psychiatry*, 66(9): 864–870.

Simeon, D., Bartz, J., Hamilton, H. *et al.* (2011). Oxytocin administration attenuates stress reactivity in borderline personality disorder: A pilot study. *Psychoneuroendocrinology*, doi: *10.1016/j.psyneuen.2011.03.013*.

Singer, T., Snozzi, R., Bird, G. *et al.* (2008). Effects of oxytocin and prosocial behavior on brain responses to direct and vicariously experienced pain. *Emotion*, 8(6): 781–791.

Stanley, B., and Siever, L. J. (2010). The interpersonal dimension of borderline personality disorder: toward a neuropeptide model. *American Journal of Psychiatry*, 167(1): 24–39.

Tansey, K. E., Brookes, K. J., Hill, M. J. *et al.* (2010). Oxytocin receptor (*OXTR*) does not play a major role in the aetiology of autism: genetic and molecular studies. *Neuroscience Letters*, 474(3): 163–167.

Taylor, S. E., Gonzaga, G. C., Klein, L. C., Hu, P., Greendale, G. A., and Seeman, T. E. (2006). Relation of oxytocin to psychological stress responses and hypothalamic-pituitary-adrenocortical axis activity in older women. *Psychosomatic Medicine*, 68(2): 238–245.

Theodoridou, A., Rowe, A. C., Penton-Voak, I. S., and Rogers, P. J. (2009). Oxytocin and social perception: oxytocin increases perceived facial trustworthiness and attractiveness. *Hormones and Behavior*, 56(1): 128–132.

Tost, H., Kolachana, B., Hakimi, S. *et al.* (2010). A common allele in the oxytocin receptor gene (*OXTR*) impacts prosocial temperament and human hypothalamic-limbic structure and function. *Proceedings of the National Academy of Sciences, USA*, 107(31): 13936–13941.

Viviani, D., Charlet, A., van den Burg, E. *et al.* (2011). Oxytocin selectively gates fear responses through distinct outputs from the central amygdala. *Science*, 333(6038): 104–107.

Winslow, J. T. and Insel, T. R. (2004). Neuroendocrine basis of social recognition. *Current Opinions in Neurobiology*, 14(2): 248–253.

Winton, E. C., Clark, D. M., and Edelmann, R. J. (1995). Social anxiety, fear of negative evaluation and the detection of negative emotion in others. *Behavioral Research and Therapy*, 33(2): 193–196.

Wu, S., Jia, M., Ruan, Y. *et al.* (2005). Positive association of the oxytocin receptor gene (*OXTR*) with autism in the Chinese Han population. *Biological Psychiatry*, 58(1):74–77.

Young, L. J. and Wang, Z. (2004). The neurobiology of pair bonding. *Nature Reviews Neuroscience*, 7(10): 1048–1054.

Zak, P. J., Kurzban, R., and Matzner, W. T. (2005). Oxytocin is associated with human trustworthiness. *Hormones and Behavior*, 48(5), 522–527.

Zak, P. J., Stanton, A. A., and Ahmadi, S. (2007). Oxytocin increases generosity in humans. *PLoS One*, 2(11): e1128.

Chapter 9

DIETARY SUPPLEMENTS

Lindsey B. DeBoer, Michelle L. Davis, Mark B. Powers, and Jasper A. J. Smits

Department of Psychology, Southern Methodist University, Dallas, TX, USA

INTRODUCTION

Anxiety disorders represent the most common class of psychological disorder in the United States (US). Lifetime prevalence estimates are 28.8%, and approximately 40 million adults (18%) suffer from an anxiety disorder in any given year (Kessler *et al.* 2005a;b). Among psychological disorders, anxiety disorders are associated with the most impairment across various domains of functioning, including life activities, communication, self-care, social relationships, and participation in society (Buist-Bowman *et al.* 2006). The societal cost of anxiety disorders is also considerable, with approximately 63.1 billion (in 1998 dollars) spent each year on psychiatric treatment, medical treatment, pharmaceutical, workplace, and mortality costs (Greenberg *et al.* 1999).

The current gold standard treatments for anxiety disorders are cognitive behavioral treatment (CBT) and pharmacotherapy (Hofmann and Smits 2008; Powers and Emmelkamp 2008; Powers *et al.* 2008; 2010). Though efficacious, 14–43% of anxiety disorder patients do not respond to treatment (Marks *et al.* 1998; Barlow *et al.* 2000; Borkovec *et al.* 2002; Davidson *et al.* 2004; Foa *et al.* 2005) and 18–48% relapse by 6 months (Barlow *et al.* 2000; Foa *et al.* 2005). These non-response and relapse rates suggest a need for augmentation or alternative approaches to treatment, as well as new approaches for maintaining treatment gains once standard interventions have ended.

Also of concern is the observation that well over half of those suffering from anxiety do not initiate or receive adequate treatment (Wang *et al.* 2002;

Psychobiological Approaches for Anxiety Disorders: Treatment Combination Strategies, First Edition. Edited by Stefan G. Hofmann.
© 2012 John Wiley & Sons, Ltd. Published 2012 by John Wiley & Sons, Ltd.

2005). The reasons for this low rate of care include a lack of access to clinicians offering empirically supported treatments (Becker et al. 2004; Freiheir et al. 2004; Rosen et al. 2004), stigma or sub-cultural disapproval of psychotherapy and psychotropic medication (Overton and Medina 2008; Hunter and Schmidt 2010), and aversive side effects of medications, including sleep disturbances, sexual side effects, gastrointestinal (GI) problems, weight gain, drug interactions, withdrawal, and dependence (Mavissakalian et al. 2002; Rivas-Vazquez 2003; Golden 2004; Choy 2007). Therefore, new treatments and treatment augmentation strategies should address both the inaccessibility and undesirability of current options. Treatment with dietary supplements may be particularly well suited to address these limitations.

THE POTENTIAL OF DIETARY SUPPLEMENTS

As defined by the Dietary Supplement Health and Education Act of 1994, dietary supplements are products taken orally that contain one or more dietary ingredients (e.g. vitamins, minerals, herbs or botanicals, amino acids, enzymes, etc.) or their constituents (US FDA 1994). Dietary supplements fall into two classes: nutritional and herbal. There are several reasons why clinicians may be inclined to suggest dietary supplements along with or in lieu of traditional approaches. For example, empirically supported supplements may be indicated for patients who cannot afford, are uncomfortable using, cannot tolerate the side effects of, or have not responded (or only partially responded) to conventional medications or psychotherapy. In addition, patients who do not have access to empirically supported conventional treatments such as CBT (e.g. those living in rural areas) may desire to use dietary supplements or other alternative treatments. Anxiety patients may perceive dietary supplements as a less stigmatized treatment option that comes with fewer side effects.

Dietary supplements are increasingly popular in the US. About 19% of Americans used herbal supplements in 2002 (Kennedy 2005), and 53% took dietary supplements in 2003–2006, a significant and steady increase since previous surveys (Bailey et al. 2011). After chronic pain, anxiety is the most frequently cited health problem treated with alternative approaches (Astin 1998). Among individuals reporting 'anxiety attacks' in the past year, 56.7% used complementary or alternative medicine, with 6.8% specifically using dietary supplements (Kessler et al. 2005). Most individuals who use alternative treatments use them alongside conventional treatment and find the two approaches equally helpful (Astin 1998; Kessler et al. 2005a), suggesting that supplement users are not necessarily dissatisfied with conventional treatment, but are instead open to using supplements as treatment augments.

Certain individuals may be inclined to try dietary supplements to alleviate their anxiety. Surveys suggest that those with more education, adults ages 45–65, and women are more likely to use herbal supplements than the less educated, younger adults, and men (Kennedy 2005). Race and ethnicity are also associated with herbal supplement use. People of mixed racial heritage are the most likely (32.2%), followed by Asians (24.6%), Native Americans and Alaskan Natives (21.9%), non-Hispanic Whites (19.1%), Hispanics (17.4%), and African Americans (14.3%). Herbal supplements are a first-line treatment in many non-Western cultures that use traditional healing practices (e.g. Ayurveda, Chinese Medicine), suggesting that clinicians should consider using empirically supported supplements when treating Asian immigrants, given an increased likelihood of familiarity with and acceptance of herbal supplements. Given the increasing popularity of supplements, there is a need for high-quality research examining their efficacy.

AIMS OF THE CURRENT REVIEW

Sixty percent of health professionals experience difficulty locating reliable sources of information on complementary and alternative medicine (Owen and Fang 2003). The availability of reliable information about supplement treatment options is critical, yet comprehensive reviews are lacking. Accordingly, the aims of this review are:

- to summarize the evidence for and side effects of each supplement that has been tested specifically for anxiety; and
- to suggest future research in light of the findings and limitations.

A description of each supplement and its proposed biological mechanism of action are provided, followed by a review of the evidence, side effects, and conclusions.

Methodology

Search Strategy

First, we searched PubMed/MEDLINE and Psycinfo databases for relevant articles written in English. Search terms included: 'alternative therapies,' 'herbal supplements,' 'nutritional supplements,' 'dietary supplements,' and individual supplement names from popular sources and scientific reviews, each crossed with one of the following terms: 'anxiety,' 'obsessive compulsive,' 'post-traumatic,' 'panic,' 'phobia,' or 'generalized anxiety.' Second, we hand-searched key articles for references.

Selection Criteria

The gold standard study design for evaluating efficacy is a double-blind, randomized, placebo-controlled trial (RCT), and we have therefore given the most weight to RCTs in this review. Open-label trials, cross-sectional studies, and case studies were included in this review for supplements that have not been subjected to evaluation using RCT methodology. Similarly, in cases where studies of clinical samples are lacking, we have reviewed studies that have examined initial efficacy in non-clinical samples. However, studies including participants with other psychological disorders or physical conditions known to impact psychological symptoms are not reviewed because treatment of comorbid disorders is beyond the scope of this review. Given that the literature on the efficacy of supplements for augmenting established psychotherapeutic and pharmacological treatments is limited, we reviewed both the singular effects of supplements in addition to their potential augmentation effects.

Effect Size Calculation

In order to facilitate the interpretation of the magnitude of observed treatment effects, we calculated effect sizes (Cohen's *d*; Cohen 1988) for significant effects if required data (i.e. means, sample sizes, and standard deviations) were reported or made available by the study authors. Cohen's *d* was calculated by dividing the differential change (i.e. treatment minus control group) in means on main outcome measures by the pooled baseline standard deviation of that measure (Cohen 1988). When standard deviations of change scores were provided, they were used instead of baseline standard deviations. We did not perform a pooled effect size analysis because of the heterogeneity among studies with respect to methodology.

NUTRITIONAL SUPPLEMENTS

Inositol

Biological Mechanism

Inositol is a glucose isomer and intracellular second messenger precursor that regulates numerous cellular functions. Inositol is found in fruit, particularly oranges and cantaloupe, and people consume about 1 g daily through a typical diet. It has been used in Europe as a remedy for neurasthenia and mild depression (Kinrys *et al.* 2009). The proposed mechanism of action is the phosphatidyl-inositol cycle, which is a second messenger system used by noradrenergic α-1 and serotonin 2 receptors (Kinrys *et al.* 2009).

Panic Disorder

In a randomized, double-blind crossover trial, 21 patients with panic disorder were randomly assigned to 4 weeks of inositol treatment (6 g/ twice daily) or placebo, and then switched to the other condition for an additional 4 weeks (Benjamin et al. 1995). Baseline number of panic attacks per week for the entire sample was 9.7. Although there were no group differences on the Hamilton Anxiety Index (HAM-A; Hamilton 1959), by week 4 the mean number of weekly panic attacks in the inositol group (3.7) was significantly lower than in the placebo group (6.3; $d = .17$), and panic attack intensity was also significantly more reduced in the inositol group ($d = -.14$). In another crossover RCT, either inositol (18 g/day) or fluvoxamine (150 mg/day of Luxov, a selective serotonin reuptake inhibitor; SSRI) was administered to 20 patients with panic disorder for 4 weeks, followed by a 1-week washout period and administration of the other substance for the next 4 weeks (Palatnik et al. 2001). Frequency and intensity of panic attacks was reduced in both groups, and anxiety scale scores and clinician-rated improvement scores were also similar. The inositol group was more effective than fluvoxamine in reducing panic attack frequency (4.1-point versus 2.4-point reduction, respectively; $d = .42$), though equally effective in reducing HAM-A scores, agoraphobia scores, and clinician-rate Clinical Global Impression (CGI; Guy 1976) severity scores. These two trials provide initial evidence suggesting that inositol may be more effective than placebo and similarly effective to an SSRI for panic disorder.

Obsessive Compulsive Disorder

The same research group conducted a double-blind crossover RCT examining the effects of inositol on symptoms for 13 obsessive compulsive disorder (OCD) patients who had either failed to respond to SSRIs or clomipramine (Anafranil) or who could not tolerate their side effects (Fux et al. 1996). Participants were administered 18 g of inositol daily or placebo for consecutive 6-week treatment intervals. Inositol resulted in significantly greater decreases in Yale-Brown Obsessive Compulsive Scale (Y-BOCS; Goodman et al. 1989a,b) scores compared to placebo (reductions of 4.6 and 0.3, respectively; $d = .30$), though HAM-A reductions were not significantly different. Although these findings may not be common to all patients with OCD, this sample may be especially representative of OCD patients who are most inclined to use dietary supplements, given their lack of success with conventional treatment. In a later trial, inositol was examined as an augment to SSRI treatment for 10 OCD patients who had not adequately responded to fluoxetine (Prozac), fluvoxamine, or clomipramine (Fux et al. 1999). These patients were given consecutive 6-week trials of inositol (18 g/day) or placebo, in addition to their SSRI medication. Although Y-BOCS scores in the inositol group decreased significantly from baseline to end of treatment (27.6 to 16.5 points), there were no significant group differences in Y-BOCS, HAM-A, or Hamilton Depression Scale (HAM-D; Hamilton 1960) scores. These results suggest that although inositol may be effective as a monotherapy for treatment-resistant OCD patients, it may not be beneficial as an augment to SSRIs for treatment-resistant OCD.

A recent open-label study involving 14 participants with OCD supported previous findings of inositol efficacy and also investigated the neurological mechanism of the effects (Carey et al. 2004). Participants administered 18 g per day of inositol for 12 weeks reported significant symptom reductions from pre- to post-treatment on the Y-BOCS (24.5 to 13.8) and CGI-severity (4.35 to 2.78). Patients also underwent single-photon emission computed tomography, and among those who responded to the inositol treatment, deactivation in the left superior temporal gyrus, middle frontal, gyrus and precuneus, and the right paramediam post-central gyrus was observed from pre- to post-treatment. The results of this small-scale study suggest that inositol may exert its influence on OCD symptomatology through altering neuronal circuitry.

Side Effects and Conclusion

The reviewed studies provide promising, though preliminary, support for the use of inositol in treating panic disorder and OCD. No significant adverse events with inositol were reported in the Benjamin et al. (1995) study, and other studies have reported only minimal side effects, including gas, loose bowels, and effects similar to SSRIs, such as nausea and tiredness (Palatnik et al. 2001; Brown et al. 2009).

Tryptophan/5-Hydroxytryptophan

Biological Mechanism

Tryptophan is an essential amino acid and a biochemical precursor to serotonin (5-HT). It is converted into 5-hydroxytryptophan (5-HTP) in the brain and eventually into serotonin (Bell et al. 2001). Dietary sources of tryptophan include chocolate, oats, dates, dairy products, red meat, eggs, fish, poultry, chickpeas, certain seeds, spirulina, and peanuts. Tryptophan depletion is associated with reductions in brain serotonin synthesis and release, causing lowered mood, memory impairment, and aggression in healthy participants (Bell et al. 2001). Tryptophan depletion in patients with clinical depression is associated with worsening of symptoms and relapse among those who have responded to SSRIs (Bell et al. 2001). Although tryptophan depletion does not cause anxiety in healthy patients or exacerbate symptoms among OCD patients, it may exacerbate anxiety and panic attacks among those with panic disorder when combined with panic-inducing agents such as yohimbine or carbon dioxide (CO_2) inhalation (Bell et al. 2001). There is preliminary evidence that tryptophan and 5-hydroxytryptophan treatment is beneficial in depression treatment (Shaw et al. 2002), but only a few trials have examined tryptophan for anxiety.

Evidence

A double-blind RCT examined the acute effects of a 200 mg dose of 5-HTP versus placebo administered 90 minutes prior to a 35% CO_2 challenge in 24 panic disorder patients (Schruers et al. 2002). 5-HTP significantly reduced panic reactions to the CO_2 challenge to the level of healthy participants, as measured by a visual analog scale of anxiety (Mann-Whitney $U = 28.5$) and a panic symptoms list ($U = 19.0$). This study demonstrates the acute effects of 5-HTP on experimentally-induced panic.

A recent pilot crossover RCT tested the acute effects of a tryptophan-rich protein (de-oiled gourd seed, 22 mg per g of protein) combined with glucose (Hudson et al. 2007). This preparation has a clinical effect similar to pharmaceutical-grade tryptophan. Seven patients with social phobia ate either the tryptophan food bar or a placebo food bar (glucose only) 1 hour before a laboratory psychosocial stressor (i.e. reading a difficult passage while being videotaped for supposed later evaluation). Following a 1-week washout, participants repeated the stressor after eating the other food bar. There were no significant condition differences in self-reported anxiety ($d = .24$) or baseline-to-stressor heart rate ($d = .25$). However, there was a significant difference in heart rate variation ratio between baseline and acute stress ($d = 7.06$), providing partial support that tryptophan diminishes the physiological anxiety response to a stressor.

There is some evidence for beneficial effects of longer-term treatment with tryptophan. A double-blind RCT involving 45 patients with various DSM-III anxiety disorders compared 8 weeks of treatment with 5-HTP to clomipramine (Anafranil) and placebo (Kahn et al. 1987). Both the tryptophan and clomipramine were titrated from 25 mg per day to a maximum of 150 mg per day. Relative to placebo, the clomipramine group showed significant reductions in HAM-A scores, whereas the tryptophan group showed only modest (i.e. not clinically meaningful), non-significant improvements. Another study examined tryptophan as an augmentation strategy in 13 OCD patients who had not responded to serotonin reuptake inhibitors (SRIs; Blier and Bergeron 1996). Although 5-hydroxytryptophan (the immediate precursor of serotonin) was not effective, tryptophan added to SRI plus pindolol (a beta-blocker) treatment resulted in significant reductions in Y-BOCS scores after 4 weeks and 36% improvement in Y-BOCS scores after 6 weeks. Pindolol alone as an augment to SRI treatment reduced only depression symptoms, suggesting that the addition of tryptophan accounted for the decreases in OCD symptoms. Limitations of this study include the open-label design and lack of a control group.

Side Effects and Conclusion

Overall, the evidence that tryptophan can reduce symptoms in patients with anxiety disorders is mixed and limited by small sample sizes. Fugh-Berman and Cott (1999) discuss potential serious but rare side effects of tryptophan, including interactions with SSRIs and monoamine oxidase (MAO) inhibitors. In 1989, three individuals developed eosinphilia-myalgia syndrome (a serious, incurable, potentially fatal neurological condition) after tryptophan supplementation (Hertzman *et al.* 1990), and serotonin precursors were thus banned in the US. Although these cases may be tied to a single contaminated brand of tryptophan, scholars have concluded that the risk outweighs any potential benefit of L-tryptophan for treating anxiety disorders (Saeed *et al.* 2007; Fugh-Berman and Cott 2009).

L-lysine and L-arginine

Biological Mechanism

Dysregulation of the neurotransmitters gamma-aminobutyric acid (GABA), serotonin, dopamine, and norepinephrine is believed to contribute to anxiety disorders (Christmas *et al.* 2008; D'Hulst *et al.* 2009; Furmark 2009). It has thus been postulated that administering precursors of neurotransmitters, such as L-tyrosine, L-tryptophan, L-lysine, and L-arginine, may influence anxiety-related neurotransmitters, thereby alleviating symptoms of anxiety (Smriga and Torii 2003; Srinongkote *et al.* 2003). L-lysine is an essential amino acid that acts as a partial benzodiazapine agonist and a partial serotonin receptor and decreases blood cortisol levels and brain-gut response to stress (Smriga *et al.* 2007). When administered with L-arginine, L-lysine blocks stress induced pathologies in animals (Smriga *et al.* 2007).

Evidence

Two RCTs have been conducted with human subjects, examining the anxiolytic effects of supplements combining L-lysine and L-arginine. One RCT examined the effects of a 10-day treatment of 3 g each of L-lysine and L-arginine in 29 healthy males high in State-Trait Anxiety Inventory (STAI; Spielberger *et al.* 1970) trait anxiety (Jezova *et al.* 2005). After the treatment, participants completed a modified Trier social stress task (i.e. a speech on an emotionally charged topic, supposedly in front of an audience), during which neuro-endocrine data was collected. Relative to the placebo group, skin conductance, epinephrine, norepinephrine, adrenocorticotropic hormone, and cortisol responses to the stressor in the supplement group were significantly increased to levels similar to those observed in non-anxious subjects. Those in the supplement group also reported less of an anxiety response to the stressor on the STAI (3.4 versus 6.7 increases; $d = 1.12$). These findings suggest that the apparently blunted hormonal response to stressors seen in high anxiety patients can be attenuated through the administration of the amino acids L-lysine and L-arginine (Jezova et al. 2005).

A recent study of 108 healthy males and females examined the effects of 1 week of L-lysine plus L-arginine treatment (2.64 g/day each) on both STAI trait and state anxiety in response to a cognitive stress battery (Smriga et al. 2007). Relative to placebo, the amino acid supplement significantly reduced both self-reported trait anxiety ($d = 4.60$) and state anxiety in response to the stressor in both genders ($d = 4.42$). Basal salivary cortisol and chromogranin-A (a protein in adrenergic neurons that reflects sympathetic stress response) levels were also significantly decreased in males relative to placebo ($d = 1.99$ for cortisol difference), though not in females ($d = .75$ for cortisol difference). The authors concluded that 1 week of L-lysine plus L-arginine treatment appears to be effective in reducing stress-induced anxiety, as well as more stable trait-like anxiety among healthy adults.

Side Effects and Conclusion

Though the extant evidence for these amino acids is promising, replication is needed, especially with clinical samples. No adverse events were reported in either of the two reviewed studies, and dietary L-lysine plus L-arginine is considered safe (Tsubuku et al. 2004a;b).

L-theanine

Biological Mechanism

Green tea has been used for centuries for its calming and medicinal effects. Its primary active ingredient is L-theanine (5-N-ethylglutamine or gamma-glutamylethylamide), an amino acid believed to reduce anxiety under stressful conditions. There is 60–160 mg of L-theanine in three to four cups of green tea (Brown et al. 2009), and it is also found in mushrooms (Lu et al. 2004). Animal studies have revealed that L-theanine perfusion into the brain increases dopamine release and may cause inhibition of excitatory neurotransmission (Yamada et al. 2005).

Evidence

Two studies have examined the anxiolytic effects of L-theanine in humans. A crossover RCT examined the acute effects of 200 mg L-theanine versus

1 mg alprazolam (a benzodoazapine) and placebo on anticipatory anxiety in 16 healthy participants (Lu et al. 2004). During the baseline relaxation condition, the L-theanine group reported greater relaxation than the alprazolam ($d = .79$) and placebo ($d = 1.06$) groups on the Visual Analogue Mood Scale (VAMS; Bond and Lader 1974) tranquil-troubled subscale. However, there was no effect of L-theanine on STAI state anxiety or the other two VAMS subscales (calm-excited and relaxed-tense). During the anticipatory anxiety condition (i.e. awaiting random electric shocks), neither L-theanine nor alprazolam had an anxiolytic effect relative to placebo. These results suggest that L-theanine may have subtle anxiolytic effects under resting conditions but not under stressful conditions.

Another double-blind crossover RCT examined the acute effects and neurological mechanism of 200 mg L-theanine administered to 12 healthy participants, either immediately before or halfway through a mental arithmetic stress task (Kimura et al. 2007). There were no significant differences between the two L-theanine groups. L-theanine administered both before and halfway through the stress task resulted in lower perceived stress ratings and STAI state anxiety ($d = 1.21$ for before, $d = .87$ for after), as well as lower heart rate and salivary IgA. The observation that heart rate variability was significantly higher in the placebo group than in the other groups (i.e. both L-theanine groups and a control group that did not undergo the stress task) suggests that the observed reductions in heart rate and IgA resulted from attenuation of sympathetic nervous activation. The authors concluded that L-theanine may cause anti-stress effects by inhibiting cortical neuron excitation (Kimura et al. 2007).

Side Effects and Conclusion

While the Kimura et al. (2007) study is suggestive of acute anxiolytic effects, the Lu et al. (2004) study provided modest support, with L-theanine reducing anxiety on only one of four scales, and only in the relaxation condition. There is currently no research on the long-term anxiolytic effects of L-theanine, nor its effect among patients with diagnosed anxiety disorders. Aside from being an anticoagulant (Brown et al. 2009), no adverse events have been reported (Lu et al. 2004). Until more research has been conducted, it is premature to recommend L-theanine for the treatment of anxiety disorders.

Magnesium

Biological Mechanism

Magnesium is a positively charged ion (cation) involved in many important molecular functions. Large amounts are found in green vegetables, nuts, seeds, dark chocolate, roasted soy beans, and some whole grains including bran. Magnesium deficiencies have been associated with anxiety-related disorders, but the physiological mechanism responsible for magnesium supplementation's proposed anxiolytic effects is uncertain (Libigerová and Holecková 1999).

Evidence

Two of the three RCTs of magnesium for anxiety have investigated magnesium in combination with other supplements, preventing linking effects specifically to magnesium. A double-blind RCT examined the effects of 4 weeks of treatment with a supplement called Berocca that included large doses of magnesium, zinc, and calcium among other vitamins versus placebo (Carroll et al. 2000). Participants were 80 healthy men, and anxiety symptoms were measured with the General Health Questionnaire-28 (GHQ-28; Goldberg and Hillier 1970), the Hospital Anxiety and Depression Scale (HADS; Zigmond and Snaith 1983), Perceived Stress Scale (PSS; Cohen et al. 1983), and rating scales. Relative to the placebo group, those who received the supplement reported decreases in perceived stress ($d = .56$) and anxiety ($d = .90$ for HADS anxiety, $d = 2.15$ for GHQ-28 anxiety and insomnia scale, $d = .54$ for anxiety rating scale). Reported physical symptoms increased over time for the placebo group but did not change for the supplement group, suggesting that there were few to no side effects of the supplement blend.

Another RCT examined the effects of Sympathyl, a supplement containing 75 mg of elemental magnesium and two plant extracts: 275 mg of hawthorn (*Crataegus oxacantha*) and 20 mg of California poppy (*Eschscholtzia californica*; Hanus et al. 2004). Participants were 264 patients with mild to moderate generalized anxiety disorder (GAD). After 3 months of treatment, there was a significant effect of treatment group on HAM-A total score (1.7-point difference; $d = 1.42$) and somatic subscale (0.8-point difference; $d = 1.14$) decreases, with the supplement group experiencing more relief.

The only RCT to investigate magnesium as a monotherapy examined its effects on pre-menstruation-related anxiety (De Souza et al. 2000). Over the course of 4 menstrual cycles, 44 women were given daily:

1) 200 mg of magnesium;
2) 50 mg of B6;
3) 200 mg of magnesium plus 50 mg of B6; and
4) placebo.

Women logged their symptoms, and results showed that the combination of magnesium plus B6 provided the greatest relief from anxiety symptoms (44% reduction from baseline; $d = .12$), but magnesium monotherapy was not more effective than placebo (25% versus 32% reduction, respectively).

Side Effects and Conclusion

Magnesium supplementation is well tolerated and incurs few side effects. Although Lakhan and Vieira (2010) concluded that magnesium supplementation is effective in treating anxiety and anxiety-related disorders when in combination with other vitamins, minerals, or herbal extracts, there is no evidence that magnesium was the active ingredient in these trials. More large-scale RCTs are needed, as well as investigations of the effects of magnesium supplementation in participants with clinical anxiety disorders.

Omega-3 Fatty Acids

Biological Mechanism

Omega-3 long-chain polyunsaturated fatty acids (n-3 PUFAs) are a type of essential fatty acid vital for normal metabolism that cannot be synthesized by the human body. The nutritionally important n-3 PUFAs are á-linolenic acid (ALA), eicosapentaenoic acid (EPA), and docosahexaenoic acid (DHA). High concentrations of n-3 PUFAs are found in fish, fish oil, walnuts, wheat germ, flax seed, and supplements derived from these foods. In addition to their many physical health benefits, n-3 PUFA supplementation, particularly EPA, appears to alleviate clinical depression (Ross *et al.* 2007). N-3 PUFA deficiency has also been related to anxiety disorders. Red blood cell membrane content of EPA and DHA was 30% lower in untreated patients with social phobia, and there was a significant inverse correlation between n-3 PUFA level and Liebowitz Social Anxiety Scale (LSAS; Liebowitz 1987) scores (Green *et al.* 2006). N-3 PUFAs may exert their effects on depression and anxiety through their role in neural structure and function. N-3 PUFAs are highly concentrated in the central nervous system and appear to be involved in neurotransmitter (specifically dopamine and serotonin) synthesis, degradation, release, reuptake, and binding (Delion *et al.* 1994). N-3 PUFA supplementation has also been found to curb the inflammatory response to stress and modulate changes in the HPA and sympathetic adrenal-medullary axes (Kiecolt-Glaser 2010).

Evidence

Relative to depression, there has been little work on n-3 PUFA supplement treatment for anxiety. One study examined the effects of n-3 PUFAs in 126 college students with significant test anxiety (Yehuda *et al.* 2005). Relative to placebo, the mixture of n-3 and n-6 PUFA containing 90 mg of ALA and 360 mg of linoleic acid (another n-3 PUFA) ingested daily for 3 weeks improved all test anxiety measures: appetite ($d = 1.06$), mood ($d = 1.39$), concentration ($d = 1.34$), fatigue ($d = 1.62$), organization ($d = 1.11$), sleep ($d = 1.82$), and cortisol levels ($d = 2.19$). In another RCT, 24 male substance abusers were given either placebo or n-3 PUFAs (2.2 g EPA plus 0.5 g DHA) daily for 3 months (Buydens-Branchey and Branchey 2006). Those given n-3 PUFAs experienced significant progressive declines in anxiety, whereas the placebo group did not ($d = 1.25$ for the between-group difference). The group differences in gains were maintained at 3- and 6-month follow-ups. Although these results are promising, individuals in these studies did not have anxiety disorders and the sample size in the later study was very small.

Only one study has examined the effects of n-3 PUFAs in participants with anxiety disorders (Fux et al. 2004). In a crossover RCT, OCD patients were given EPA (2 g/day) in addition to SSRIs for 6 weeks. Changes in Y-BOCS scores did not differ from the placebo group, and there were no significant group differences or changes over time in HAM-A or HAM-D scores. Weaknesses of this study include a small sample (n = 11) and a shorter treatment period than what has been used in depression trials (Ross 2009). Given that combining EPA with DHA was effective in reducing anxiety among substance abusers (Buydens-Branchey and Branchey 2006), it is possible that adding DHA to EPA may yield benefits.

Side Effects and Conclusion

Despite theoretical and circumstantial evidence supporting n-3 PUFA supplementation for anxiety disorder treatment (Ross 2009), the evidence is limited at this time given that the positive RCTs used non-clinical and substance abuse samples. Longer-term RCTs with large samples of patients diagnosed with anxiety disorders are needed. Given the theoretical evidence for their anxiolytic effect, general health benefits, and negligible side effects (e.g. 'fishy breath, belching, and mild nausea and GI distress) (Fugh-Berman and Cott 1999; Brown et al. 2009), more research on n-3 PUFAs for anxiety is warranted.

GABA

Biological Mechanism

GABA is a major inhibitory neurotransmitter involved in cardiovascular regulation, pituitary function, immunity, fertilization, and renal function. Compounds that enhance GABA have been found to reduce anxiety and stabilize mood (Brown et al. 2009). Many foods contain small amounts of GABA, and some fermented foods contain high levels. Natural GABA is produced through fermentation and is widely used as a functional food supplement in Japan. Importantly, GABA has been found to modulate levels of immunoglobulin A (IgA; Abdou et al. 2006). Highly anxious individuals have low levels of salivary IgA, and levels drop even further in highly stressful situations, whereas relaxation results in increases in IgA. Salivary IgA levels have therefore been used as a marker of stress and immune response in anxious patients (Abdou et al. 2006).

Evidence

Although several studies support the anxiolytic effects (particularly for GAD) of pregabalin, a synthetic structural analog of GABA (Owen 2007), only one study has examined the effects of GABA produced by natural fermentation (specifically PharmaGABA®, which is produced with a specific strain of lactic acid bacteria). One small study randomized 8 acrophobia patients to receive either 100 mg of GABA or placebo prior to walking across a narrow pedestrian suspension bridge (Abdou et al. 2006). Salivary immunoglobulin A (IgA) was measured halfway across the bridge and at the end of the bridge. The placebo group showed substantial drops in IgA both halfway and at the end, whereas the GABA group's IgA levels dropped only slightly at halfway and rose above baseline at the end. The GABA group showed significantly less reduction in salivary IgA than the placebo group, demonstrating that GABA may have a physiological anxiolytic effect when individuals are in phobic situations. Limitations of this study include a small sample and no self-reports of anxiety.

Side Effects and Conclusion

There are no known significant adverse effects or drug interactions associated with GABA supplement treatment (Yoshikuni 2008). Further research is needed to replicate this effect in larger samples and with participants diagnosed with other anxiety disorders. In addition, work is needed to determine the anxiolytic effects and side effects of long-term GABA use. Nonetheless, the study provides preliminary evidence that oral administration of 100 mg of GABA produced by natural fermentation results in decreased anxiety and physiological stress in response to feared situations within 1 hour of administration.

7-keto DHEA

Biological Mechanism

7-keto DHEA (3-acetyl-7-oxo-dehydroepiandrosterone) is a metabolite of dehydroepiandrosterone (DHEA), a 'parent hormone' produced by glands near the kidneys. 7-keto DHEA increases resting metabolic rate and has been marketed as a weight loss aid (Zenk et al. 2007). 7-keto DHEA is believed to decrease psychological symptoms through its anti-glucocorticoid effects (Hampl *et al.* 2000; Morfin and Stárka 2001; Liu *et al.* 2003). Several RCTs have supported DHEA's efficacy for treating depression (Wolkowitz *et al.* 1995; 1999; Schmidt *et al.* 2005).

Evidence

A case series of five women with severe post-traumatic stress disorder (PTSD), who had not responded to psychotherapy or medication, showed clinically meaningful decreases in PTSD symptoms within a few days of beginning 7-keto DHEA treatment (Sageman and Brown 2006).

Side Effects and Conclusion

Further research using randomized controlled designs is needed to determine the efficacy of 7-keto DHEA for treating PTSD and other anxiety disorders. Here, it is important to include placebo comparators (Smits and Hofmann 2009). When taken by mouth, 7-keto DHEA is not converted to steroid hormones (unlike DHEA), and no side effects have been reported (Sageman and Brown 2006; Zenk *et al.* 2007). However, Brown *et al.* (2009) report that bipolar patients taking 7-keto DHEA may become agitated, irritable, or anxious, and patients with estrogen-sensitive cancers or prostate cancer should also avoid 7-keto DHEA.

HERBAL AND BOTANICAL SUPPLEMENTS

Kava

Biological Mechanism

Kava (also called kava kava) is made from the *Piper methysticum* plant, a perennial shrub originating in the South Pacific traditionally taken as a ceremonial drink. Kava has sedative and anesthetic properties as apparent in its long history of use for anxiety, restlessness, and insomnia. It is approved in Germany for anxiety treatment in doses of 60 to 120 mg (Fugh-Berman and Cott 1999). Kava's intoxicating, anxiolytic, sedative, anticonvulsant, and analgesic properties have been attributed to its alpha-pyrones (kavalactones), which are a class of skeletal muscle relaxants believed to enhance ligand binding to GABA-A receptors, block violated-gated sodium channels and calcium ion channels, inhibit norepinephrine and dopamine reuptake, and inhibit monoamine oxidase B (Singh and Singh 2002).

Non-Clinical Anxiety and Mixed Anxiety Disorders

Among dietary supplements purported to relieve anxiety, kava has been the most studied. A meta-analysis of seven double-blind RCTs (n = 380) of

Table 9.1. Nutritional supplements for anxiety

Supplement	Structure	Reported Side Effects	Total Number of Studies (N)	Study Designs	Studies with Positive Support
Inositol	Glucose isomer	Minimal	5 (N = 78)	4 RCTs, 1 Open-label	4 (Panic disorder; OCD)
Tryptophan/ 5-Hydroxytryprophan	Amino acid	Rare but serious interactions	4 (N = 91)	3 RCTs, 1 Open-label	2 (Panic disorder; OCD)
L-lysine and L-arganine	Amino acid	None	2 (N = 157)	RCTs	2 (High trait anxiety; non-clinical)
L-theanine	Amino acid	None; anticoagulant effects	2 (N = 28)	RCTs	1 (Non-clinical)
Magnesium (Mg)/Magnesium blends	Cation	Minimal	3 (N = 388)	RCTs	2 (Healthy men; mild to moderate GAD; no support for Mg monotherapy)
Omega-3 fatty acids	Fatty acid	Negligible	3 (N = 161)	RCTs	2 (High test anxiety; substance dependence)
GABA	Neurotransmitter	None	1 (N = 8)	RCT	1 (Acrophobia)
7-keto DHEA	Hormone	Minimal; patients with certain cancers should avoid	1 (N = 5)	Case study	1 (PTSD)

kava for non-clinical anxiety and anxiety disorders revealed significant improvement in HAM-A scores relative to placebo (Pittler and Ernst 2003). The weighted mean difference between kava and placebo was 3.9 scale points (95% confidence interval (CI): 0.1 to 7.7; $p = .05$), suggesting that kava outperforms placebo in producing small reductions in anxiety. The five additional RCTs (n = 320), which could not be included in the meta-analysis due to use of different outcome measures, largely supported the results of the meta-analysis. A second meta-analysis of 6 placebo-controlled RCTs (n = 345) of kava for anxiety disorders replicated these results (Witte et al. 2005). A specific kava extract (WS1490) was used in these trials, only three of which were included in the Pittler and Ernst (2003) meta-analysis. The mean HAM-A score change of −5.94 was marginally greater than placebo (95% CI: −0.86 to 12.8; $p = .07$). Success rates in the trials ranged from 53–85% for kava and 20–50% for placebo, and the overall odds ratio was 3.3 (95% CI: 2.09–5.22) demonstrating superiority of kava to placebo in treating anxiety. In addition, this meta-analysis found non-significant but greater response to kava for females and younger adults (below the combined studies' median age of 53 years).

Generalized Anxiety Disorder

One meta-analysis examined the anxiolytic effects of three 4-week kava treatments (Connor et al. 2006). They found no benefits of kava over placebo for GAD. These null effects could be due to small samples (n = 64 for the meta-analysis), as well as relatively short trial durations. A 24-week double-blind RCT of kava for various anxiety disorders (n = 101), including agoraphobia, specific phobia, social phobia, GAD, and adjustment disorder, found significant reductions in HAM-A and CGI scores beginning in the eighth week ($d = .39$) and continuing through week 24 ($d = .67$; Volz and Kieser 1997). An 8-week RCT of kava (120 mg/day) for GAD (n = 127) found significant HAM-A improvement at post-treatment, with 76.7% of participants responding (i.e. 50% score reduction) and 65.1% achieving full remission (i.e. score < 9; Boerner et al. 2003).

A preliminary RCT of the physiological correlates associated with kava's anxiolytic effects showed that improvements in GAD symptoms were associated with improved reflex vagal control of heart rate, a physiological change that the placebo group did not experience (Watkins et al. 2001).

Only two studies were found comparing kava to a conventional medication. In one study, GAD remission rates were lower for kava (n = 28) than venlafaxine-XR (n = 6), a serotonin-norepinephrine reuptake inhibitor (25% versus 33%; Connor et al. 2006). However, a much larger trial (n = 127) found that response rates for kava were indistinguishable from buspirone and opipramol among participants with GAD, with HAM-A scores decreasing from 23 to about 8 in all groups (Boerner et al. 2003).

Side Effects and Conclusion

Unlike benzodiazapines, there are no sedating effects or cognitive impairment associated with kava use. There have been historical reports and correlation studies describing adverse physiological effects of daily long-term kava use (see Brown *et al*. 2009, for a review). Concerns of potential liver toxicity resulted in the US Food and Drug Administration (FDA) issuing a warning of potential for severe liver damage (e.g. hepatitis, cirrhosis, liver failure) for kava supplements in 2002 (US FDA 2002), and Canada and the UK have banned kava for this reason. However, the reported cases of liver problems are thought to be the result of poor-quality kava, overdose, prolonged therapy, or medication interactions (Teschke *et al*. 2008). Recent evidence suggests that the frequency of serious side effects is low. Indeed, side effects reported in each of the reviewed meta-analyses and trials were mild, transient, and uncommon, and no serious adverse events have been reported in trials with doses under 400 mg/per day (Lakhan and Vieira 2010). In recent studies of kava, which have examined changes in hepatic enzymes, no patients (of 64) experienced significant alteration of liver function (Connor *et al*. 2006). In 5 of 7 studies reviewed by Pittler and Ernst (2000), mild side effects including GI complaints, restlessness, drowsiness, tremor, headache, and tiredness were reported. In addition, there is a risk of drug interactions with kava. Kava may seriously interact with alprazolam and reduce the effectiveness of other medications because it inhibits the cytochrome P450 enzyme used by the liver to metabolize many medications (Almeida and Grimsey 1996; Singh and Singh 2002).

Overall, there is good evidence for the use of kava for treatment of GAD and other anxiety-related disorders, and it appears that the benefits outweigh the risks (Saeed *et al*. 2007; Lakhan and Vieira 2010). Not only has kava demonstrated efficacy in short trials, but there is also evidence for improvements with longer-term use (Volz and Kieser 1997). Given that its effects are often small and that it may interact with some medications, kava may be ideal for use as an adjunctive treatment to CBT, as opposed to being combined with other anxiolytic medications or used as a singular treatment. More research is needed on kava's effects on specific anxiety disorders other than GAD, as well as its comparability to other medications.

Lavender

Biological Mechanism

Lavender (*Lavandula*) is a flowering plant of the mint family traditionally used for relaxation and to aid sleep, as well as for its antiseptic and anti-inflammatory properties. Lavender oil has many constituents, but the active component is believed to be linalool (a naturally occurring terpene alcohol chemical), which has been found to inhibit the glutamate binding in the cerebral cortex, possibly explaining lavender oil's effects on the central nervous system (Elizabetsky et al. 1995).

Evidence

Lavender oil has most commonly been used in aromatherapy and massage, but an oral capsule form of lavender oil called Silexan has recently been investigated for treatment of anxiety (Woelk and Schläfke 2010). An RCT examined the effects 80 mg of Silexan versus 0.5 mg of lorazepam on anxiety symptoms in 77 patients with GAD (Woelk and Schläfke 2010). After 6 weeks of treatment, HAM-A scores were significantly and similarly reduced in both groups (45% reduction for Silexan and 46% for lorazepam). Improvements in clinician-rated CGI severity scores and other assessments of worry, anxiety, and sleep were also similar in both groups.

A review of 3 RCTs found beneficial effects of 80 mg per day of Silexan in 509 participants with GAD (versus lorazepam for 10 weeks), sub-clinical anxiety disorders (versus placebo for 6 weeks), or high levels of restlessness and agitation (versus placebo for 10 weeks; Kasper et al. 2010). At 6 weeks, Silexan-treated patients (n = 180) showed significant decreases in HAM-A scores relative to placebo at week 6 ($d = .52$ for trial 1; $d = .31$ for trial 2), as well as week 10 ($d = .75$; $d = .27$). For the GAD group, Silexan and lorazepam resulted in similar improvements.

Side Effects and Conclusion

The only reported side effects of lavender oil supplementation have been belching and mild GI discomfort (Kasper et al. 2010). As opposed to benzodiazapines, lavender oil is well tolerated and has shown no sedative effects or potential for dependence and withdrawal (Woelk and Schläfke 2010). These well-controlled initial studies with large samples suggest that supplementation with 80 mg daily of lavender oil may be effective in reducing anxiety in patients with GAD. Future work should examine the effects of lavender oil in samples with other anxiety diagnoses.

Passionflower

Biological Mechanism

Passionflower (*Passiflora incarnata* Linneaus) is a plant indigenous to Argentina, Brazil, and the Southern US, which has been used as an herbal remedy for anxiety and as a sedative in many cultures (especially among Native Americans). It has been traditionally used to treat insomnia, hysteria, epilepsy, and pain, and it has a long and global history of use as an anxiolytic (Dhawan *et al.* 2001). Passionflower is listed as an official plant drug by the pharmacopoeias of the US, Britain, Germany, France, Switzerland, Egypt, and India (Dhawan *et al.* 2001). It is approved in Germany for treatment of nervousness and restlessness and in Britain for sleep disorders, restlessness, nervous stress, and anxiety. As is the case with many herbal remedies, passionflower contains numerous phytochemicals, and the specific anxiolytic agents are therefore not clear (Lakhan and Vieira 2010). However, passionflower does contain chrysin, a flavone with anxiolytic effects, which binds to benzodiazepine receptors (Brown *et al.* 2009). Passionflower is also involved in monoamine oxidase inhibition and activation of GABA receptors (Kinrys *et al.* 2009).

Evidence

To date, three trials have been conducted examining the effects of passionflower for anxiety and anxiety disorders. An RCT with a non-clinical sample of 60 patients about to undergo surgery found that those who took 500 mg passionflower reported significantly less preoperative anxiety than those who took the placebo (Movafegh *et al.* 2008). Two studies have examined passionflower in clinical samples. A double-blind RCT with 36 GAD patients demonstrated that passionflower was as effective as a benzodiazepine in reducing anxiety (Akhondzadeh *et al.* 2001). For 4 weeks, patients were given 45 drops of passionflower extract daily plus a placebo tablet, or 30 mg per day of oxazepam (a benzodiazepine) plus placebo drops. Although the oxazepam had more rapid effects, passionflower was as effective in reducing anxiety (both groups dropped from a mean HAM-A of 20 at baseline to 6 at post-treatment). Importantly, passionflower resulted in less self-reported cognitive and functional impairment related to job performance. Limitations of the study were the small sample size and lack of a placebo-only group. A larger double-blind RCT (n = 182) of patients with adjustment disorder with anxious mood found that passionflower in combination with other herbal supplements (*Crataegus oxyacantha, Ballota foetida, Valeriana officinalis, Cola nitida,* and *Paullinia cupana*) was significantly more effective than placebo in reducing anxiety (Bourin *et al.* 1997). After 4 weeks of treatment, HAM-A scores decreased to below 10 for 43.9% of the treatment group but only 25.3% of the placebo group. Because passionflower was combined with several other herbal supplements, it is impossible to know which herb accounted for the effects or whether there was a synergistic effect of the combined supplements.

Side Effects and Conclusion

Passionflower appears to be well-tolerated and safe for use. Only one study reported mild side effects which included drowsiness, confusion, and dizziness; however, the reports of side effects did not differ from the oxazepam control group (Akhondzadeh *et al.* 2001). Because each study was conducted with a different patient population, replication and trials examining effects on other anxiety disorders is needed. Although all three studies have shown significant anxiolytic effects of passionflower (or its combination with other herbs), larger studies of passionflower monotherapy in clinical samples are needed in order to determine its potential for anxiety disorder treatment.

St John's Wort

Biological Mechanism

St John's Wort (SJW; *Hypericum perforatum*) is derived from a flowering perennial shrub native to Europe, West Asia, and North Africa. It has been used in folk medicine for centuries for a number of problems and is an efficacious herbal treatment for depression (Linde *et al.* 1996). It is currently approved in Germany for the treatment of depression, anxiety, and sleep problems. Although SJW has numerous potentially active compounds, hypericin and hyperforin are believed to be the two primary compounds, and they act on the hypothalamic-pituitary adrenal axis and inhibit neurotransmitter reuptake (for a description of the physiological mechanism, see Kinrys *et al.* 2009). Several studies have examined the effects of SJW for comorbid anxiety and depression, but only a few studies have examined its effects specifically on anxiety disorders.

Obsessive Compulsive Disorder

One open-label uncontrolled study showed support for SJW (450 mg with 0.3% hypericin, twice daily) in reducing symptoms in 12 patients with OCD (Taylor and Kobak 2000). The patients experienced significant reductions in Y-BOCS scores after 1 week (2.1-point decrease), with symptom decreases continued through to week 12 (7.4-point decrease). These gains are similar to those found in clinical trials with SSRIs (Kinrys *et al.* 2009). However, this evidence is severely limited by the small sample and lack of a control group. In a later 12-week double-blind RCT, the same group tested the effects of SJW (flexible dose, 600–1800 mg per day) on 60 OCD patients and found no differences relative to placebo in Y-BOCS scores at post-treatment (3.43 and 3.60 score reduction, respectively; Kobak *et al.* 2005).

Social Phobia

A double-blind RCT examined the effects of a 12-week SJW treatment (flexible dose, 300–1800 mg/day) in 40 patients with social phobia (Kobak *et al.* 2005). They found no post-treatment differences in symptoms between SJW and placebo; both groups showed significant declines in LSAS scores (11.40 and 13.15 score reduction, respectively).

Generalized Anxiety Disorder

Only case reports are available for the effects of SJW on GAD. These studies have reported significant improvement in GAD symptoms in a total of 6 patients who were administered between 900 mg and 1800 mg per day of SJW (Davidson and Connor 2001; Kobak *et al.* 2003).

Side Effects and Conclusion

Given that the only available RCTs have not supported SJW as an effective treatment for anxiety disorders, there is no support to recommend it for anxiety disorders. SJW causes some mild symptoms including GI symptoms, dizziness, confusion, jitteriness, insomnia, fatigue, and photosensitivity (Fugh-Berman and Cott 1999; Brown *et al.* 2009). Agitation side effects were more common in the SJW group than placebo (Kobak *et al.* 2005). SJW also interacts with anticoagulants, reduces effectiveness of some contraceptives, and should not be taken with SSRIs due to risk of serotonin syndrome (Fugh-Berman and Cott 1999).

Valerian

Biological Mechanism

Valerian (*Valeriana officinalis*) is a perennial flowering plant that grows in temperate to temperate-to-warm climates worldwide. Supplements derived from its root have traditionally been used to treat insomnia and nervousness, and it has more recently been applied to anxiety and epilepsy. Valerian contains arginine, glutamine, alanine, and GABA, and possible mechanisms of action include GABA transmission enhancement (Yuan *et al.* 2004; Awad *et al.* 2007) and serotonin modulation (Dietz *et al.* 2005).

Evidence

A double-blind crossover RCT with a 1-week washout examined the combination of valerian plus lemon balm in 24 healthy participants (Kennedy *et al.* 2006). Participants were administered placebo or one of three doses of the supplement (600, 1200, or 1800 mg) before a laboratory stressor. The 600 mg dose significantly reduced STAI state anxiety after 3 hours ($d = 2.42$) and 6 hours ($d = 2.65$) relative to placebo, whereas the

1800 mg dose increased state anxiety ($d = 2.94$). All three doses led to decrements in performance on a series of cognitive and psychomotor tasks. Although this study offers some support for acute anxiolytic effects of a 600 mg dose, higher doses may actually exacerbate anxiety and any dose appears to negatively impact cognitive and psychomotor performance. Furthermore, it is impossible to determine whether the observed effects in these studies resulted from valerian, lemon balm, or their unique combination.

Two studies have investigated valerian monotherapy for anxiety. An RCT examined the acute stress-reducing effects of valerian alone (100 mg), propranolol (a beta-blocker; 20 mg) alone, valerian and propranolol combined (100 mg and 20 mg, respectively), versus placebo in 48 healthy participants (Kohnen and Oswald 1988). Valerian did not have an effect on state anxiety or heart rate, but alone and in combination with propranolol, it led to decreased subjective somatic arousal in response to a laboratory stressor. Another double-blind RCT with 36 patients diagnosed with GAD compared 4 weeks of treatment with valerian (mean dose of 81.3 mg valepotriates per day) to diazepam (mean dose 6.5 mg/day) and placebo (Andreatini et al. 2002). There were significant decreases in HAM-A scores for all groups (mean decrease of 9.27), but no condition differences on HAM-A or STAI trait anxiety changes. However, the diazepam and valerian groups did show significant reductions on the HAM-A psychic subscale (i.e. psychological as opposed to somatic symptoms) relative to placebo ($d = .35$).

Side Effects and Conclusion

Side effects of valerian are minimal and include unpleasant taste and odor, occasional GI discomfort, headaches, and minor hangover on doses over 600 mg (Brown et al. 2009). Andreatini et al. (2002) reported no differences in side effects from placebo, and there have been no cases of habituation or abuse. The available evidence for the anxiolytic effects of valerian is limited and mixed, and future research should examine valerian monotherapy using adequately powered designs. There is currently not sufficient evidence to recommend valerian for the treatment of anxiety disorders.

Less Studied Herbal Supplements

Ginkgo Biloba

Ginkgo (*Ginkgo biloba*) is a species of tree with a long history of use in Chinese and Japanese traditional medicine (Ernst 2002). It has primarily been used to treat memory problems and dementia (Søholm 1998). Ginkgo appears to reduce anxiety in addition to other emotional and cognitive

Table 9.2. Herbal and botanical supplements for anxiety

Supplement	Plant Species	Reported Side Effects	Total Number of Studies (N)	Study Designs	Studies with Positive Support
Kava	*Piper methysticum*	Mild; reports of liver damage may be due to poor drug quality	4 (N = 1109)	Meta-analyses	3 (Sub-clinical anxiety; mixed anxiety disorders; GAD)
Lavender	*Lavandula*	Mild	4 (N = 586)	RCTs	3 (Sub-clinical anxiety; GAD)
Passionflower	*Passiflora incarnata* L.	Mild	3 (N = 278)	RCTs	3 (GAD; adjustment disorder with anxious mood; non-clinical)
St. John's Wort	*Hypericum perforatum*	Mild; some medication interactions	5 (N = 118)	2 RCTs, 1 Open-label, 2 Case studies	3 (OCD; GAD; no RCT evidence)

Valerian	Valeriana officinalis	Mild	3 (N = 108)	RCTs	2 (Non-clinical; partial support for GAD)
Ginkgo biloba anticoagulant effects	Ginkgo biloba 1 (N = 170)	Mild; RCT			1 (GAD and adjustment disorder with anxious mood)
Chamomile	Matricaria recutita	Minimal	1 (N = 57)	RCT	1 (GAD)
Galphimia glauca	Galphimia gracilis	Some excessive sedation	1 (N = 114)	RCT	1 (GAD)
Rhodiola rosea	Rhodiola rosea	Minimal	1 (N = 10)	Open-label	1 (GAD)

symptoms in dementia patients (Scripnikov *et al.* 2007), and one study has specifically examined the anxiolytic effects of Ginkgo. In a double-blind RCT, 170 adults with GAD or adjustment disorder with anxious mood were given either 480 mg Ginkgo, 240 mg Ginkgo, or placebo daily for 4 weeks (Woelk *et al.* 2007). Relative to placebo, HAM-A scores decreased significantly with both doses of Ginkgo, with a slight advantage of higher dose. The mean change was −14.3 points for the high dose ($d = .75$) and −12.1 for the low dose ($d = .42$). Ginkgo also outperformed placebo on the Erlangen Anxiety Tension and Aggression Scale ($d = .53$ for high dose; $d = .41$ for low dose), list of complaints ($d = .64; d = .21$), patients' ratings of change, and CGI improvement scores. Clinician-reported response rates (i.e. much or very much improved) were 81, 67, and 38% of the high dose, low dose, and placebo groups, respectively.

These results suggest that Ginkgo may be an effective treatment for GAD, but replication is needed. Given its anticoagulant effects, Ginkgo should not be consumed by patients with bleeding disorders, taking anticoagulant medication, or having surgery within 2 weeks (Fugh-Berman and Cott 1999; Ernst 2002; Brown *et al.* 2009). Other potential side effects are mild and transient, including mild GI discomfort, headaches, dizziness, heart palpitations, and restlessness.

Chamomile

Chamomile (*Matricaria recutita*) is a flower that has been used for centuries as a relaxation agent. The active component of chamomile is thought to be apigenin, a flavone that has high affinity for benzodiazepine receptors. Chamomile also inhibits glutamic acid decarboxylase, which influences brain GABA levels and neurotransmission (Awad *et al.* 2007). Although several studies have examined chamomile aromatherapy for anxiety and chamomile as a dietary supplement for sleep disorders (Cauffield and Forbes 1999; Larzelere and Wiseman 2002), only one study has examined it as a dietary supplement for anxiety (Amsterdam *et al.* 2009). A double-blind RCT (n = 57) found that 8 weeks of treatment with chamomile extract (220 mg, 1.2% apigenin) resulted in significantly greater reduction in HAM-A scores in GAD patients relative to placebo, but there were no significant differences in improvement on the Beck Anxiety Inventory (Beck *et al.* 1988), CGI-severity, or general psychological well-being. Chamomile is well tolerated with minimal side effects, including drowsiness and rare allergic reaction.

Galphimia Glauca

Galphimia glauca (*Galphimia gracilis*) is a flowering plant used in traditional Mexican medicine (Herrera-Arellano *et al.* 2007). Its anxiolytic properties are attributed to its methanol content. The only RCT to examine its anxiolytic effects found that 4 weeks of Galphimia glauca treatment (310 mg daily, with 0.35 mg of galphamine B, the active component) resulted in significant decreases in anxiety symptoms in 114 GAD patients (Herrera-Arellano et al. 2007). The anxiolytic effects were comparable to lorazepam: Galphimia glauca reduced HAM-A scores by 61.2% and lorazepam reduced scores by 60.3%. Significant improvements were also found for clinician-rated CGI and patients' evaluations of symptom severity. However, patients tolerated Galphimia glauca better than lorazepam. Excessive sedation was reported by 6.8% and 21.3%, respectively.

Rhodiola Rosea

Rhodiola rosea is a plant used in traditional Chinese medicine for depression. Root extracts from *Rhodiola rosea* contain phenolic compounds that are structurally related to catecholamines and involved in sympathetic nervous system activation during stress response (Brown et al. 2009). *Rhodiola rosea* is considered a plant adaptogen, which is a compound that increases an organism's ability to adapt to and avoid the damages of stress (Panossian and Wagner 2005). A small, uncontrolled trial examined the effects of a 10-week treatment of *Rhodiola rosea* (340 mg/day) in 10 GAD patients (Bystritsky et al. 2008). Half of participants responded with a 50% or greater reduction on the HAM-A, with an average decrease of 9.3 points. Reported side effects were dizziness (20%) and dry mouth (40%).

CONCLUSION

This chapter reviewed eight nutritional supplements and nine herbal supplements that have been studied for their anxiolytic effects. Of these dietary supplements, only two, namely kava and inositol, have demonstrated significant anxiolytic effects in several placebo-controlled RCTs, including trials with clinically anxious samples. These supplements therefore appear to have an adequate evidence base to justify use for anxiety disorder treatment. Other supplements that have preliminary support from RCTs include lavender, passionflower, the combination of L-lysine and L-arginine, *Ginkgo biloba*, chamomile, and Galphimia glauca. However, there have been too few trials to draw conclusions on their efficacy.

There are several limitations to the extant work on the efficacy of nutritional and herbal supplements for anxiety disorders. First, there is often variability in supplement quality and lack of standardization among studies. The purity and potency of dietary supplements vary based on where they are grown, when they were harvested, and the type of extraction technique (Brown et al. 2009). There is therefore a need for research to determine appropriate dosages and possible side effects. Although the FDA tracks consumer reports of side effects and intervenes after an unsafe supplement is already on the market, supplement manufacturers do not need to register or seek approval of their supplements with the FDA (US FDA 1994). Unlike other over-the-counter and prescription medications, dietary supplements sold in the US are not subject to safety and ingredient testing.

Second, for many supplements, studies are either too few in number or lacking appropriate control procedures. Future work in this area should focus on replication, using large samples, and evaluating effects for each of the different anxiety disorders separately. Similarly, it would be beneficial to examine supplements as monotherapies first, as opposed to in combination with other supplements. Once the singular effects of a supplement are determined, it will be beneficial to examine possible synergistic effects of combining with other dietary supplements. Likewise, we did not find any RCTs examining the effects of supplements for augmenting psychotherapy. Hence, future research may focus on the utility of using supplements for augmenting the effects of established interventions.

Finally, it may be worthwhile to investigate the anxiolytic effects of supplements that have been shown to alleviate other psychiatric problems such as depression (e.g. folate, vitamins D and B_{12}), as well as supplements that may increase anxiety or otherwise be detrimental to mental health (e.g. S-adenosyl-methionine (SAMe), omega-6, and trans-isomer fatty acids). Here, it is important to also mention macronutrient and overall dietary approaches, such as the Mediterranean diet. Indeed, dietary supplementation for anxiety disorder treatment is a promising field, given the positive findings for kava and inositol and the preliminary results for many other supplements.

REFERENCES

Abdou, A. M., Higashiguchi, S., Horie, K., Kim, M., Hatta, H., and Yokogoshi, H. (2006). Relaxation and immunity enhancement effects if gamma-aminobutyric acid (GABA) administration in humans. *Biofactors*, 26(3): 201–208.

Akhondzadeh, S., Naghavi, H. R., Vazirian, M., Shayeganpour, A. Rashidi, H., and Khani, M. (2001). Passionflower in the treatment of generalized anxiety disorder: A pilot double-blind randomized controlled trial with oxazepam. *Journal of Clinical Pharmacy and Therapeutics*, 26(5): 363–367.

Almeida, J. C. and Grimsley, E. W. (1996). Coma from the health food store: Interaction between kava and alprazolam. *Annals of Internal Medicine*, 125(11): 940–941.

Amsterdam, J. D., Li, Y., Soeller, I., Rockwell, K., Mao, J. J., and Shults, J. (2009). A randomized, double-blind, placebo-controlled trial or oral *Matricaria recutita* (chamomile) extract therapy for generalized anxiety disorder. *Journal of Clinical Psychopharmacology*, 29(4): 378–382.

Andreatini, R., Sartori, V. A., Seabra, M. L., and Leite, J. R. (2002). Effect of valepotriates (valerian extract) in generalized anxiety disorder: A randomized placebo-controlled pilot study. *Phytotherapy Research*, 16(6): 650–654.

Astin, J. A. (1998). Why patients use alternative medicine: Results of a national study. *Journal of the American Medical Association,* 279: 1548–1553.

Awad, R., Levac, D., Cybulska, P., Merali, Z., Trudeau, V. L., and Arnason, J. T. (2007). Effects of traditionally used anxiolytic botanicals on enzymes of the gamma-aminobutyric acid (GABA) system. *Canadian Journal of Physiology and Pharmacology,* 85(9): 933–942.

Bailey, R. L., Gahche, J. J., Lentino, C. V. et al. (2011). Dietary supplement use in the United States, 2003–2006. *The Journal of Nutrition,* 141(2): 261–266.

Barlow, D. H., Gorman, J. M., Shear, M. K., and Woods, S. W. (2000). Cognitive-behavioral therapy, imipramine, and their combination for panic disorder: A randomized controlled trial. *Journal of the American Medical Association,* 283(19): 2529–2536.

Beck, A. T., Epstein, N., Brown, G., and Steer, R. A. (1988). An inventory for measuring clinical anxiety: Psychometric properties. *Journal of Consulting and Clinical Psychology,* 56(6): 893–897.

Becker, C. B., Zayfert, C., and Anderson, E. (2004). A survey of psychologists' attitudes towards and utilization of exposure therapy for PTSD. *Behaviour Research and Therapy,* 42(3): 277–292.

Bell, C., Abrams, J., and Nutt, D. (2001). Tryptophan depletion and its implications for psychiatry. *The British Journal of Psychiatry,* 178: 399–405.

Benjamin, J., Levine, J., Fux, M., Aviv, A., Levy, D., and Belmaker, R. H. (1995). Double-blind, placebo-controlled, crossover trial of inositol treatment for panic disorder. *American Journal of Psychiatry,* 152: 1084–1086.

Blier, P. and Bergeron, R. (1996). Sequential administration of augmentation strategies in treatment-resistant obsessive-compulsive disorder: Preliminary findings. *International Clinical Psychopharmacology,* 11(1): 37–44.

Boerner, R., Sommer, H., Berger, W., Kuhn, U., Schmidt, U., and Mannel, M. (2003). Kava-kava extract LI 150 is as effective as opipramol and buspirone in generalized anxiety disorder: An 8-week randomized, double-blind multi-centre clinical trial in 129 outpatients. *Phytomedicine,* 10: 1–5.

Bond, A. and Lader, M. (1974). The use of analogue scales in rating subjective feelings. *British Journal of Medical Psychology,* 80: 1–46.

Borkovec, T. D., Newman, M. G., Pincus, A. L., and Lytle, R. J. (2002). A component analysis of cognitive-behavioral therapy for generalized anxiety disorder and the role of interpersonal problems. *Journal of Consulting and Clinical Psychology,* 70(2): 288–298.

Bourin, M., Bougerol, T., Guitton, B., and Broutin, E. (1997). A combination of plant extracts in the treatment of outpatients with adjustment disorder with anxious mood: Controlled study versus placebo. *Fundamental and Clinical Pharmacology,* 11(2): 127–132.

Brown, R. P., Gerbard, P. L., and Muskin, P. R. (2009). How to use herbs, nutrients and yoga in mental health care. New York: W. W. Norton and Co., Inc.

Buist-Bowman, M. A., De Graaf, R., Vollebergh, W. A. M., Alonso, J., Bruffaerts, R., and Ormel, J. (2006). Functional disability of mental disorders and comparison with physical disorders: a study among the general population of six European countries. *Acta Psychiatrica Scandinavica,* 113: 492–500.

Buydens-Branchey, L. and Branchey, M. (2006). n-3 polyunsaturated fatty acids decrease anxiety feelings in a population of substance abusers. *Journal of Clinical Psychopharmacology,* 26(6): 661–665.

Bystritsky, A., Kerwin, L., and Feusner, J. D. (2008). A pilot study of *Rhodiola rosea* (Rhodax) for generalized anxiety disorder. *Journal of Alternative and Complementary Medicine*, 14: 175–180.

Carey, P. D., Warwick, J., Harvey, B. H., Stein, D. J., and Seedat, S. (2004). Single photon emission computed tomography (SPECT) in obsessive-compulsive disorder before and after treatment with inositol. *Metabolic Brain Disease*, 19(2): 135–144.

Carroll, D., Ring, C., Suter, M., and Willemsen, G. (2000). The effects of an oral multivitamin combination with calcium, magnesium, and zinc on psychological well-being in healthy young male volunteers; a double-blind placebo-controlled trial. *Psychopharmacology*, 150: 220–225.

Cauffield, J. J., and Forbes, H. J. (1999). Dietary supplements used in the treatment of depression, anxiety, and sleep disorders. *Lippincott's Primary Care Practice*, 3(3): 290–204.

Choy, Y. (2007). Managing side effects of anxiolytics. *Primary Psychiatry*, 14(7): 68–76.

Christmas, D., Hood, S., and Nutt, D. (2008). Potential novel anxiolytic drugs. *Current Pharmaceutical Design*, 195(6): 483–490.

Cohen, J. (1988). *Statistical Power Analysis for the Behavioral Sciences*, 2nd edn. Hillsdale, NJ: Lawrence Erlbaum Associates.

Cohen, S., Kamarck, T., and Mermelstein, R. (1983). A global measure of perceived stress. *Journal of Health and Social Behavior*, 24: 385–396.

Connor, K. M., Payne, V., and Davidson, J. R. (2006). Kava in generalized anxiety disorder: Three placebo-controlled trials. *International Clinical Psychopharmacology*, 21(5): 249–253.

Davidson, J. R. T., and Connor, K. M. (2001). St John's Wort in generalized anxiety disorder: three case reports. *Journal of Clinical Psychopharmacology*, 21: 635–636.

Davidson, J. R., Foa, E. B., Huppert, J. D. et al. (2004). Fluoxetine, comprehensive cognitive behavioral therapy, and placebo in generalized social phobia. *Archives of General Psychiatry*, 61(10): 1005–1013.

Delion, S., Chalon, S., Hérault, S., Guilloteau, D., Besnard, J. C., and Durand, G. (1994). Chronic dietary alpha-Linolenic acid deficiency alters dopaminergic and serotonergic neurotransmission in the rats. *The Journal of Nutrition*, 124(12): 2466–2477.

De Souza, M. C., Walker, A. F., Robinson, P. A. and Bolland, K. (2000). A synergistic effect of a dietary supplement for one month of 200 mg magnesium plus 50 mg vitamin B6 for the relief of anxiety-related presmentrual symptoms: a double-blind, crossover study. *Journal of Women's Health and Gender-Based Medicine*, 9(2): 131–139.

Dhawan, K., Kumar, S., and Sharma, A. (2001). Anti-anxiety studies on extracts of Passiflora incarnata Linneaus. *Journal of Ethnopharmacology*, 78, 165–170.

D'Hulst, C., Atack, J. R., Kooy, R. F. (2009). The complexity of the GABAA receptor shapes unique pharmacological profiles. *Drug Discovery Today*, 14: 866–875.

Dietz, B. M., Mahady, G. B., Pauli, G. F., and Farnsworth, N. (2005). Valerian extract and valerenic acid are partial agonists of the 5-HT5a receptor *in vitro*. *Molecular Brain Research*, 138: 191–197.

Elizabetsky, E., Marschner, J., and Souza, D. O. (1995). Effects of linalool on glutamatergic system in the rat cerebral cortex. *Neurochemistry Research*, 20: 461–465.

Ernst, E. (2002). The risk-benefit profile of commonly used herbal therapies: Ginkgo, St John's wort, ginseng, echinacea, saw palmetto, and kava. *Annals of Internal Medicine*, 136(1): 42–53.

Foa, E. B., Liebowitz, M. R., Kozak, M. J. *et al.* (2005). Randomized, placebo-controlled trial of exposure and ritual prevention, clomipramine, and their combination in the treatment of obsessive-compulsive disorder. *The American Journal of Psychiatry*, 162(1): 151–161.

Freiheir, S. R., Vye, C., Swan, R., and Cady, M. (2004). Cognitive-behavioral therapy for anxiety: Is dissemination working? *The Behavior Therapist*, 27(2): 25–32.

Fugh-Berman, A. and Cott, J. M. (1999). Dietary supplements and natural products as psychotherapeutic agents. *Psychosomatic Medicine*, 61: 712–728.

Furmark, T. (2009). Neurobiological aspects of social anxiety disorder. *The Israel Journal of Psychiatry and Related Sciences*, 46(1): 5–12.

Fux, M., Levine, J., Aviv, A., and Belmaker, R. H. (1996). Inositol treatment of obsessive-compulsive disorder. *American Journal of Psychiatry*, 153(9): 1219–1221.

Fux, M., Benjamin, J., and Belmaker, R. H. (1999). Inositol versus placebo augmentation of serotonin reuptake inhibitors in the treatment of obsessive-compulsive disorder: A double-blind crossover study. *International Journal of Neuropsychopharmacology*, 2: 193–195.

Fux, M., Benjamin, J., and Nemets, B. (2004). A placebo-controlled cross-over trial of adjunctive EPA in OCD. *Journal of Psychiatric Research*, 38(3): 323–325.

Goldberg, D. and Hillier, V. F. (1970). A scaled version of the General Health Questionnaire. *Psychological Medicine*, 9: 139–145.

Golden, R. N. (2004). Making advances where it matters: Improving outcomes in mood and anxiety disorders. *CNS Spectrums*, 9(6) Supplement 4: 14–22.

Goodman, W. K., Price, L. H., Rasmussen, S. A. *et al.* (1989a). The Yale-Brown Obsessive Compulsive Scale: 2. Validity. *Archives of General Psychiatry*, 46: 1012–1016.

Goodman, W. K., Price, L. H., Rasmussen, S. A. (1989b). The Yale-Brown Obsessive Compulsive Scale: I. Development, use, and reliability. *Archives of General Psychiatry*, 46: 1006–1011.

Green, P., Hermesh, H., Monselise, A., Marom, S., Presburger, G., and Weizman, A. (2006). Red cell membrane omega-3 fatty acids are decreases in nondepressed patients with social anxiety disorder. *European Neuropsychopharmacology*, 16(2): 107–113.

Greenberg, P. E., Sisitsky, T., Kessler, R. C. *et al.* (1999). The economic burden of anxiety disorders in the 1990s. *Journal of Clinical Psychiatry*, 60: 427–435.

Guy, W. (1976). Clinical global impression. In W. Guy (ed.), *ECDEU Assessment manual for psychopharmacology* Rockville, MD, National Institute of Mental Health: 217–222.

Hamilton, M. (1959). The assessment of anxiety states by rating. *British Journal of Medical Psychology*, 32: 50–55.

Hamilton, M. (1960). A rating scale for depression. *Journal of Neurology, Neurosurgery, and Psychiatry*, 23: 56–62.

Hampl, R., Lapcik, O., Hill, M. *et al.* (2000). 7–hydroxydehydroepiandrosterne: A natural antiglucocorticoid and a candidate for steroid replacement therapy? *Physiological Research*, 49 (Supplement 1): S107–S112.

Hanus, M., Lafon, J., and Mathieu, M. (2004). Double-blind, randomized, placebo-controlled study to evaluate the efficacy and safety of a fixed combination containing two plant extracts (*Crataegus oxyacantha* and *Eschscholtzia californica*) and magnesium in mild-to-moderate anxiety disorders. *Current Medical Research and Opinion*, 20(1): 63–71.

Herrera-Arellano, A., Jiménez-Ferrer, E., Zamilpa, A., Morales-Valdéz, M., García-Valencia, C. E., and Tortoriello, J. (2007). Efficacy and tolerability of a standardized herbal product from Galphimia glauca on generalized anxiety disorder: A randomized double-blind clinical trial controlled with lorazepam. *Planta Medica*, 73(8): 713–717.

Hertzman, P. A., Blevins, W. I., Mayer, J., Greenfield, B., Ting, M., and Gleich, G. J. (1990). Association of the eosinophilia-myalgia syndrome with ingestion of tryptophan. *New England Journal of Medicine*, 322: 869–873.

Hofmann, S. G. and Smits, J. A. (2008). Cognitive-behavioral therapy for adult anxiety disorders: a meta-analysis of randomized placebo-controlled trials. *Journal of Clinical Psychiatry*, 69(4): 621–632.

Hudson, C., Hudson, S., and MacKenzie, J. (2007). Protein-source tryptophan as an efficacious treatment for social anxiety disorder: a pilot study. *Canadian Journal of Physiology and Pharmacology*, 85(9): 928–932.

Hunter, L. R. and Schmidt, N. B. (2010). Anxiety psychopathology in African American adults: Literature review and development of an empirically informed sociocultural model. *Psychological Bulletin*, 136(2): 211–235.

Jezova, D., Makatsori, A., Smriga, M., Morinaga, Y., and Duncko, R. (2005). Subchronic treatment with amino acid mixture of L-lysine and L-arginine modifies neuroendocrine activation during psychosocial stressing subjects with high trait anxiety. *Nutritional Neuroscience*, 8: 155–160.

Kahn, R. S., Westenberg, H. G., Verhoeven, W. M., Gispen-De Wied, C. C., and Kamerbeek, W. D. (1987). Effect of serotonin precursor and uptake inhibitor in anxiety disorders: A double-blind comparison of 5-hydroxytryptophan, clomipramine and placebo. *International Clinical Psychopharmacology*, 2(1): 33–45.

Kasper, S., Gastpar, M., Müller, W. E. *et al.* (2010). Efficacy and safety of Silexan, a new, orally administered lavender oil preparation, in subthreshold anxiety disorder – Evidence from clinical trials. *Wiener Medizinische Wochenschrift*, 160: 547–556.

Kennedy, D. O., Little, W., Haskell, C. F., and Scholey, A. B. (2006). Anxiolytic effects of a combination of *Melissa officinalis* and *Valerian officinalis* during laboratory induced stress. *Phytotherapy Research*, 20(2): 96–102.

Kennedy, J. (2005). Herb and supplement use in the US adult population. *Clinical Therapeutics*, 27(11): 1847–1858.

Kessler, R. C., Chiu, W. T., Demler, O., Merikangas, K. R., and Walters, E. E. (2005a). Prevalence, severity, and comorbidity of 12-month DSM-IV disorders in the National Comorbidity Survey Replication. *Archives of General Psychiatry*, 62(7): 617–627.

Kessler, R. C., Chiu, W. T., Demler, O., and Walters, E. E. (2005b). Lifetime prevalence and age-of-onset distributions of DSM-IV disorders in the national comorbidity survey replication. *Archives of General Psychiatry*, 62(7): 593–602.

Kiecolt-Glaser, J. K. (2010). Stress, food, and inflammation: Psychoneuroimmunology and nutrition at the cutting edge. *Psychosomatic Medicine*, 72: 365–369.

Kimura, K., Ozeki, M., Juneja, L. R., and Ohira, H. (2007). L-Theanine reduces psychological and physiological stress responses. *Biological Psychology*, 74(1): 39–45.

Kinrys, G., Coleman, E., and Rothstein, E. (2009). Natural remedies for anxiety disorders: potential use and clinical applications. *Depression and Anxiety*, 26(3): 259–265.
Kobak, K. A., Taylor, L. V., Futterer, R., and Warner, G. (2003). St John's Wort in generalized anxiety disorder: Three more case reports. *Journal of Clinical Pscyhopharmacology*, 23(5): 531–532.
Kobak, K. A., Taylor, L. V., Bystritsky, A. *et al.* (2005a). St John's Wort versus placebo in obsessive-compulsive disorder: Results from a double-blind study. *International Clinical Psychopharmacology*, 20(6): 299–304.
Kobak, K. A., Taylor, L. V., Warner, G., and Futterer, R. (2005b). St. John's Wort versus placebo in social phobia: Results from a placebo-controlled pilot study. *Journal of Clinical Psychopharmacology*, 25(1): 51–58.
Kohnen, R. and Oswald, D. (1988). The effects of valerian, propranolol, and their combination on activation, performance, and mood of healthy volunteers under social stress conditions. *Pharmacopsychiatry*, 21: 447–448.
Lakhan, S. E. and Vieira, K. F. (2010). Nutritional and herbal supplements for anxiety and anxiety-related disorders. *Nutrition Journal*, 9(42): 1–14.
Larzelere, M. and Wiseman, P. (2002). Anxiety, depression, and insomnia. *Primary Care*, 29: 339–360.
Libigerová, E. and Holecková, M. (1999). Magnesium deficiency in anxiety disorders. *Homeostasis in Health and Disease*, 39: 124–125.
Liebowitz, M. R. (1987). Social phobia. *Modern Problems of Pharmacopsychiatry*, 22: 141–173.
Linde, K., Ramirez, G., Mulrow, C. D., Pauls, A., Weidenhammer, W., and Melchart, D. (1996). St. John's Wort for depression: An overview and meta-analysis of randomized clinical trials. *British Medical Journal*, 313(7052): 253–258.
Liu, Y. Y., Yang, N., Kong, L. N., and Zuo, P. P. (2003). Effects of 7-oxo-DHEA treatment on the immunoreactivity of BALB/c mice subjected to chronic mild stress. *Acta Pharmaceutica Sinica (Yao Xue Xue Bao)*, 38(12): 881–884.
Lu, K., Gray, M. A., Oliver, C. *et al.* (2004). The acute effects of L-theanine in comparison with alprazolam on anticipatory anxiety in humans. *Human Psychopharmacology*, 19(7): 457–465.
Marks, I., Lovell, H., Noshirvani, M., Livanou, M., and Thrasher, S. (1998). Treatment of post-traumatic stress disorder by exposures and/or cognitive restructuring: A controlled study. *Archives of General Psychiatry*, 55(4): 317–325.
Mavissakalian, M., Perel, J., and Guo, S. (2002). Specific side effects of long-term imipramine management of panic disorder. *Journal of Clinical Psychopharmacology*, 22(2): 155–161.
Morfin, R. and Stárka, L. (2001). Neurosteroid 7-hydroxylation products in the brain. *International Review of Neurobiology*, 46: 79–95.
Movafegh, A., Alizadeh, R., Hajimohamadi, F. Esfehani, F., and Nejatfar, M. (2008). Preoperative oral Passiflora incarnata reduces anxiety in ambulatory surgery patients: A double-blind, placebo-controlled study. *Anesthesia and Analgesia*, 106 (6): 1728–1732.
Overton, S. L. and Medina, S. L. (2008). The stigma of mental illness. *Journal of Counseling and Development*, 86(2): 143–151.
Owen, D. J. and Fang, M. L. (2003). Information-seeking behavior in complementary and alternative medicine (CAM): An online survey of faculty at a health sciences campus. *Journal of the Medical Library Association*, 91(3): 311–321.

Owen, R. T. (2007). Pregabalin: Its efficacy, safety and tolerability profile in generalized anxiety. *Drugs Today*, 43(9): 601.

Palatnik, A., Frolov, K., Fux, M., and Benjamin, J. (2001). Double-blind, crossover trial of inositol versus fluvoxamine for the treatment of panic disorder. *Journal of Clinical Psychopharmacology*, 21: 335–339.

Panossian, A. and Wagner, H. (2005). Stimulating effects of adaptogens: An overview with particular reference to their efficacy following single dose administration. *Phytotherapy Research*, 19(10): 819–838.

Pittler, M. H. and Ernst, E. (2000). Efficacy of kava extract for treating anxiety: Systematic review and meta-analysis. *Journal of Clinical Psychopharmacology*, 20 (1): 84–89.

Pittler, M. H. and Ernst, E. (2003). Kava extract versus placebo for treating anxiety. *Cochrane Database of Systematic Reviews*, 2003(1): CD003383.

Powers, M. B. and Emmelkamp, P. M. G. (2008). Virtual reality exposure therapy for anxiety disorders: A meta-analysis. *Journal of Anxiety Disorders*, 22: 561–569.

Powers, M. B., Halpern, J. M., Ferenschak, M. P., Gillihan, S. J., and Foa, E. B. (2010). A meta-analytic review of prolonged exposure for post-traumatic stress disorder. *Clinical Psychology Review*, 30(6): 635–641.

Rivas-Vazquez, R. A. (2003). Benzodiazepines in contemporary clinical practice. *Professional Psychology: Research and Practice*, 34(3): 324–328.

Rosen, C. S., Chow, H. C., Finney, J. F. *et al.* (2004). VA practice patterns and practice guidelines for treating post-traumatic stress disorder. *Journal of Traumatic Stress*, 17(3): 213–222.

Ross, B. M. (2009). Omega-3 polyunsaturated fatty acids and anxiety disorders. *Prostaglandins, Leukotrienes, and Essential Fatty Acids*, 81: 309–312.

Ross, B. M., Sunguin, J., and Sieswerda, L. (2007). Omega-3 fatty acids as treatments for mental illness: Which disorder and which fatty acid? *Lipids in Health and Disease*, 6: 1–19.

Saeed, S. A., Bloch, R. M., and Antonacci, D. J. (2007). Herbal and dietary supplements for treatment of anxiety disorders. *American Family Physician*, 76(4): 549–556.

Sageman, S. and Brown, R. P. (2006). 3-acetyl-7-oxo-dehydroepiandrosterone for healing treatment resistant post-traumatic stress disorder in women: 5 case reports. *Journal of Clinical Psychiatry*, 67(3): 493–496.

Schmidt, P. J., Daly, R. C., Bloch, M. *et al.* (2005). Dehydroepiandrosterone monotherapy in midlife-onset major and minor depression. *Archives of General Psychiatry*, 62(2): 154–162.

Schruers, K., van Diest, R., Overbek, T., and Griez, E. (2002). Acute L-5-hydroxytryptophan administration inhibits carbon dioxide-induced panic in panic disorder patients. *Psychiatry Research*, 113: 237–243.

Scripnikov, A., Khomenko, A., and Napryeyenko, O. (2007). Effects of Ginkgo biloba extract EGb 761 on neuropsychiatric symptoms of dementia: Findings from a randomized controlled trial. *Wien Medizin Wochenschrift*, 157: 295–300.

Shaw, K., Turner, J., and Del Mar, C. (2002). Are tryptophan and 5-hydroxytryptophan effective treatments for depression: A meta-analysis. *The Australian and New Zealand Journal of Psychiatry*, 36(4): 488–491.

Singh, Y. N. and Singh, N. N. (2002). Therapeutic potential of kava in the treatment of anxiety disorders. *CNS Drugs*, 16(11): 731–743.

Smits, J. A. J. and Hofmann, S. G. (1998). A meta-analytic review of the effects of psychotherapy control conditions for anxiety disorders. *Psychological Medicine*, 39: 229–239.
Smits, J. A. J. and Hofmann, S. G. (2009). A meta-analytic review of the effects of psychotherapy control conditions. *Psychological Medicine*, 39(2), 229–239.
Smigra, M. and Torii, K. (2003). L-Lysine acts like a partial serotonin receptor 4 antagonist and inhibits serotonin-mediated intestinal pathologies and anxiety in rats. *Proceedings of the National Academy of Sciences of the United States of America*, 100(26), 15370–15375.
Smriga, M., Ando, T., Akutsu, M., Furukawa, Y., Miwa, K., and Morinaga, Y. (2007). Oral treatment with L-lysine and L-arginine reduces anxiety and basal cortisol levels in healthy humans. *Biomedical Research*, 28: 85–90.
Søholm, B. (1998). Clinical improvement of memory and other cognitive functions by Ginkgo biloba: Review of relevant literature. *Advances in Therapy*, 15(1): 54–65.
Spielberger, C. D., Gorsuch, R. L., and Lushene, R. E. (1970). *Manual for the State-Trait Anxiety Inventory*. Palo Alto, CA: Consulting Psychologists Press.
Srinongkote, S. Smriga, M., Nakagawa, K., and Toride, Y. (2003). A diet fortified with L-lysine and L-arginine reduces plasma cortisol and blocks anxiogenic response to transportation in pigs. *Nutritional Neuroscience*, 6(5): 283–289.
Taylor, L. V., and Kobak, K. A. (2000). An open-label trial of St John's wort (Hypericum perforatum) in obsessive-compulsive disorder. *Journal of Clinical Psychiatry*, 61: 575–578.
Teschke, R., Schwarzenboeck, A., and Akinci, A. (2008). Kava hepatotoxicity: A European view. *New Zealand Medical Journal*, 121: 90–98.
Tsubuku, S., Hatayama, K., Mawatari, K., Smriga, M., and Kimura, T. (2004a). Thirteen-week oral toxicity study of L-arginine in rats. *International Journal of Toxicology*, 23(2): 101–105.
Tsubuku, S., Mochizuki, M., Mawatari, K., Smriga, M., and Kimura, T. (2004b). Thirteen-week oral toxicity study of L-lysine hydrochloride in rats. *International Journal of Toxicology*, 23(2): 113–118.
US Food and Drug Administration. (1994). Dietary Supplement Health and Education Act of 1994. http://www.fda.gov/Food/DietarySupplements/ConsumerInformation/ucm110417.htm#what
US Food and Drug Administration Center for Safety and Applied Nutrition (2002). Letter to health care professionals: FDA issues consumer advisory that Kava products may be associated with severe liver injury. http://www.fda.gov/Food/ResourcesForYou/Consumers/ucm085482.htm
Volz, H. P. and Kieser, M. (1997). Kava-kava extract WS 1490 versus placebo in anxiety disorders: A randomized placebo-controlled 25-week outpatient trial. *Pharmacopsychiatry*, 30: 1–5.
Wang, P. S., Demler, O., and Kessler, R. C. (2002). Adequacy of treatment for serious mental illness in the United States. *American Journal of Public Health*, 92(1): 92–98.
Wang, P. S., Lane, M., Olfson, M., Pincus, H. A., Wells, K. B., and Kessler, R. C. (2005). Twelve-month use of mental health services in the United States: Results from the National Comorbidity Survey Replication. *Archives of General Psychiatry*, 62: 629–640.
Watkins, L. L., Connor, K. M., and Davidson, J. R. (2001). Effect of kava extract on vagal cardiac control in generalized anxiety disorder: preliminary findings. *Journal of Psychopharmacology*, 15(4): 283–286.

Witte, S., Loew, D., and Gaus, W. (2005). Meta-analysis of the efficacy of the acetonic kava-kava extract WS1490 in patients with non-psychotic anxiety disorders. *Phytotherapy Research*, 19: 138–188.

Woelk, H., and Schläfke, S. (2010). A multi-center, double-blind, randomized study of the lavender oil preparation Silexan in comparison to Lorazepam for generalized anxiety disorder. *Phytomedicine*, 17(2): 94–99.

Woelk, H., Arnoldt, K. H., Kieser, M., and Hoerr, R. (2007). Ginkgo biloba special extract EGb761 in generalized anxiety disorder and adjustment disorder with anxious mood: A randomized, double-blind, placebo-controlled trial. *Journal of Psychiatric Research*, 41(6): 472–480.

Wolkowitz, O. M., Reus, V. I., Roberts, E. *et al.* (1995). Antidepressant and cognition-enhancing effects of DHEA in major depression. *Annals of the New York Academy of Sciences*, 29(774): 337–339.

Wolkowitz, O. M., Reus, V. I., Keebler, A. *et al.* (1999). Double-blind treatment of major depression with dehydroepiandrosterone. *The American Journal of Psychiatry*, 156(4): 646–649.

Yamada, T., Terashima, T., Okubo, T., Juneja, L. R., and Yokogoshi, H. (2005). Effects of theanine, r-glutamylethylamide, on neutrotransmitter release and its relationship with glutamic acid neurotransmission. *Nutrition and Neuroscience*, 8 (4): 219–226.

Yehuda, S., Rabinovitz, S., and Mostofsky, D. I., (2005). Mixture of essential fatty acids lowers test anxiety. *Nutrition and Neuroscience*, 8(4): 265–267.

Yoshikuni, Y. (2008). GRAS (generally recognized as safe) notice for gamma-amino butyric acid (GABA). www.accessdata.fda.gov/scripts/fcn/gras_notices/807973A.pdf

Yuan, C. S., Mehendale, S., Xiao, Y., Aung, H. H., Xie, J. T., and Ang-Lee, M. K. (2004). The gamma-aminobutyric acidergic effects of valerian and valerenic acid on rat brainstem neuronal activity. *Anesthesia and Analgesia*, 17(1): 63–68.

Zenk, J. L., Frestedt, J. L., and Kuskowski, M. A. (2007). HUM5007, a novel combination of thermogenic compounds, and 3-acetyl-7-oxo-dehydroepiandrosterone: Each increases the resting metabolic rate of overweight adults. *The Journal of Nutritional Biochemistry*, 18(9): 629–634.

Zigmond, A. S. and Snaith, R.P. (1983) The Hospital Anxiety and Depression Scale. *Acta Psychiatrica Scandinavica*, 67: 361–370.

Chapter 10

A ROADMAP FOR THE RESEARCH AND PRACTICE OF COMBINATION STRATEGIES

Stefan G. Hofmann
Department of Psychology, Boston University, Boston, MA, USA

The most effective psychological treatment for anxiety disorders is cognitive-behavioral therapy (CBT). This treatment is typically administered in the form of 12 to 15 weekly 1-hour individual or group treatment sessions (Hofmann and Smits 2008; Stewart and Chambless 2009; Cape *et al.* 2010). The intervention consists of several distinct but interwoven treatment components. At its core, it combines cognitive restructuring techniques and exposure techniques. As part of the cognitive techniques, patients practice identifying maladaptive cognitions (automatic thoughts), observing the covariation between anxious mood and automatic thoughts, examining the errors of logic, and formulating rational alternatives to their automatic thoughts. As part of the exposure practices, patients are asked to identify avoidance strategies and to eliminate them while exposing themselves to anxiety-provoking situations that appear to violate their personal social standards. During the course of treatment, patients typically confront increasingly difficult feared situations while applying cognitive restructuring techniques and eliminating any forms of avoidance strategies. In addition, behavioral experiments are utilized to confront specific reactions to exposure experiences.

As summarized in Chapters 2–4, other common therapies include traditional (anxiolytic) pharmacological agents, including benzodiazepines, selective serotonin reuptake inhibitors (SSRIs), monoamine oxidase inhibitors (MAOIs), and tricyclic antidepressants, among other drugs. Although both treatment modalities (CBT and traditional anxiolytic

---

Psychobiological Approaches for Anxiety Disorders: Treatment Combination Strategies, First Edition. Edited by Stefan G. Hofmann.
© 2012 John Wiley & Sons, Ltd. Published 2012 by John Wiley & Sons, Ltd.

pharmacological agents) are more efficacious than placebo, there is clearly still room for further improvement. For example, a more complete analysis of placebo-controlled CBT trials showed an average placebo-controlled treatment effect size of only 0.73 (Hofmann and Smits 2008). Similarly, pharmacotherapy trials consistently report modest effects of anxiolytics for treating anxiety disorders (Roy-Byrne and Cowley 2002). Surprisingly, combining these two treatment modalities is not consistently more effective than the monotherapies (Otto *et al.* 2006).

This disappointing state of affairs raises a number of important theoretical and practical questions. Instead of presenting yet another critical review of the existing treatment literature, I will outline a roadmap describing some promising new and fruitful avenues for future research. This roadmap is intended to encourage the field to move into some new research directions. These directions include the following:

- a move beyond the traditional horse race comparison of clinical trials and toward translational medicine;
- a move toward understanding the mechanism of treatment change; and
- a move toward personalized medicine to identify biomarkers for maximizing treatment outcome.

MOVING BEYOND THE HORSE RACE COMPARISON OF CLINICAL TRIALS AND TOWARD TRANSLATIONAL MEDICINE

In an attempt to maximize treatment efficacy, a number of studies have examined the efficacy of combining CBT and conventional anxiolytic medications. This strategy was based on the presumption that combining two mediocre treatment strategies might somehow lead to improved efficacy, either by acting synergistically through different mechanisms or by adding their efficacy through the same mechanism.

However, clinical trials examining the efficacy of such combination treatments yielded disappointing results. For example, a meta-analysis comparing CBT plus anxiolytic medication with CBT plus pill placebo only showed modest benefits of combination strategies immediately after treatment and no added benefit at 6-month follow-up (Hofmann *et al.* 2009). Moreover, clinical trials often report that over half of patients do not respond fully to CBT or pharmacologic interventions. In virtually all studies, a large proportion of patients remain symptomatic after the initial intervention, and the combination between CBT and the active drug usually does not outperform the combination between CBT and a pill placebo. These data question the notion that combination therapy has a clear advantage over CBT alone or CBT plus pill placebo.

The reason for this disappointing finding is not clear. It is possible that the affect modulating properties of pharmacotherapy and their associated side effects may interfere with CBT by providing conditions for state-dependent learning during the exposure-based therapy sessions. In other words, discontinuing the medication may alter the internal state, which may in turn interfere with the learning during exposure-based therapy that happens during an internal state due to the influence of the pharmacological agent. This perspective receives some support from animal studies, suggesting that extinction learning from exposure to feared cues is sensitive to context effects (Bouton 2002; 2004). It is also possible that the anxiolytic effect of pharmacotherapy inhibits the full activation of the fear structure, leading to a suppression of emotion processing of the feared stimuli (Foa and Kozak 1986). This account is consistent with studies, suggesting that strategies to decrease the perceived threat of exposure lead to less fear reduction (Powers *et al.* 2004). Finally, it is possible that the fear reduction during exposure-based therapy are attributed to the pill rather than the exposure practices during combined treatment, which may negatively affect the person's perception of self-efficacy with regards to the treatment gains.

Whatever the reason for these puzzling results, it has become apparent that simple randomized controlled trials that directly pitch CBT against pharmacotherapy typically yield disappointing results, and a combination strategy between CBT and anxiolytic medications does not reliably lead to a more efficacious intervention than the monotherapies. The reason is not certain and it is not easy to explain these results, in part because the theoretical model to justify a combination between two monotherapies has been underdeveloped in the first place, to say the least. Therefore, future research studies will need to move away from a simple head-to-head horse race comparison toward developing a heuristically valuable treatment change model that would explain why a combination strategy should produce better effects than the monotherapies. Instead, clinical trials should be informed by basic neuroscience research that examines the mechanism and biological correlates of behavior change. However, in order to accomplish this, researchers and funding agencies alike will need to spend more time and energy to investigate the mechanisms through which the treatments are supposed to work.

MOVING TOWARD UNDERSTANDING THE MECHANISM OF TREATMENT CHANGE

The mechanism of treatment change in psychiatry is poorly understood. It could be argued that the treatment mechanism model of CBT might be more developed than the model of anxiolytic medications. The CBT model assumes that dysfunctional cognitions are causally linked to emotional distress. Correcting these dysfunctional cognitions is assumed to result in improvement of emotional distress and maladaptive behaviors. Therefore, the core model of CBT holds that cognitions causally influence emotions and behaviors and, in the case of dysfunctional thoughts and cognitive distortions, contribute to the maintenance of psychopathology.

A core element of CBT is cognitive reappraisal, and effective emotion regulation strategies. Although CBT places a focus on the cognitive realm, the physiological, emotional, and behavioral components are also clearly recognized for the role that they play in the disorder. In short, from the CBT perspective, it is the way one thinks about a situation or experience that influences the way he or she feels and behaves in the context of that situation or experience. Negative emotions – such as fear, panic, and anxiety – as well as harmful behaviors, are products of dysfunctional thoughts and cognitive distortions.

Recent mediation studies support this model. The methodological procedures to investigate mediation are complicated and have only recently been developed. Examples include regression discontinuation and interrupted time series for single-group study designs (Doss and Atkins 2006), structural equation modeling procedures for longitudinal tests (Cole and Maxwell 2003), multilevel models (Kenny *et al.* 2003), and linear regression models for randomized controlled trials (Kraemer *et al.* 2002). Data have since accumulated to support the CBT model for the treatment of panic disorder (Hofmann *et al.* 2007), social anxiety disorder (Hofmann 2004; Smits *et al.* 2006), obsessive-compulsive disorder (Moore and Abramowitz 2007), depression (Kaysen *et al.* 2005; Tang *et al.* 2005), and pain (Price 2000), to name only a few.

Similarly, it will be important to understand the treatment mechanisms of anxiolytic medications. In the case of agents that act on the dopamine system, it has been shown that catecholamine modulation, especially prefrontal cortex dopamine, is implicated in higher cognition, such as working memory. For example, the D1 receptor in the dorsolateral prefrontal cortex appears to be critically involved in spatial working memory performance in monkeys (Sawaguchi and Goldman-Rakic 1991). D1 receptor activation appears to attenuate the recurrent excitation, probably by presynaptic inhibition of glutamate release (Seamans and Yang 2004). There is evidence to suggest that D1 receptor activation adjusts the gain (i.e. the strength of the representation) of the glutamate-encoded information in the prefrontal cortex, which includes a depression of background prefrontal cortex activity, making the self-sustained activity robust to noise and distractors (Durstewitz and Seamans 2002).

Aside from working memory and cognition, dopamine has been implicated in various other brain processes, such as motivation and reward seeking. Neuro-imaging and lesion studies suggest that a high binding potential at dopamine receptors in brain areas, such as the mesolimbic and striatal regions, seem to be related to a greater frequency of anxiety and compulsion-related disorders (Stein and Ludik 2000; Olver *et al.* 2009; de la Mora *et al.* 2010). Similar patterns in dopaminergic receptors have been observed in these brain regions in individuals reporting symptoms of generalized social anxiety disorder (Sareen *et al.* 2007; van der Wee *et al.* 2008; Furmark 2009). Given the observation of higher binding potential of dopamine to its receptors in the striatal regions of the brain, direct methods that target the blockade of these dopamine receptors by dopamine antagonists to ideally produce anxiolytic effects would be a promising area to explore further, particularly for reduction in symptoms of OCD and social anxiety disorder.

Other agents, such as D-cycloserine (DCS: Chapter 5), yohimbine (Chapter 6), and cortisol (Chapter 7), have been classified as cognitive enhancers (for a review, see also Hofmann 2007; Hofmann *et al.* 2011) based on their assumed mechanism through which the drugs augment learning during CBT (Hofmann 2008). Oxytocin (Chapter 8), propranolol (Chapter 9), and various nutritional supplements (Chapter 10) are other agents that might head a paradigm shift when it comes to combination strategies. Neither of these agents is used as a stand-alone anxiolytic medication. Instead, the agents are used to augment a process that is believed to be critical in CBT. In the case of DCS, the agent acts as a partial agonist of the glycine recognition site of the glutamatergic N-methyl-D-aspartate receptor complex to facilitate extinction learning in animals and exposure therapy in humans. The infrahuman and clinical studies are examples of new approaches in combination strategies. This approach is genuinely translational in nature and not only points to new drug targets, but may also clarify the basic biological mechanisms of therapy.

MOVING TOWARD PERSONALIZED MEDICINE USING BIOMARKERS

Future research needs to focus on the basic mechanisms of treatment change and the factors that account for individual differences in these mechanisms. Treatment failures should not be considered a nuisance but as opportunities to refine existing disease models, nosology, improve the treatment options, and identify the biological markers that predict treatment response to pharmacotherapy, psychotherapy, and combination therapy. Promising research to identify such biomarkers comes from neuro-imaging and EEG experiments (neuromarkers) and genetic studies.

Evidence for the existence of neuromarkers has been reported in studies on dyslexia. It has been shown that evoked-response potentials (ERP) measured in newborns that were at risk for developing reading difficulty based on their family history correlated with language and reading scores years later (Molfese *et al.* 2001). Moreover, ERP assessed at a very young age and before children learned how to read was the best and only predictor of reading ability 5 years later (Maurer et al. 2009). Similarly, certain fMRI patterns of activation were 92% accurate in predicting reading gains among dyslexic children over a 2.5 year period (Hoeft et al. 2007).

Neuromarkers have also been found to predict clinical outcome and response to treatment in various psychiatric disorders. For example, neuro-imaging data predicted recovery from depression 8 months later (Canli et al. 2005), relapse in methamphetamine-dependence 1 year later (Paulus et al. 2005), response to drug treatment for depression (Davidson et al. 2003; Fu et al. 2004) and anxiety (Whalen et al. 2008), CBT response in schizophrenia (Kumari et al. 2009), and onset of psychosis in at-risk individuals (Koutsouleris et al. 2009). In many cases, the neuromarkers were more predictive than commonly-used self-report scales and structured interviews. For example, pre-treatment fMRI activation in the subgenual cingulate cortex in depression (Siegle et al. 2006) and the dorsolateral prefrontal cortex in schizophrenia (Kumari et al. 2009) accounted for more than half of the between-subjects variance after CBT. In one study with methamphetamine-dependent patients, the fMRI data gathered early in recovery and after a 28-day treatment program correctly predicted 20 of 22 subjects who did not relapse and 17 of 18 subjects who did relapse 1 year later (Paulus et al. 2005).

Future studies should, therefore, examine whether there are neuromarkers that predict differential response to CBT versus pharmacotherapy. One possible concern that could be raised regarding the practical application of fMRI for identifying neuromarkers to guide treatment choice might be related to financial costs. However, the cost of gathering neuroimaging data might outweigh the cost associated with a failed course of treatment, both in terms of the financial and emotional burden. Furthermore, structural fMRI data and functional connectivity data, which are considerably less costly than fMRI data, might also be useful for identifying neuromarkers.

Another potential concern might be that fMRI and other imaging techniques, which are useful research tools for comparing average group differences, may not offer reliable information about single patients to match them to specific treatment modalities due to the low signal/noise ratios that make precise measurement difficult. However, the existing methods, such as clinical interviews, self-report measures, and behavioral assessment, have had very limited success in predicting treatment outcome, let alone differential treatment outcomes. Therefore, exploring neuromarkers would be extremely valuable for matching patients to a specific treatment modality, in line with a personalized medicine approach.

A related question would be whether CBT and pharmacotherapy in a particular psychiatric disorder alter brain function in similar, dissimilar, or partially overlapping ways. For example, in depression, most studies have found at least partially different brain changes associated with behavioral therapy versus pharmacotherapy (Martin et al. 2001; Goldapple et al. 2004; Kennedy et al. 2007).

Another promising avenue for treatment prediction offers genes as possible biomarkers for treatment. One such biomarker might be the brain-derived neurotrophic factor (BDNF), which is part of the neurotrophin family of growth factors, and is a biological substrate of certain anxiety disorders (Kaplan et al. 2010). It also plays an important role in synaptic plasticity of neurons involved in learning and memory (Egan et al. 2003; Hariri et al. 2003), possibly by mediating consolidation of extinction memory within the infralimbic medial prefrontal cortex (Nestler et al. 2002; Charney and Maniji 2004; Yu et al. 2009). A study by Kobayashi et al. (2005) examined 42 outpatients with panic disorder with manualized CBT and found that patients with poor response to CBT had significantly lower serum BDNF levels (25.9 ng/ml (S.D. 8.7]) relative to patients with good response to CBT (33.7 ng/ml (S.D. 7.5]). It has been shown that a single nucleotide polymorphism in the BDNF gene (Val66Met) influences hippocampal volume and hippocampal dependent memory (Egan et al. 2003; Hariri et al. 2003; Bueller et al. 2006). It has also been shown that $BDNF_{Met}$ allele carriers exhibit less ventromedial prefrontal cortical activity and greater amygdala activation (Soliman et al. 2010), suggesting a hypo-responsiveness in $BDNF_{Met}$ allele carriers in brain regions crucial for extinction learning. Thus, it is possible that $BDNF_{Met}$ allele carriers might respond more poorly to CBT than to pharmacotherapy.

Similarly, KIBRA might serve as a biomarker that might determine a differential response to CBT versus pharmacotherapy. KIBRA is a molecule that is involved with the postsynaptic protein dendrin (Kremerskothen et al. 2003) and has been shown to play a key genetic role in memory and cognition (Papassotiropoulos et al. 2006). Carriers of certain KIBRA T alleles (rs17070145, rs6439886) perform significantly better in tasks involving multiple episodic memories compared to individuals that are homozygous for the C allele at either polymorphism (Schneider et al., 2010). Furthermore, fMRI studies have found greater activation in brain areas associated with memory retrieval in the rs17070145 T-allele-noncarriers as compared to T-allele carriers on an episodic memory task, suggesting a strong effect of a genetic contribution to certain types of memory. To date, no studies have examined KIBRA in anxiety or mood disorders.

Another candidate biomarker and genetic predictor for differential treatment response include the serotonin transporter gene (5HTTLPR), which has been linked to amygdala activation (Hariri et al. 2002; Furmark et al. 2004; Heinz et al. 2005; Smolka et al. 2007; Dannlowski et al. 2008), anxiety sensitivity (Stein et al. 2008), HPA axis activation (Gotlib et al. 2008), and attentional vigilance to threat (Beevers et al. 2007; Hayden et al. 2008). Other possible genetic treatment predictors include the dopamine transporter gene, the D2 dopamine receptor gene, and the monoamine oxidase A gene.

CONCLUSION

As proposed in this chapter, I recommend that the field of psychiatry and pharmacology explores new avenues of combination research, which will:

- move us beyond the traditional horse race comparison of clinical trials and toward translational research from 'bench to bedside;'
- move us closer toward understanding the mechanism of treatment change; and
- move us closer toward personalized medicine by tailoring the treatment to the client based on certain biomarkers.

Exploring such avenues could open up enormous opportunities for new drug targets, new indications for existing drugs, and new psychological strategies.

Psychiatry and neuroscience has been poorly integrated with little cross-fertilization; and within psychiatry, assessments and treatment strategies have been poorly connected. In other words, diagnosis does not directly translate to specific treatment strategies. Although some strategies are clearly more suitable than others for a given diagnosis, there are usually multiple possible treatment option for any particular disorder and patient. Yet, contemporary treatment models of anxiety disorders, which are aligned with the medical classification system of mental disorders, assume the same underlying disease model for patients sharing the same diagnoses. In essence, treatment models have been limited by the categories of the Diagnostic and Statistical Manual of Mental Disorders, 4th Edition Text Revision (DSM-IV-TR; American Psychiatric Association 2000) and the International Classification of Diseases-10 (ICD-10; World Health Organization 1992; 1993). Although, contemporary disease models most typically focus on understanding and explaining psychopathology reflected by specific DSM/ICD diagnostic categories, it would be more fruitful to adopt an integrative approach that accounts for the complex interplay between genetic, biological, cognitive, behavioral, neurobiological, and sociocultural mechanisms beyond a purely symptom-based conceptualization.

The NIMH Research Domain Criteria (RDoC), http://www.nimh.nih.gov/research-funding/rdoc/nimh-research-domain-criteria-rdoc.shtml is an attempt to develop a new way of classifying individuals based on behavioral measures and neurobiological dimensions. Approaches such as these have substantial potential for further enhancing our understanding of presenting problems, clarifying the treatment models, and increasing the effectiveness of the treatments available for various disorders.

ACKNOWLEDGMENT

Work on this manuscript was supported in part by MH078308. Dr Hofmann has received consulting and/or research support from Organon (Merck/Schering-Plough).

REFERENCES

American Psychiatric Association (2000). *Diagnostic and statistical manual of mental disorders* (4th ed., text revision; DSM-IV-TR). Washington DC.

Beevers, C. G., Gibb, B. E., McGeary, J. E., and Miller, I. W. (2007). Serotonin transporter genetic variation and biased attention for emotional word stimuli among psychiatric inpatients. *Journal of Abnormal Psychology*, 116: 208–212.

Bouton, M. E. (2002). Context, ambiguity, and unlearning: Sources of relapse after behavioral extinction. *Biological Psychiatry*, 52: 976–986.

Bouton, M. E. (2004). Context and behavioral processes in extinction. *Learning and Memory*, 11: 485–494.

Bueller, J. A., Aftab, M., Sen, S., Gomez-Hassan, D., Burmeister, M., and Zubieta, J. K. (2006). BDNF Val66Met allele is associated with reduced hippocampal volume in healthy subjects. *Biological Psychiatry*, 599: 812–815.

Canli, T., Cooney, R. E., Goldin, P. *et al.* (2005). Amygdala reactivity to emotional faces predicts improvement in major depression. *Neuroreport*, 16: 1267–1270.

Cape, J., Whittington, C., Buszewicz, M., Wallace, P., and Underwood, L. (2010). Brief psychological therapies for anxiety and depression in primary care: Meta-analysis and meta-regression. *BMC Medicine*, 25: 38.

Charney, D. S. and Manji, H. K. (2004). Life stress, genes, and depression: multiple pathways lead to increased risk and new opportunities for intervention. *Science STKE*, 225: re5.

Cole, D. A. and Maxwell, S. E. (2003). Testing mediational models with longitudinal data: Questions and tips in the use of structural equation modeling. *Journal of Abnormal Psychology*, 112: 558–577.

Dannlowski, U., Ohrmann, P., Bauer, J. *et al.* (2008). 5-HTTLPR biases amygdala activity in response to masked facial expressions in major depression. *Neuropsychopharmacology*, 33: 418–424.

Davidson, R. J., Irwin, W., Anderle, M. J., and Kalin, N. H. (2003). The neural substrates of affective processing in depressed patients treated with venlafaxine. *American Journal of Psychiatry*, 160: 64–75.

de la Mora, M. P., Gallegos-Cari, A., Arizmendi-García, Y., Marcellino, D., and Fuxe, K. (2010). Role of dopamine receptor mechanisms in the amygdaloid modulation of fear and anxiety: Structural and functional analysis. *Progress in Neurobiology*, 90: 198–216.

Doss, B. D. and Atkins, D. C. (2006). Investigating treatment mediators when simple random assignment to a control group is not possible, *Clinical Psychology: Science and Practice*, 13: 321–336.

Durstewitz, D. and Seamans, J. K. (2002). The computational role of dopamine D1 receptors in working memory. *Neural Networks*, 15: 561–72.

Egan, M. F., Kojima, M., Callicott, J. H. *et al.* (2003). The BDNF val66met polymorphism affects activity-dependent secretion of BDNF and human memory and hippocampal function. *Cell*, 112: 257–269.

Foa, E. B., and Kozak, M. J. (1986). Emotional processing of fear: Exposure to corrective information. *Psychological Bulletin*, 99: 20–35.

Fu, C. H., Williams, S. C., Cleare, A. J. *et al.* (2004). Attenuation of the neural functional magnetic resonance imaging study. *Archives of General Psychiatry*, 61: 877–889.

Furmark, T. (2009). Neurobiological aspects of social anxiety disorder. *Journal of Psychiatry and Related Sciences*, 46: 5–12.

Furmark, T., Tillfors, M., Garpenstrand, H. *et al.* (2004). Serotonin transporter polymorphism related to amygdala excitability and symptom severity in patients with social phobia. *Neuroscience Letters*, 362: 189–192.

Goldapple, K., Segal, Z., Garson, C. *et al.* (2004). Modulation of cortical-limbic pathways in major depression: treatment-specific effects of cognitive behavior therapy. *Archives of General Psychiatry*, 61: 34–41.

Gotlib, I. H., Joormann, J., Minor, K. L., and Hallmayer, J. (2008). HPA axis reactivity: A mechanism underlying the associations among 5-HTTLPR, stress, and depression. *Biological Psychiatry*, 63: 847–851.

Hariri, A. R., Mattay, V. S., Tessitore, A. *et al.* (2002). Serotonin transporter genetic variation and the response of the human amygdala. *Science*, 297: 400–403.

Hariri, A. R., Goldberg, T. E., Mattay, V. S. *et al.* (2003). Brain-derived neurotrophic factor val66met polymorphism affects human memory-related hippocampal activity and predicts memory performance. *Journal of Neuroscience*, 23: 6690–6694.

Hayden, E. P., Dougherty, L. R., Maloney, B. *et al.* (2008). Early-emerging cognitive vulnerability to depression and the serotonin transporter promoter region polymorphism. *Journal of Affective Disorders*, 107: 227–230.

Heinz, A., Braus, D. F., Smolka, M. N. *et al.* (2005). Amygdala-prefrontal coupling depends on a genetic variation of the serotonin transporter. *Nature Neuroscience*, 8: 20–21.

Hoeft, F., Ueno, T., Reiss, A. L. *et al.* (2007). Prediction of children's reading skills using behavioral, functional, and structural neuro-imaging measures. *Behavioral Neuroscience*, 121: 602–613.

Hofmann, S. G. (2004). Cognitive mediation of treatment change in social phobia. *Journal of Consulting and Clinical Psychology*, 72: 392–399.

Hofmann, S. G. (2007). Enhancing exposure-based therapy from a translational research perspective. *Behaviour Research and Therapy*, 45: 1987–2001.

Hofmann, S. G. (2008). Cognitive processes during fear acquisition and extinction in animals and humans: Implications for exposure therapy of anxiety disorders. *Clinical Psychology Review*, 28: 199–210.

Hofmann, S. G. and Smits, J. A. (2008). Cognitive-behavioral therapy for adult anxiety disorders: a meta-analysis of randomized placebo-controlled trials. *Journal of Clinical Psychiatry*, 69: 621–632.

Hofmann, S. G., Meuret, A. E., Rosenfield, D. *et al.* (2007). Preliminary evidence for cognitive mediation during cognitive behavioral therapy for panic disorder. *Journal of Consulting and Clinical Psychology*, 75: 374–379.

Hofmann, S. G., Sawyer, A. T., Korte, K. J., and Smits, J. A. J. (2009). Is it beneficial to add pharmacotherapy to cognitive-behavioral therapy when treating anxiety disorders? A meta-analytic review. *International Journal of Cognitive Therapy*, 2: 160–175.

Hofmann, S. G., Smits, J. A. J., Asnaani, A., Gutner, C. A., and Otto, M. W. (2011). Cognitive enhancers for anxiety disorders. *Pharmacology, Biochemistry, and Behavior*, 99: 275–284.

Kaplan, G. B., Vasterling, J. J., and Vedak, P. C. (2010). Brain-derived neurotrophic factor in traumatic brain injury, post-traumatic stress disorder, and their comorbid conditions: role in pathogenesis and treatment. *Behavioral Pharmacology*, 21: 427–437.

Kaysen, D., Scher, C. D., Mastnak, J., and Reich, P. (2005). Cognitive mediation of childhood maltreatment and adult depression in recent crime victims. *Behavior Therapy*, 36: 235–244.

Kennedy, S. H., Konarski, J. Z., Segal, Z. V. et al. (2007). Differences in brain glucose metabolism between responders to CBT and venlafaxine in a 16-week randomized controlled trial. *American Journal of Psychiatry*, 164: 778–788.

Kenny, D. A., Korchmaros, J. D., and Bolger, N. (2003). Lower level mediation in multilevel models. *Psychological Methods*, 8: 115–28.

Kobayashi, K., Shimizu, E., Hashimoto, K. et al. (2005). Serum brain-derived neurotrophic factor (BDNF) levels in patients with panic disorder: as a biological predictor of response to group cognitive behavioral therapy. *Progress in Neuropsychopharmacology and Biological Psychiatry*, 29: 658–63.

Koutsouleris, N., Meisenzahl, E. M., Davatzikos, C. et al. (2009). Use of neuroanatomical pattern classification to identify subjects in at-risk mental states of psychosis and predict disease transition. *Archives of General Psychiatry*, 66: 700–712.

Kraemer, H. C., Wilson, T., Fairburn, C. G., and Agras, W. S. (2002). Mediators and moderators of treatment effects in randomized clinical trials. *Archives of General Psychiatry*, 59: 877–883.

Kremerskothen, J., Plaas, C., Büther, K. et al. (2003). Characterization of KIBRA, a novel WW domain-containing protein. *Biochemical and Biophysical Research Communications*, 300: 862–867.

Kumari, V., Peters, E. R., Fannon, D. et al. (2009). Dorsolateral prefrontal cortex activity predicts responsiveness to cognitive-behavioral therapy in schizophrenia. *Biological Psychiatry*, 66: 594–602.

Martin, S. D., Martin, E., Rai, S. S. Richardson, M. A., and Royall, R. (2001). Brain blood flow changes in depressed patients treated with interpersonal psychotherapy or venlafaxine hydrochloride: preliminary findings. *Archives of General Psychiatry*, 58: 641–648.

Maurer, U., Bucher, K., Brem, S. et al. (2009). Neurophysiology in preschool improves behavioral prediction of reading ability throughout primary school. *Biological Psychiatry*, 66: 341–348.

Molfese, V. J., Molfese, D. L., and Modgline, A. A. (2001). Newborn and preschool predictors of second-grade reading scores: an evaluation of categorical and continuous scores. *Journal of Learning Disabilities*, 34: 545–554.

Moore, E. L. and Abramowitz, J. S. (2007). The cognitive mediation of thought-control strategies. *Behaviour Research and Therapy*, 45: 1949–1955.

Nestler, E. J., Barrot, M., DiLeone, R. J., Eisch, A. J., Gold, S. J., and Monteggia, L. M. (2002). Neurobiology of depression. *Neuron*, 34: 13–25.

Olver, J. S., O'Keefe, G., Jones, G. R. et al. (2009). Dopamine D1 receptor binding in the striatum of patients with obsessive-compulsive disorder. *Journal of Affective Disorders*, 114: 321–326.

Otto, M. W., Smits, J. A. J., and Reese, H. E. (2006). Combined psychotherapy and pharmacotherapy for mood and anxiety disorders in adults: Review and analysis. *Clinical Psychology: Science and Practice*, 12: 72–86.

Papassotiropoulos, A., Stephan, D. A., Huentelman, M. J. et al. (2006). Common Kibra alleles are associated with human memory performance. *Science*, 314: 475–478.

Paulus, M. P., Tapert, S. F., and Schuckit, M. A. (2005). Neural activation patterns of methamphetaminedependent subjects during decision making predict relapse. *Archives of General Psychiatry*, 62: 761–768.

Powers, M. B., Smits, J. A., and Telch, M. J. (2004). Disentangling the effects of safety-behavior utilization and safety-behavior availability during exposure-based treatment: a placebo-controlled trial. *Journal of Consulting and Clinical Psychology*, 72: 448–454.

Price, D. D. (2000). Psychological and neural mechanisms of the affective dimension of pain, *Science*, 288: 1769–1772.

Sareen, J., Campbell, D. W., Leslie, W. D. et al. (2007). Striatal function in generalized social phobia: a functional magnetic resonance imaging study. *Biological Psychiatry*, 61: 396–404.

Sawaguchi, T. and Goldman-Rakic, P. S. (1991). D1 dopamine receptors in prefrontal cortex: involvement in working memory. *Science*, 251: 947–950.

Schneider, A., Huentelman, M. J., Kremerskothen, J., Duning, K., Spoelgen, R., and Nikolich, K. (2010). KIBRA: A New Gateway to Learning and Memory? *Frontiers in Aging Neuroscience*, 2: 4.

Seamans, J. K. and Yang, C. R. (2004). The principal features and mechanisms of dopamine modulation in the prefrontal cortex. *Progress in Neurobiology*, 74: 1–58.

Siegle, G. J., Carter, C. S., and Thase, M. E. (2006). Use of FMRI to predict recovery from unipolar depression with cognitive behavior therapy. *American Journal of Psychiatry*, 163: 735–738.

Smits, J. A. J., Rosenfield, D., Telch, M. J., and McDonald, R. (2006). Cognitive mechanisms of social anxiety reduction: An examination of specificity and temporality. *Journal of Consulting and Clinical Psychology*, 74: 1203–1212.

Smolka, M. N., Buhler, M., Schumann, G. et al. (2007). Gene-gene effects on central processing of aversive stimuli. *Molecular Psychiatry*, 12: 307–317.

Soliman, F., Glatt, C. E., Bath, K. G. et al. (2010). A genetic variant BDNF polymorphism alters extinction learning in both mouse and human. *Science*, 327: 863–866.

Stein, D. J. and Ludik, J. (2000). A neural network of obsessive-compulsive disorder: modeling cognitive disinhibition and neurotransmitter dysfunction. *Medical Hypotheses*, 55: 168–176.

Stein, M. B., Schork, N. J., and Gelernter, J. (2008). Gene-by-environment (serotonin transporter and childhood maltreatment) interaction for anxiety sensitivity, an intermediate phenotype for anxiety disorders. *Neuropsychopharmacology*, 33: 312–319.

Stewart, R. E. and Chambless, D. L. (2009). Cognitive-behavioral therapy for adult anxiety disorders in clinical practice: a meta-analysis of effectiveness studies. *Journal of Consulting and Clinical Psychology*, 77: 595–606.

Tang, T. Z., DeRubeis, R. J., Beberman, R., and Pham, T. (2005). Cognitive changes, critical sessions, and sudden gains in cognitive-behavioral therapy for depression. *Journal of Consulting and Clinical Psychology*, 73: 168–172.

van der Wee, N. J., van Veen, J. F., Stevens, H., van Vliet, I.M., van Rijk, P.P., and Westenberg, H. G. (2008). Increased serotonin and dopamine transporter binding in psychotropic medication-naive patients with generalized social anxiety disorder shown by 123I-beta-(4-iodophenyl)-tropane SPECT. *Journal of Nuclear Medicine*, 49: 757–763.

Whalen, P. J., Johnstone, T., Somerville, L. H. *et al.* (2008). A functional magnetic resonance imaging predictor of treatment response to venlafaxine in generalized anxiety disorder. *Biological Psychiatry*, 63: 858–863.

World Health Organization (1992). The ICD-10 classification of mental and behavioural disorders: Clinical descriptions and diagnostic guidelines. Geneva: World Health Organization.

World Health Organization (1993). The ICD-10 classification of mental and behavioural disorders: Diagnostic criteria for research. Geneva: World Health Organization.

Yu, H., Wang, Y., Pattwell, S. *et al.* (2009). Variant BDNF Val66Met polymorphism affects extinction of conditioned aversive memory. *Journal of Neuroscience*, 29: 4056–4064.

INDEX

absolute meta-analysis method   64–5
acrophobia   8
agoraphobia
　antidepressants   41–3, 45–51, 54–5
　D-cycloserine   83–4
alpha2-adrenoreceptor antagonists *see* yohimbine hydrochloride
alprazolam   12, 29, 162
alternative medicines   146
amygdala
　biomarkers   187
　combination strategies   7–8, 11
　cortisol   111–12
　D-cycloserine   77
　oxytocin   124–5, 134
　yohimbine hydrochloride   94–5
antidepressants
　agoraphobia   41–3, 45–51, 54–5
　clinical experience   43–4
　combination strategies   12–13, 26, 41–5, 47–57
　dietary supplements   149–50, 152
　discontinuation effects   43, 48, 52
　obsessive-compulsive disorder   41, 46, 51–4
　panic disorder   41–3, 45–51, 54–5, 57
　social anxiety disorder   41, 55–6
　see also individual drugs/drug classes
antipsychotics   135
L-arginine   152–3, 160
arginine vasopressin (AVP)   11
ASD *see* autism spectrum disorders
attention placebos   62
autism spectrum disorders (ASD)   123, 124, 127, 133
aversive memory   114, 117

avoidance of fear cues   27
AVP *see* arginine vasopressin

BAT *see* behavioral approach tasks
BDNF *see* brain-derived neurotrophic factor
Beck Anxiety Inventory   171
behavioral approach tasks (BAT)   98
benzodiazepines
　clinical experience   26–7
　combination strategies   12–13, 14–15, 25–33
　dietary supplements   163–5
　discontinuation effects   29–31, 32–3
　efficacy for anxiety disorders   25–6
　memory effects and cognitive behavioral therapy (CBT)   27–9, 31–3
　model cognitive behavioral therapy (CBT) combination strategy   31–2
biomarkers   185–8
borderline personality disorder (BPD)   123, 127, 129, 134–6
botanical supplements   146, 159–72
BPD *see* borderline personality disorder
brain-derived neurotrophic factor (BDNF)   187
brief dynamic psychotherapy   42, 50–1
buspirone
　combination strategies   12–13
　generalized anxiety disorder   69
　panic disorder   67, 68

caffeine   9, 30
CBT *see* cognitive behavioral therapy
central nervous system (CNS)   124, 156
cerebrospinal fluid (CSF)   125

Psychobiological Approaches for Anxiety Disorders: Treatment Combination Strategies, First Edition.   Edited by Stefan G. Hofmann.
© 2012 John Wiley & Sons, Ltd. Published 2012 by John Wiley & Sons, Ltd.

CGI *see* Clinical Global Impressions Scale
chamomile 169, 170
claustrophobia 98–9, 102
Clinical Global Impressions Scale (CGI) 64, 163, 170–1
clomipramine
　combination strategies 15–16, 42–3, 46, 50–4, 57
　dietary supplements 149–50, 151
CNS *see* central nervous system
cognitive behavioral therapy (CBT)
　antidepressants 42–5, 47–51, 55–7
　basic learning processes 75–7, 85–7
　benzodiazapines 25–39
　clinical experience 26–7, 43–4
　combination strategies 5–6, 7–8, 12–16
　cortisol 113–16, 118
　dietary supplements 146, 162
　discontinuation effects 29–31, 32–3
　efficacy and clinical trials 61–3
　follow-up studies 63–4, 68, 71
　generalized anxiety disorder 68–72
　mechanism of treatment change 183–5
　memory effects of benzodiazepines 27–9, 33
　meta-analyses 64–5
　model benzodiazepines (BZ) combination strategy 31–2
　panic disorder 65–8
　personalized medicine 186–7
　research and practice roadmap 181–8
　social anxiety disorder 69–72
　translational medicine 182–3
　yohimbine hydrochloride 91
cognitive restructuring 62
Cohen's *d* 148
combination strategies 5–24
　antidepressants 41–5, 47–57
　benzodiazepines and cognitive behavioral therapy (CBT) 25–39
　biomarkers 185–8
　clinical experience 26–7
　context 5–6
　cortisol 113–16, 118
　D-cycloserine 81–3, 84–7

developmental psychobiology 10
discontinuation effects 29–31, 32–3
generalized anxiety disorder 14, 68–72
mechanism of treatment change 183–5
memory effects 27–9, 33
model of benzodiazepines (BZ) and cognitive behavioral therapy (CBT) 31–2
neuroendocrine systems 10
neurotransmitters 7, 8–9
obsessive-compulsive disorder 15–16, 81–3, 84–5
oxytocin 132–5
panic disorder 12–13, 65–8
personalized medicine 185–8
post-traumatic stress disorder 11, 14–15
psychobiology 7–8, 17
research and practice roadmap 181–8
social anxiety disorder 8, 13–14, 69–72
social neuropeptides 11
translational medicine 182–3
yohimbine hydrochloride 91, 93, 97–100
comorbid disorders 5
compassion-focused imagery 129
complementary medicines 146
conditioned feared responses (CR) 76, 93–5
conditioned stimuli (CS) 76–7, 93–5
consolidation of memory 110–11, 114, 117
cortisol 109–22
　benzodiazepines 27–8, 33
　combination strategies 113–16, 118
　dietary supplements 153
　exposure therapy 113–16
　fear memories 113, 115
　hypothalamus-pituitary-adrenal axis 109
　memory consolidation 110–11, 114, 117
　memory regulation 110–15
　memory retrieval 111–12, 113–14, 116

social stress and anxiety   125–7
stress hormone activation   109–10, 115–16
underlying mechanisms for fear reduction   116–17
working memory   112–13
CR *see* conditioned feared responses
CS *see* conditioned stimuli
CSF *see* cerebrospinal fluid
cyberball paradigm   130, 133
D-cycloserine (DCS)   75–89
   agoraphobia   83–4
   animal models   78–9
   basic learning processes in cognitive behavioral therapy   75–7
   clinical applications in humans   79–84
   combination strategies   8–9, 13–16, 81–3, 84–7
   fear extinction   77–9
   implications for clinical practice   84–6
   obsessive-compulsive disorder   81–3, 84–5
   panic disorder   83–4
   post-traumatic stress disorder   79–80
   social anxiety disorder   80–1, 84
   specific phobias   80, 84

data search strategies   147
DCS *see* d-cycloserine
depression
   biomarkers   186–7
   combination strategies   5
   D-cycloserine   77
   oxytocin   124
developmental psychobiology   10–11
DHA *see* docosahexaenoic acid
diazepam   167
dietary supplements   145–80
   L-arginine   152–3, 160
   biological mechanisms   148, 150–6, 158–9, 162–4, 166
   chamomile   169, 170
   clinical potential   146–7
   context   145–6
   data search strategies   147
   effect size calculations   148

Galphimia glauca   169, 170–1
gamma-aminobutyric acid   157–8, 160, 166
generalized anxiety disorder   155, 161–2, 166, 170–1
Ginkgo biloba 167, 169–70
herbal supplements   146, 159–72
inositol   148–50, 160
kava   159–62, 168
7-keto dehydroepiandrosterone   158–9, 160
lavender   162–3, 168
L-lysine   152–3, 160
magnesium   154–6, 160
methodology   146–7
nutritional supplements   146, 148–59
obsessive-compulsive disorder   149–50, 165
omega-3 fatty acids   156–7, 160
panic disorder   149
passionflower   163–5, 168
review aims   147–8
Rhodiola rosea   171
St John's Wort   165–6, 168
side effects   150, 152–4, 156–9, 162–7
social phobia   165–6
L-theanine   153–4, 160
trial selection criteria   148
tryptophan/5-hydroxytryptophan   150–2, 160
valerian   166–7, 169
discontinuation effects
   antidepressants   43, 48, 52, 54
   combination strategies   29–31, 32–3
docosahexaenoic acid (DHA)   156–7
dopamine system   184–5, 187–8
double placebos   69
drop-out response   29
dyslexia   185–6

effect size calculations   148
eicosapentaenoic acid (EPA)   156–7
Emotion-Processing Theory   75–7
emotion recognition   127–9, 133, 135
emotional arousal   112–13
emotional consolidation   27
emotional learning   95–6

empathic accuracy 127–8
EPA *see* eicosapentaenoic acid
Erlangen Anxiety Tension and Aggression Scale 170
ERP *see* evoked-response potentials; exposure and response prevention
ethnicity 147
evoked-response potentials 185–6
exposure and response prevention 81–3
exposure therapy 63
   antidepressants 43, 46–7, 50, 52–4
   benzodiazepines and cognitive behavioral therapy 29–31
   cortisol 113–16
   D-cycloserine (DCS) 75–6, 84–7
   generalized anxiety disorder 69
   panic disorder 66–7
   translational medicine 183
   yohimbine hydrochloride 91, 93, 97–100
extinction learning
   benzodiazepines and cognitive behavioral therapy 27, 30
   cortisol 110–11, 113–15, 117
   D-cycloserine (DCS) 77–9, 86
   yohimbine hydrochloride 93–5, 96–7, 101, 103

facial expressions 128–30, 133
fear extinction
   benzodiazepines and cognitive behavioral therapy 27, 30
   cortisol 110–11, 113–15, 117
   D-cycloserine 77–9, 86
   yohimbine hydrochloride 93–5, 96–7, 101, 103
fear of flying 99–100, 102
flooding *see* therapist-directed exposure
fluoxetine 13, 69–70
fluvoxamine 15–16, 65–6, 68
fMRI *see* functional magnetic resonance imaging
follow-up studies 63–4, 68, 71
functional magnetic resonance imaging (fMRI) 94, 95, 186

GABA *see* gamma-aminobutyric acid
GAD *see* generalized anxiety disorder

Galphimia glauca 169, 170–1
gamma-aminobutyric acid (GABA) 157–8, 160, 166
General Health Questionnaire-28 (GHQ-28) 155
generalized anxiety disorder (GAD)
   antidepressants 44
   benzodiazepines and cognitive behavioral therapy 25–6, 33
   combination strategies 14–15, 68–72
   dietary supplements 155, 161–2, 166, 170–1
   selective serotonin reuptake inhibitors 68–72
   yohimbine hydrochloride 91
generosity 130
genetic factors 100
GHQ-28 *see* General Health Questionnaire-28
Ginkgo biloba 167, 169–70
glucocorticoid receptor (GR) agonist/antagonists 10–11
glucocorticoids 27
   see also cortisol
GR *see* glucocorticoid receptor

HADS *see* Hospital Anxiety and Depression Scale
Hamilton Anxiety Scale
   dietary supplements 149–52, 157, 161, 163–4, 167, 170–1
   selective serotonin reuptake inhibitors 64
Hamilton Depression Scale 150, 157
herbal supplements 30, 146, 159–72
Hospital Anxiety and Depression Scale (HADS) 155
HPA *see* hypothalamus-pituitary-adrenal
hydrocortisone 96
5-hydroxytryptophan (5-HT) 150–2, 160
Hypericum perforatum 165–6, 168
hypothalamus-pituitary-adrenal (HPA) axis 109, 125–6, 134, 187

imipramine 42–3, 45–50, 57, 79
immunoglobulin A 157–8

inositol 148–50, 160
insomnia 33

kava 159–62, 168
7-keto
    dehydroepiandrosterone 158–9,
    160
KIBRA 187

lavender 162–3, 168
Liebowitz Social Anxiety Scale
    (LSAS) 156
linolenic acid 156–7
long-term memory 110–11
lorazepam 163
LSAS see Liebowitz Social Anxiety Scale
L-lysine 152–3, 160

magnesium 154–6, 160
magnetic resonance imaging
    (MRI) 94, 95, 186
MAOI see monoamine oxidase
    inhibitors
MAPK see mitogen-activated protein
    kinase
memory effects
    benzodiazepines and cognitive
        behavioral therapy 27–9, 33
    consolidation 110–11, 114, 117
    cortisol 110–15
    oxytocin 129
    retrieval 111–12, 113–14, 116
    working memory 112–13
    yohimbine hydrochloride 95–6
menstruation-related anxiety 155
meta-analyses 64–5
methamphetamine-dependence 186
methoxy-4-hydroxyphenylglycol
    (MHPG) 95–6
N-methyl-D-aspartate (NMDA)
    receptor/agonists see D-cycloserine
metoprolol 95
MHPG see methoxy-4-
    hydroxyphenylglycol
midazolam 28
mitogen-activated protein kinase
    (MAPK) 9
mixed anxiety disorders 159–61
moclobemide

generalized anxiety disorder 69–72
panic disorder 66, 68
social anxiety disorder 13–14
monoamine oxidase inhibitors
    (MAOI) 41, 54–6, 152
MRI see magnetic resonance imaging
Multicenter Comparative Treatment
    Study of Panic Disorder 48–50

N3-PUFA see omega-3 fatty acids
neuroendocrine systems 10
neuroimaging 7–8
neuropeptides 124–5, 132, 136
neuroplasticity 14
neuroscience 6
neurotransmitters
    combination strategies 7, 9, 10
    dietary supplements 152, 156
nicotine replacement therapy
    (NRT) 31
NMDA see methyl-D-aspartate
non-clinical anxiety 159–61
non-inferiority trials 62–3
norepinephrine 110, 112
NRT see nicotine replacement therapy
nutritional supplements 146, 148–59

obsessive-compulsive disorder (OCD)
    antidepressants 41, 46, 51–4
    combination strategies 15–16,
        29–30, 81–3, 84–5
    D-cycloserine 81–3, 84–5
    dietary supplements 149–50, 165
    selective serotonin reuptake
        inhibitors 62
    yohimbine hydrochloride 91
omega-3 fatty acids (N3-
    PUFA) 156–7, 160
oxazepam 164–5
OXTR polymorphisms 132
oxytocin (OXT) 10–11, 123–43
    combination strategies 132–5
    context 123
    emotion recognition 127–9
    human social behavior 124
    methodological issues 124–5
    neurophysiological bases 123–4
    prosocial behavior 130–2
    social cognition and memory 129

oxytocin (OXT) (*Continued*)
  social disorders   123, 127–9, 132–6
  social stress and anxiety   125–7

panic disorder (PD)
  antidepressants   41–3, 45–51, 54–5, 57
  combination strategies   12–13, 26, 28, 30, 32–3, 65–8
  D-cycloserine   83–4
  dietary supplements   149
  selective serotonin reuptake inhibitors   65–8
  yohimbine hydrochloride   91
paroxetine   15, 66
passionflower   163–5, 168
patient drop-out   29
PD *see* panic disorder
Perceived Stress Scale (PSS)   155
peripheral nervous system (PNS)   124–5
personalized medicine   185–8
phenelzine   13, 55–6
phosphatidylinositol 3-kinase (PI-3K)   9
phosphatidylinositol cycle   148
pindolol   151–2
Piper methysticum   159–62, 168
PNS *see* peripheral nervous system
polyunsaturated fatty acids (PUFA)   156–7
post-traumatic stress disorder (PTSD)
  antidepressants   41
  combination strategies   8, 10, 15, 29, 30
  cortisol   110, 114–17
  D-cycloserine   79–80
  dietary supplements   159
  selective serotonin reuptake inhibitors   62
  yohimbine hydrochloride   91, 93, 100
pre-menstruation-related anxiety   155
pregabalin   72
propranolol   96, 167
prosocial behavior   130–2
PSS *see* Perceived Stress Scale
psychological placebos   62, 69
PUFA *see* polyunsaturated fatty acids

Reading the Mind in the Eyes Test (RMET)   128
rebound anxiety   43
reconsolidation of memory   114
relationship stress   124
relative meta-analysis method   64
relaxation training
  antidepressants   52
  combination strategies   29–30, 32–3
resistance to treatment *see* treatment resistance
retrieval of memory   111–12, 113–14, 116
return of fear (ROF)   76–7
reversible inhibitors of monoamine oxidase A (RIMA)   41
  generalized anxiety disorder   69–72
  panic disorder   66, 68
  social anxiety disorder   13–14
Rhodiola rosea   171
RIMA *see* reversible inhibitors of monoamine oxidase A
ritual prevention   53–4
RMET *see* Reading the Mind in the Eyes Test
ROF *see* return of fear

SAD *see* social anxiety disorder
St John's Wort   165–6, 168
salivary alpha amylase analysers   99
schizophrenia
  biomarkers   186
  oxytocin   124, 127, 135
selective serotonin reuptake inhibitors (SSRI)   61–74
  acute studies   65
  combination strategies   5–6, 7–8, 10–11, 15, 26
  context   61
  dietary supplements   149–50, 152
  efficacy and clinical trials   61–3
  follow-up studies   63–4, 68, 71
  generalized anxiety disorder   68–72
  long-term effects   65, 68
  meta-analyses   64–5
  methodological issues   61–4
  panic disorder   65–8
  social anxiety disorder   69–72
self-directed exposure   42, 47

serotonin (5-HT) 150–2, 160
serotonin norepinephrine reuptake
    inhibitors (SNRI) 61
serotonin reuptake inhibitors (SRI) 41, 57
sertraline 13–15, 66, 71
sexual dysfunction 92
short-term memory 110–11
sildenafil 92
silexan 163
smoking cessation 31
SNRI *see* serotonin norepinephrine reuptake inhibitors
social anxiety disorder (SAD)
    antidepressants 41, 55–6
    benzodiazepines and cognitive behavioral therapy 25–6
    combination strategies 8, 13–14, 69–72
    D-cycloserine 80–1, 84
    oxytocin 123, 127–9, 132–3
    selective serotonin reuptake inhibitors 69–72
    yohimbine hydrochloride 91
social cognition 129
social neuropeptides 11
social phobia 165–6
social stress 115–16, 125–7
specific phobias
    antidepressants 41
    combination strategies 8
    cortisol 110
    D-cycloserine 80, 84
    yohimbine hydrochloride 98–100, 102
spontaneous panic attacks 51
SRI *see* serotonin reuptake inhibitors
SSRI *see* selective serotonin uptake inhibitors
State-Trait Anxiety Inventory (STAI) 152–4, 166–7
substance abuse disorders 5
suicidality 77
supportive therapy 43, 45–6, 55

TCA *see* tricyclic antidepressants
L-theanine 153–4, 160
therapist-directed exposure 42, 47, 52–3

translational medicine 182–3
treatment resistance 6
trial selection criteria 148
tricyclic antidepressants (TCA) 41–54
    agoraphobia 41–3, 45–51
    combination strategies 41–4, 47–54
    obsessive-compulsive disorder 41, 46, 51–4
    panic disorder 41–3, 45–51, 57
Trier Social Stress Test (TSST) 115–16, 125–6, 134, 152
trust 130–1
tryptophan 150–2, 160
TSST *see* Trier Social Stress Test

unconditioned stimuli (US) 76–7, 93–5
underdiagnosis 6
undertreatment 6
US *see* unconditioned stimuli

valerian 166–7, 169
Visual Analogue Mood Scale (VAMS) 154

wait-list controls 64–5
working memory 112–13

Yale-Brown Obsessive Compulsive Scale (Y-BOCS) 54, 149–50, 150–1, 157, 165
yohimbine hydrochloride (YOH) 9, 91–107
    animal studies of extinction 96–7
    augmentation of exposure treatment in humans 91, 93, 97–100
    combination strategies 91, 93, 97–100
    context 91–2
    dietary supplements 151
    emotional learning 95–6
    fear conditioning and extinction learning 93–5, 96–7, 101, 103
    historical context 92
    memory effects 95–6
    preclinical and clinical studies 101–2
    safety and tolerability 92–3